AF531301

SCIENCE OF MUSHROOMS

SCIENCE OF MUSHROOMS

By

Dr. Shubhrata R. Mishra

Deptt. of Botany
Vikram University
Ujjain (M.P.)
(India)

DISCOVERY PUBLISHING HOUSE PVT. LTD.
NEW DELHI-110 002

Published by:
Tilak Wasan
DISCOVERY PUBLISHING HOUSE PVT. LTD.
4383/4B, Ansari Road, Darya Ganj
New Delhi-110 002 (India)
Phone : +91-11-23279245, 43596064-65
Fax : +91-11-23253475
E-mail : parul.wasan@gmail.com
discoverypublishinghouse@gmail.com
web : www.discoverypublishinggroup.com

***First Edition:* 2013**

ISBN: 978-93-5056-301-4

Science of Mushrooms

Printed at:
Dynamic Printers
Delhi

Preface

A mushroom is the fleshy, spore-bearing fruiting body of a fungus, typically produced above ground on soil or on its food source. Like all fungi, mushrooms are not plants and do not undergo photosynthesis. The standard for the name "mushroom" is the cultivated white button mushroom, *Agaricus bisporus*; hence the word "mushroom" is most often applied to those fungi (Basidiomycota, Agaricomycetes) that have a stem (stipe), a cap (pileus), and gills (lamellae, sing. lamella) or pores on the underside of the cap.

"Mushroom" describes a variety of gilled fungi, with or without stems, and the term is used even more generally, to describe both the fleshy fruiting bodies of some Ascomycota and the woody or leathery fruiting bodies of some Basidiomycota, depending upon the context of the word.

Forms deviating from the standard morphology usually have more specific names, such as "puffball", "stinkhorn", and "morel", and gilled mushrooms themselves are often called "agarics" in reference to their similarity to *Agaricus* or their place *Agaricales*. By extension, the term "mushroom" can also designate the entire fungus when in culture; the thallus (called a mycelium) of species forming the fruiting bodies called mushrooms; or the species itself.

Identifying mushrooms requires a basic understanding of their macroscopic structure. Most are Basidiomycetes and gilled. Their spores, called basidiospores, are produced on the gills and fall in a fine rain of powder from under the caps as a result. At the microscopic level the basidiospores are shot off basidia and then fall between the gills in the dead air space. As a result, for most mushrooms, if the cap is cut off and placed gill-side-down overnight, a powdery impression reflecting the shape of the gills (or pores, or spines, etc.) is formed (when the fruit body is sporulating). The color of the powdery print, called a spore print, is used to help classify mushrooms and can help to identify them. Spore print colors include white (most common), brown, black, purple-brown, pink, yellow, and cream, but almost never blue, green, or red.

While modern identification of mushrooms is quickly becoming molecular, the standard methods for identification are still used by most and have developed into a fine art harking back to medieval times and the Victorian era, combined with microscopic examination. The presence of juices upon breaking, bruising reactions, odors, tastes, shades of color, habitat, habit, and season are all considered by both amateur and professional mycologists. Tasting and smelling mushrooms carries its own hazards because of poisons and allergens. Chemical tests are also used for some genera.

People who collect mushrooms for consumption are known as mycophagists, and the act of collecting them for such is known as mushroom hunting, or simply "mushrooming".

China is the world's largest edible mushroom producer. The country produces about half of all cultivated mushrooms, and around 2.7 kilograms (6.0 lb) of mushrooms is consumed per person per year by over a billion people.

Many mushroom species produce secondary metabolites that can be toxic, mind-altering, antibiotic, antiviral, or bioluminescent. Although there are only a small number of deadly species, several others can cause particularly severe and unpleasant symptoms. Toxicity likely plays a role in protecting the function of the basidiocarp: the mycelium has expended considerable energy and protoplasmic material to develop a structure to efficiently distribute its spores.

—Author

Contents

Preface

1. **Introduction** 1
   Psychoactive Mushrooms

2. **Sporocarp** 13
   Characteristics; Shared Futures; Unique Features; Reproduction; Asexual Reproduction; Sexual Reproduction; Other Sexual Processes; Evolution; Taxonomic Groups; Symbiosis; With Plants; Drugs; Cultured Foods; Edible and Poisonous Species; Pest Control; Model Organisms; Others; Mycotoxins; Mycology; History

3. **Yeast** 41
   Alcoholic Beverages; Bioremediation; Probiotics; Aquarium Hobby; Food Spoilage

4. **Ascocarp** 54
   Classification of Ascocarps; Basidiocarp

5. **Basidiomycota** 58
   Agaricomycotina; Pucciniomycotina; Ustilaginomycotina; Typical Life-cycle; Variations in Life-cycles; Rusts; Smuts

6. **Puffball** 67
Stalked Puffballs; True Puffballs; False Puffballs; Classification; Lycoperdales, Tulostomatales; Nidulariales (Related to Agaricales); Geastrales and Phallales (Related to Cantharellales); Agaricus; Phylogenetics; Sections; Edibility

7. **Mycelium** 74
Phallaceae

8. **Edible Mushrooms** 81
Current Culinary Use; Commercially Cultivated; Other Edible Wild Species; Conditionally Edible Species; Current Medical Use; Preparing Wild Edibles

9. **Mushrooming** 89
Little Brown Mushrooms; Psychotropics; Radiation; Guidelines for Mushroom Picking; Eating Poisonous Species; Commonly Gathered Mushrooms; Agaricaceae; Boletaceae; Cantharellus Cibarius; Helvellaceae; Lepiotaceae; A Basket of Morels; Lactarius; Russulaceae; Tricholomataceae

10. **Mushroom Poisoning** 100
Folk Traditions; Causes of Poisonings; Toxins and Their Symptoms; Poisonous Mushrooms; Other Causes of Poisoning

11. **Medicinal Mushrooms** 113
Immune System and Cancer; Statins; Effect on Cholesterol; Effect on Cognition; *In vitro* Antiviral, Antibacterial, Antifungal and Antimicrobial Activities; *In Vitro* Antihormone Activity; Anti-inflammatory Activity; Effect on Blood Sugar; Vitamin D_2 and Conjugated Linoleic Acid (CLA); Antioxidant Activity; Epidemiological Research; Edible Species; Species Used by Tea or Extraction; *Cordyceps spp.*, (Caterpillar Fungus); *Fomes Fomentarious* (Ice man Fungus); *Ganoderma Lucidum*

(Lingzhi, Reishi, Mannentake); *Inonotus Obliquus* (Chaga Mushroom); *Peziza Vesiculosa; Phellinus Linteus* (Mesima); *Piptoporus Betulinus* (Birch Polypore); *Polyporus Umbellatus* (Zhu-ling); *Trametes Gibbosa* (Daedelea Gibbosa); *Trametes Versicolor* (Coriolus Versicolor, Turkey, Tail, Kawaratake, Yun-zhi); *Claviceps Purpurea* (Ergot); Heavy Metals

12. Fungiculture **126**
Introduction; Techniques; Wild Harvesting; Outdoor Logs; Indoor Trays; Substrates; Pests and Diseases; Commercially Cultivated Fungi; Friendly Fungi; Fungal Enemies; Fungal Growth and Reproduction

13. Psilocybin Mushroom **137**
Sensory; Emotional; Spiritual and Well-being; Legality

14. Fomes Fomentarius (*Tinder Fungus*) **145**
Similar Species; Habitat and Distribution; Amadou

15. Ascomycota **151**
Modern Classification of Ascomycota; Outdated Taxon Names; Morphology; Asexual Reproduction; Asexual Spores; Conidiogenesis and Dehiscence; Sexual Reproduction; Heterokaryosis and Parasexuality; Formation of Sexual Spores; Ecology; Lichens; Mycorrhizal Fungi and Endophytes; Symbiotic Relationships with Animals; Importance for Humans; Harmful Interactions; Positive Effects

16. Mushroom Cultivation **168**
Selection of Strains; Maintenance of Strains; Spawn; Manure Spawn; Grain Spawn; Perlite Spawn; Compost; Materials and Their Functions; Carbohydrate Nutrients; Wheat Straw; Composting Theory; Formulations; Method of Composting; Composting by Short Method

17. **Different Types of Mushrooms** **179**
Saprotrophs–Thriving on Decay; Mycorrhizae–Successful Partnering with Plants; Parasites–Feeding on the Weak; Endophytes–A Mysterious Symbiosis

18. **Nutritive Value of Mushrooms** **187**
Cultivation Technologies of Edible Mushrooms; Cultivation of White Button Mushroom (*Agaricus Bisporus*); Cultivation of Oyster or Tropical Mushroom (*Pleurotus* spp.)

19. **Mushroom Industry in India** **200**
Benefits of Oyster Mushroom Growing; Substrate Preparation and Treatment; Spawn Preparation; Substrate Inoculation; Spawn Run and Pin Initiation; Canning; Drying

Bibliography **213**

Index **215**

CHAPTER 1 Introduction

A mushroom is the fleshy, spore-bearing fruiting body of a fungus, typically produced above ground on soil or on its food source. Like all fungi, mushrooms are not plants and do not undergo photosynthesis. The standard for the name "mushroom" is the cultivated white button mushroom, *Agaricus bisporus*; hence the word "mushroom" is most often applied to those fungi (Basidiomycota, Agaricomycetes) that have a stem (stipe), a cap (pileus), and gills (lamellae, sing. lamella) or pores on the underside of the cap.

"Mushroom" describes a variety of gilled fungi, with or without stems, and the term is used even more generally, to describe both the fleshy fruiting bodies of some Ascomycota and the woody or leathery fruiting bodies of some Basidiomycota, depending upon the context of the word.

Forms deviating from the standard morphology usually have more specific names, such as "puffball", "stinkhorn", and "morel", and gilled mushrooms themselves are often called "agarics" in reference to their similarity to *Agaricus* or their place *Agaricales*. By extension, the term "mushroom" can also designate the entire fungus when in culture; the thallus (called a mycelium) of species forming the fruiting bodies called mushrooms; or the species itself.

Identifying mushrooms requires a basic understanding of their macroscopic structure. Most are Basidiomycetes and gilled. Their spores, called basidiospores, are produced on the gills and fall in a fine rain of powder from under the caps as a result. At the microscopic level the basidiospores are shot off basidia and then fall between the gills in the dead air space. As a result, for most mushrooms, if the cap is cut off and placed gill-side-down overnight, a powdery impression reflecting the shape of the gills (or pores, or spines, etc.) is formed (when the fruit body is sporulating). The colour of the powdery print, called a spore print, is used to help classify mushrooms and can help to identify them. Spore print colours include white (most common), brown, black, purple-brown, pink, yellow, and cream, but almost never blue, green, or red.

While modern identification of mushrooms is quickly becoming molecular, the standard methods for identification are still used by most and have developed into a fine art harking back to medieval times and the Victorian era, combined with microscopic examination. The presence of juices upon breaking, bruising reactions, odors, tastes, shades of colour, habitat, habit, and season are all considered by both amateur and professional mycologists. Tasting and smelling mushrooms carries its own hazards because of poisons and allergens. Chemical tests are also used for some genera.

In general, identification to genus can often be accomplished in the field using a local mushroom guide. Identification to species, however, requires more effort; one must remember that a mushroom develops from a button stage into a mature structure, and only the latter can provide certain characteristics needed for the identification of the species. However, over-mature specimens lose features and cease producing spores. Many novices have mistaken humid water marks on paper for white spore prints, or discoloured paper from oozing liquids on lamella edges for coloured spored prints.

Typical mushrooms are the fruit bodies of members of the order Agaricales, whose type genus is *Agaricus* and type species is the field mushroom, *Agaricus campestris*. However, in modern molecularly-defined classifications, not all members of the order Agaricales produce mushroom fruit bodies, and many other gilled fungi, collectively called mushrooms, occur in other orders of the class Agaricomycetes. For example, chanterelles are in the Cantharellales, false chanterelles like *Gomphus* are in the Gomphales, milk mushrooms (*Lactarius*) and russulas (*Russula*) as well as *Lentinellus* are in the Russulales, while the tough leathery genera *Lentinus* and *Panus* are among the Polyporales, but *Neolentinus* is in the Gloeophyllales, and the little pin-mushroom genus, *Rickenella*, along with similar genera, are in the Hymenochaetales.

Within the main body of mushrooms, in the Agaricales, are common fungi like the common fairy-ring mushroom (*Marasmius oreades*), shiitake, enoki, oyster mushrooms, fly agarics, and other amanitas, magic mushrooms like species of *Psilocybe*, paddy straw mushrooms, shaggy manes, etc.

An atypical mushroom is the lobster mushroom, which is a deformed, cooked-lobster-coloured parasitized fruitbody of a *Russula* or *Lactarius*, coloured and deformed by the mycoparasitic Ascomycete *Hypomyces lactifluorum*.

Other mushrooms are not gilled and then the term "mushroom" is loosely used, so it is difficult to give a full account of their classifications. Some have pores underneath (and are usually called boletes), others have spines, such as the hedgehog mushroom and other tooth fungi, and so on. "Mushroom" has been used for polypores, puffballs, jelly fungi, coral fungi, bracket fungi, stinkhorns, and cup fungi. Thus, the term is more one of common application to macroscopic fungal fruiting bodies than one having precise taxonomic meaning. There are approximately 14,000 described species of mushrooms.

The terms "mushroom" and "toadstool" go back centuries and were never precisely defined, nor was there consensus on application. The term "toadstool" was often, but not exclusively, applied to poisonous mushrooms or to those that have the classic umbrella-like cap-and-stem form. Between AD 1400 and AD 1600, the terms *tadstoles, frogstooles, frogge stoles, tadstooles, tode stoles, toodys hatte, paddockstool, puddockstool, paddocstol, toadstoole, and paddockstooles* sometimes were used synonymously with *mushrom, mushrum, muscheron, mousheroms, mussheron, or musserouns.*

The word has apparent analogies in Dutch *padde(n)stoel* (*toad-stool/chair*, mushroom) and German *Krötenschwamm* (*toad-fungus*, alt. word for panther cap). Others have proposed a connection with German "Todesstuhl" (lit. "death's chair"). Since *Tod* is a direct cognate to *death*, in that case it would be a German borrowing. However, there is no common word akin to "Todesstuhl" used in German referring to mushrooms, poisonous or not.

The term "mushroom" and its variations may have been derived from the French word *mousseron* in reference to moss (*mousse*). The toadstool's connection to toads may be direct, in reference to some species of poisonous toad, or may just be a case of phono-semantic matching from the German word. However, there is no clear-cut delineation between edible and poisonous fungi, so that a "mushroom" may be edible, poisonous, or unpalatable. The term "toadstool" is nowadays used in storytelling when referring to poisonous or suspect mushrooms. The classic example of a toadstool is *Amanita muscaria.*

A mushroom develops from a nodule, or pinhead, less than two millimeters in diameter, called a primordium, which is typically found on or near the surface of the substrate. It is formed within the mycelium, the mass of threadlike hyphae that make up the fungus. The primordium enlarges into a roundish structure of interwoven hyphae roughly resembling an egg, called a "button". The button has a cottony roll of mycelium, the universal veil, that surrounds the developing fruit body. As the egg expands, the universal veil ruptures and may remain as a cup, or volva, at the base of the stalk, or as warts or volval patches on the cap. Many mushrooms lack a universal veil and therefore do not have either a volva or volval patches. Often there is a second layer of tissue, the partial veil, covering the bladelike gills that bear spores. As the cap expands, the veil breaks, and remnants of the partial veil may remain as a ring, or annulus, around the middle of the stalk or as fragments hanging from the margin of the cap. The ring may be skirt-like as in some species of *Amanita*, collar-like as in many species of *Lepiota*, or merely the faint remnants of a cortina (a partial veil composed of filaments resembling a spiderweb), which is typical of the genus *Cortinarius*. Mushrooms that lack a partial veil do not form an annulus.

The stalk (also called the stipe, or stem) may be central and support the cap in the middle, or it may be off-centre and/or lateral, as in species of *Pleurotus* and *Panus*. In other mushrooms, a stalk may be absent, as in the polypores that form shelf-like brackets. Puffballs lack a stalk but may have a supporting base. Other mushrooms, like truffles, jellies, earthstars, bird's nests, usually do not have stalks, and a specialized mycological vocabulary exists to describe their parts.

The way that gills attach to the top of the stalk is an important feature of mushroom morphology. Mushrooms in the genera *Agaricus*, *Amanita*, *Lepiota* and *Pluteus*, among others, have free gills that do not extend to the top of the stalk. Others have decurrent gills that extend down the stalk, as in the genera *Omphalotus* and *Pleurotus*. There are a great number of variations between the extremes of free and decurrent, collectively called attached gills. Finer distinctions are often made to distinguish the types of attached gills: adnate gills, which adjoin squarely to the stalk; notched gills, which are notched where they join the top of the stalk; adnexed gills, which curve upward to meet the stalk, and so on. These distinctions between attached gills are sometimes difficult to interpret, since gill attachment may change as the mushroom matures, or with different environmental conditions.

A hymenium is a layer of microscopic spore-bearing cells that covers the surface of gills. In the non-gilled mushrooms, the hymenium lines the inner surfaces of the tubes of boletes and polypores, or covers the teeth of spine fungi and the branches of corals. In the Ascomycota, spores develop within a microscopic elongated, saclike cell called an ascus, which typically contains eight spores. The Discomycetes—which contains the cup, sponge, brain, and some club-like fungi—develop an exposed layer of asci, as on the inner surface of cup fungi or within the pits of morels. The Pyrenomycetes, tiny dark-coloured fungi that live on a wide range of substrates including soil, dung, leaf litter, decaying wood, as well as other fungi, produce minute flask-shaped structures called perithecia, within which the asci develop.

In the Basidiomycetes, usually four spores develop on the tips of thin projections called sterigmata, which extend from a club-shaped cell called a basidium. The fertile portion of the Gasteromycetes, called a gleba, may become powdery as in the puffballs or slimy as in the stinkhorns. Interspersed among the asci are threadlike sterile cells called paraphyses. Similar structures called cystidia often occur within the hymenium of the Basidiomycota. Many types of cystidia exist and assessing their presence, shape, and size is often used to verify the identification of a mushroom.

The most important microscopic feature for identification of mushrooms is the spores themselves. Their colour, shape, size, attachment, ornamentation, and reaction to chemical tests often can be the crux of an identification. Spores often have a protrusion at one end, called an apiculus, which is the point of attachment to the basidium, termed the apical germ pore, from which the hypha emerges when the spore germinates.

Many species of mushrooms seemingly appear overnight, growing or expanding rapidly. This phenomenon is the source of several common expressions in the English language including "to mushroom" or "mushrooming" (expanding rapidly in size or scope) and "to pop up like a mushroom" (to appear unexpectedly and quickly). In reality all species of mushrooms take several days to form primordial mushroom fruit bodies, though they do expand rapidly by the absorption of fluids.

The cultivated mushroom as well as the common field mushroom initially form a minute fruiting body, referred to as the pin stage because of their small size. Slightly expanded they are called buttons, once again because of the relative size and shape. Once such stages are formed, the mushroom can rapidly pull in water from its mycelium and expand, mainly by inflating preformed cells that took several days to form in the primordia.

Similarly, there are even more ephemeral mushrooms, like *Parasola plicatilis* (formerly *Coprinus plicatlis*), that literally appear overnight and may disappear by late afternoon on a hot day after rainfall. The primordia form at ground level in lawns in humid spaces under the thatch and after heavy rainfall or in dewy conditions balloon to full size in a few hours, release spores, and then collapse. They "mushroom" to full size.

Not all mushrooms expand overnight; some grow very slowly and add tissue to their fruitbodies by growing from the edges of the colony or by inserting hyphae. For example *Pleurotus nebrodensis* grows slowly, and because of this combined with human collection, it is now critically endangered.

Though mushroom fruiting bodies are short-lived, the underlying mycelium can itself be long-lived and massive. A colony of *Armillaria solidipes* (formerly known as *Armillaria ostoyae*) in Malheur National Forest in the United States is estimated to be 2400 years old, possibly older, and spans an estimated 2200 acres (8.9 km^2). Most of the fungus is underground and in decaying wood or dying tree roots in the form of white mycelia combined with black shoelace-like rhizomorphs that bridge colonized separated woody substrates.

Mushrooms are a low-calorie food usually eaten raw or cooked to provide garnish to a meal. Raw dietary mushrooms are a good source of B vitamins, such as riboflavin, niacin and pantothenic acid, and the essential minerals, selenium, copper and potassium. Fat, carbohydrate and calorie content are low, with absence of vitamin C and sodium.

NUTRITIONAL VALUE PER 100 G (3.5 OZ)	
Energy	113 kJ (27 kcal)
Carbohydrates	4.1 g
Fat	0.1 g
Protein	2.5 g
Thiamine (Vit. B_1)	0.1 mg (8%)
Riboflavin (Vit. B_2)	0.5 mg (33%)
Niacin (Vit. B_3)	3.8 mg (25%)
Pantothenic acid (B_5)	1.5 mg (30%)
Vitamin C	0 mg (0%)
Calcium	18 mg (2%)
Phosphorus	120 mg (17%)
Potassium	448 mg (10%)
Sodium	6 mg (0%)
Zinc	1.1 mg (11%)

When exposed to ultraviolet light, natural ergosterols in mushrooms produce vitamin D^2, a process now exploited for the functional food retail market.

Known as the meat of the vegetable world, edible mushrooms are used extensively in cooking, in many cuisines (notably Chinese, Korean, European, and Japanese).

Most mushrooms that are sold in supermarkets have been commercially grown on mushroom farms. The most popular of these, *Agaricus bisporus*, is generally considered safe for most people to eat because it is grown in controlled, sterilized environments, though some individuals do not tolerate it well. Several varieties of *A. bisporus* are grown commercially, including whites, crimini, and portobello. Other cultivated species now available at many grocers include shiitake, maitake or hen-of-the-woods, oyster, and enoki. In recent years increasing affluence in developing countries has led to a considerable growth in interest in mushroom cultivation, which is now seen as a potentially important economic activity for small farmers.

There are a number of species of mushroom that are poisonous, and although some resemble certain edible species, consuming them could be fatal. Eating mushrooms gathered in the wild is risky and should not be undertaken by individuals not knowledgeable in mushroom identification, unless the individuals limit themselves to a relatively small number of good edible species that are visually distinctive. *A. bisporus* contains carcinogens called hydrazines, the most abundant of which is agaritine. However, the carcinogens are destroyed by moderate heat when cooking.

More generally, and particularly with gilled mushrooms, separating edible from poisonous species requires meticulous attention to detail; there is no single trait by which all toxic mushrooms can be identified, nor one by which all edible mushrooms can be identified. Additionally, even edible mushrooms may produce an allergic reaction in susceptible individuals, from a mild asthmatic response to severe anaphylactic shock.

People who collect mushrooms for consumption are known as mycophagists, and the act of collecting them for such is known as mushroom hunting, or simply "mushrooming".

China is the world's largest edible mushroom producer. The country produces about half of all cultivated mushrooms, and around 2.7 kilograms (6.0 lb) of mushrooms is consumed per person per year by over a billion people.

Many mushroom species produce secondary metabolites that can be toxic, mind-altering, antibiotic, antiviral, or bioluminescent. Although there are only a small number of deadly species, several others can cause particularly severe and unpleasant symptoms. Toxicity likely plays a role in protecting the function of the basidiocarp: the mycelium has expended considerable energy and protoplasmic material to develop a structure to efficiently distribute its spores. One defense against consumption and premature destruction is the evolution of chemicals that render the mushroom inedible, either causing the consumer to vomit the meal , or to learn to avoid consumption altogether. In addition, due to the ability of mushrooms to absorb heavy metals, including those that are radioactive, European mushrooms may, to date, include toxicity from the 1986 Chernobyl disaster and continue to be studied.

Psychoactive Mushrooms

Mushrooms that have psychoactive properties have long played a role in various native medicine traditions in cultures all around the world. They have been used as sacrament in rituals aimed at mental and physical healing, and to facilitate visionary states. One such ritual is the *velada* ceremony. A practitioner of traditional mushroom use is the shaman and *curandera* (priest-healer).

Psilocybin mushrooms possess psychedelic properties. Commonly known as "magic mushrooms" or "shrooms," they are openly available in smart shops in many parts of the world, or on the black market in those countries that have outlawed their sale. Psilocybin mushrooms have been reported as facilitating profound and life-changing insights often described as mystical experiences. Recent scientific work has supported these claims, as well as the long-lasting effects of such induced spiritual experiences.

Psilocybin, a naturally occurring chemical in certain psychedelic mushrooms like *Psilocybe cubensis*, is being studied for its ability to help people suffering from psychological disorders, such as obsessive-compulsive disorder. Minute amounts have been reported to stop cluster and migraine headaches. A double-blind study, done by the Johns Hopkins

Hospital, showed that psychedelic mushrooms could provide people an experience with substantial personal meaning and spiritual significance. In the study, one third of the subjects reported that ingestion of psychedelic mushrooms was the single most spiritually significant event of their lives. Over two-thirds reported it among their five most meaningful and spiritually significant events. On the other hand, one-third of the subjects reported extreme anxiety. However, the anxiety went away after a short period of time.

Amanita muscaria pictured above is also psychoactive. The active constituents are ibotenic acid and muscimol. The Muscaria chemotaxonomic group of Amanitas contain no amatoxins or phallotoxins, and are not hepatoxic.

Medicinal mushrooms are mushrooms or extracts from mushrooms that are used or studied as possible treatments for diseases. Some mushroom materials, including polysaccharides, glycoproteins and proteoglycans, modulate immune system responses and inhibit tumor growth. Some medicinal mushroom isolates that have been identified also show cardiovascular, antiviral, antibacterial, antiparasitic, anti-inflammatory, and antidiabetic properties. Currently, several extracts have widespread use in Japan, Korea and China, as adjuncts to radiation treatments and chemotherapy.

Historically, mushrooms have long had medicinal uses, especially in traditional Chinese medicine. Mushrooms have been a subject of modern medical research since the 1960s, where most modern medical studies concern the use of mushroom extracts, rather than whole mushrooms. Only a few specific mushroom extracts have been extensively tested for efficacy. Polysaccharide-K and lentinan are among the mushroom extracts with the firmest evidence. The available results for most other extracts are based on *in vitro* data, effects on isolated cells in a lab dish, animal models like mice, or underpowered clinical human trials. Studies show that glucan-containing mushroom extracts primarily change the function of the innate and adaptive immune systems, functioning as bioresponse modulators, rather than by directly killing bacteria, viruses, or cancer cells as cytocidal agents. In some countries, extracts like polysaccharide-K, schizophyllan, polysaccharide peptide, and lentinan are government-registered adjuvant cancer therapies.

Mushrooms can be used for dyeing wool and other natural fibers. The chromophores of mushroom dyes are organic compounds and produce strong and vivid colours, and all colours of the spectrum can be achieved with mushroom dyes. Before the invention of synthetic dyes mushrooms were the source of many textile dyes.

Some fungi, types of polypores loosely called mushrooms, have been used as fire starters (known as tinder fungi).

Mushrooms are currently being employed by the company Ecovative Design LLC to make biodegradable packaging, a direct replacement for the petroleum based styrofoam.

Mushrooms and other fungi play a role in the development of new biological remediation techniques (e.g., using mycorrhizae to spur plant growth) and filtration technologies (e.g. using fungi to lower bacteria levels in contaminated water). The US Patent and Trademark Office can be searched for patents related to the latest developments in mycoremediation and mycofiltration.

Sporocarp

In fungi, the sporocarp (also known as fruiting body or fruit body) is a multicellular structure on which spore-producing structures, such as basidia or asci, are borne. The fruiting body is part of the sexual phase of a fungal life cycle, with the rest of the life cycle being characterized by vegetative mycelial growth and asexual spore production.

The sporocarp of a basidiomycete is known as a basidiocarp, while the fruiting body of an ascomycete is known as an ascocarp. A significant range of different shapes and morphologies is found in both basidiocarps and ascocarps.

Fruiting bodies are termed epigeous if they grow on the ground, as with ordinary mushrooms, while ones which grow underground are hypogeous. Epigeous sporocarps that are visible to the naked eye, especially fruiting bodies of a more or less agaricoid morphology, are often referred to as mushrooms, while hypogeous fungi are usually called truffles or false truffles. During their evolution truffles lost the ability to disperse their spores via air currents, instead propagating by animal consumption and subsequent dispersal of their spores.

In amateur mushroom hunting, and to a large degree in academic mycology as well, identification of higher fungi is based on the features of the sporocarp.

A fungus (pl. fungi or funguses) is a member of a large group of eukaryotic organisms that includes microorganisms such as yeasts and molds (British English: moulds), as well as the more familiar mushrooms. These organisms are classified as a kingdom, Fungi, which is separate from plants, animals, and bacteria. One major difference is that fungal cells have cell walls that contain chitin, unlike the cell walls of plants, which contain cellulose. These and other differences show that the fungi form a single group of related organisms, named the *Eumycota* (*true fungi* or *Eumycetes*), that share a common ancestor (a *monophyletic group*). This fungal group is distinct from the structurally similar myxomycetes (slime molds) and oomycetes (water molds). The discipline of biology devoted to the study of fungi is known as mycology, which is often regarded as a branch of botany, even though genetic studies have shown that fungi are more closely related to animals than to plants.

Abundant worldwide, most fungi are inconspicuous because of the small size of their structures, and their cryptic lifestyles in soil, on dead matter, and as symbionts of plants, animals, or other fungi. They may become noticeable when fruiting, either as mushrooms or molds. Fungi perform an essential role in the decomposition of organic matter and have fundamental roles in nutrient cycling and exchange. They have long been used as a direct source of food, such as mushrooms and truffles, as a leavening agent for bread, and in fermentation of various food products, such as wine, beer, and soy sauce. Since the 1940s, fungi have been used for the production of antibiotics, and, more recently, various enzymes produced by fungi are used industrially and in detergents. Fungi are also used as biological pesticides to control weeds, plant diseases and insect pests. Many species produce bioactive compounds called mycotoxins, such as alkaloids and polyketides, that are toxic to animals including humans. The fruiting structures of a few species contain psychotropic compounds and are consumed recreationally or in traditional spiritual ceremonies. Fungi can break down manufactured materials and buildings, and become significant pathogens of humans and other animals. Losses of crops due to fungal diseases (e.g. rice blast disease) or food spoilage can have a large impact on human food supplies and local economies.

The fungus kingdom encompasses an enormous diversity of taxa with varied ecologies, life cycle strategies, and morphologies ranging from single-celled aquatic chytrids to large mushrooms. However, little is known of the true biodiversity of Kingdom Fungi, which has been estimated at around 1.5 million species, with about 5 per cent of these having been formally classified. Ever since the pioneering 18th and 19th century taxonomical works of Carl Linnaeus, Christian Hendrik Persoon, and Elias Magnus Fries, fungi have been classified according to their morphology (e.g., characteristics such as spore colour or microscopic features) or physiology. Advances in molecular genetics have opened the way for DNA analysis to be incorporated into taxonomy, which has sometimes challenged the historical groupings based on morphology and other traits. Phylogenetic studies published in the last decade have helped reshape the classification of Kingdom Fungi, which is divided into one subkingdom, seven phyla, and ten subphyla.

The English word *fungus* is directly adopted from the Latin *fungus* (mushroom), used in the writings of Horace and Pliny. This in turn is derived from the Greek word *sphongos*/ ("sponge"), which refers to the macroscopic structures and morphology of mushrooms and molds; the root is also used in other languages, such as the German *Schwamm* ("sponge"), *Schimmel* ("mold"), and the French *champignon* and the Spanish *champiñon* (which both mean "mushroom"). The use of the word *mycology*, which is derived from the Greek *mykes*/ (mushroom) and *logos*/ (discourse), to denote the scientific study of fungi is thought to have originated in 1836 with English naturalist Miles Joseph Berkeley's publication *The English Flora of Sir James Edward Smith*, Vol. 5.

Characteristics

Before the introduction of molecular methods for phylogenetic analysis, taxonomists considered fungi to be members of the Plant Kingdom because of similarities in lifestyle: both fungi and plants are mainly immobile, and have similarities in general morphology and growth habitat. Like plants, fungi often grow in soil, and in the case of mushrooms form conspicuous fruiting bodies, which sometimes bear resemblance to plants such as mosses. The fungi are now considered a separate kingdom, distinct from both plants and animals, from which they appear to have diverged around one billion years ago. Some morphological, biochemical, and genetic features are shared with other organisms, while others are unique to the fungi, clearly separating them from the other kingdoms.

Shared Features

With other eukaryotes: As other eukaryotes, fungal cells contain membrane-bound nuclei with chromosomes that contain DNA with noncoding regions called introns and coding regions called exons. In addition, fungi possess membrane-bound cytoplasmic organelles such as mitochondria, sterol-containing membranes, and ribosomes of the 80S type. They have a characteristic range of soluble carbohydrates and storage compounds, including sugar alcohols (e.g., mannitol), disaccharides, (e.g., trehalose), and polysaccharides (e.g., glycogen, which is also found in animals).

With animals: Fungi lack chloroplasts and are heterotrophic organisms, requiring preformed organic compounds as energy sources.

With plants: Fungi possess a cell wall and vacuoles. They reproduce by both sexual and asexual means, and like basal plant groups (such as ferns and mosses) produce spores. Similar to mosses and algae, fungi typically have haploid nuclei.

With euglenoids and bacteria: Higher fungi, euglenoids, and some bacteria produce the amino acid L-lysine in specific biosynthesis steps, called the a-aminoadipate pathway.

The cells of most fungi grow as tubular, elongated, and thread-like (filamentous) structures and are called hyphae, which may contain multiple nuclei and extend at their tips. Each tip contains a set of aggregated vesicles—cellular structures consisting of proteins, lipids, and other organic molecules—called Spitzenkörper. Both fungi and oomycetes grow as filamentous hyphal cells. In contrast, similar-looking organisms, such as filamentous green algae, grow by repeated cell division within a chain of cells.

In common with some plant and animal species, more than 60 fungal species display the phenomenon of bioluminescence.

Unique Features

Some species grow as single-celled yeasts that reproduce by budding or binary fission. Dimorphic fungi can switch between a yeast phase and a hyphal phase in response to environmental conditions.

The fungal cell wall is composed of glucans and chitin; while the former compounds are also found in plants and the latter in the exoskeleton of arthropods, fungi are the only organisms that combine these two structural molecules in their cell wall. In contrast to plants and the oomycetes, fungal cell walls do not contain cellulose.

Most fungi lack an efficient system for long-distance transport of water and nutrients, such as the xylem and phloem in many plants. To overcome these limitations, some fungi, such as *Armillaria*, form rhizomorphs, that resemble and perform functions similar to the roots of plants. Another characteristic shared with plants includes a biosynthetic pathway for producing terpenes that uses mevalonic acid and pyrophosphate as chemical building blocks. However, plants have an additional terpene pathway in their chloroplasts, a structure fungi do not possess. Fungi produce several secondary metabolites that are similar or identical in structure to those made by plants. Many of the plant and fungal enzymes that make these compounds differ from each other in sequence and other characteristics, which indicates separate origins and evolution of these enzymes in the fungi and plants.

Fungi have a worldwide distribution, and grow in a wide range of habitats, including extreme environments such as deserts or areas with high salt concentrations or ionizing radiation, as well as in deep sea sediments. Some can survive the intense UV and cosmic radiation encountered during space travel. Most grow in terrestrial environments, though several species live partly or solely in aquatic habitats, such as the chytrid fungus *Batrachochytrium dendrobatidis*, a parasite that has been responsible for a worldwide decline in amphibian populations. This organism spends part of its life cycle as a motile zoospore, enabling it to propel itself through water and enter its amphibian host. Other examples of aquatic fungi include those living in hydrothermal areas of the ocean.

Around 100,000 species of fungi have been formally described by taxonomists, but the global biodiversity of the fungus kingdom is not fully understood. On the basis of observations of the ratio of the number of fungal species to the number of plant species in selected environments, the fungal kingdom has been estimated to contain about 1.5 million species. In mycology, species have historically been distinguished by a variety of methods and concepts. Classification based on morphological characteristics, such as the size and shape of spores or fruiting structures, has traditionally dominated fungal taxonomy. Species may also be distinguished by their biochemical and physiological characteristics, such as their ability to metabolize certain biochemicals, or their reaction to chemical tests. The biological species concept discriminates species based on their ability to mate. The application of molecular tools, such as DNA sequencing and phylogenetic analysis, to study diversity has greatly enhanced the resolution and added robustness to estimates of genetic diversity within various taxonomic groups.

Most fungi grow as hyphae, which are cylindrical, thread-like structures 2-10 µm in diameter and up to several centimeters in length. Hyphae grow at their tips (apices); new hyphae are typically formed by emergence of new tips along existing hyphae by a process called *branching*, or occasionally growing hyphal tips bifurcate (fork) giving rise to two parallel-growing hyphae. The combination of apical growth and branching/forking leads to the development of a mycelium, an interconnected network of hyphae. Hyphae can be either septate or coenocytic: septate hyphae are divided into compartments separated by cross walls (internal cell walls, called septa, that are formed at right angles to the cell wall giving the hypha its shape), with each compartment containing one or more nuclei; coenocytic hyphae are not compartmentalized. Septa have pores that allow cytoplasm, organelles, and sometimes nuclei to pass through; an example is the dolipore septum in the fungi of the phylum Basidiomycota. Coenocytic hyphae are essentially multinucleate supercells.

Many species have developed specialized hyphal structures for nutrient uptake from living hosts; examples include haustoria in plant-parasitic species of most fungal phyla, and arbuscules of several mycorrhizal fungi, which penetrate into the host cells to consume nutrients.

Although fungi are opisthokonts—a grouping of evolutionarily related organisms broadly characterized by a single posterior flagellum—all phyla except for the chytrids have lost their posterior flagella. Fungi are unusual among the eukaryotes in having a cell wall that, in addition to glucans (e.g., ß-1,3-glucan) and other typical components, also contains the biopolymer chitin.

Fungal mycelia can become visible to the naked eye, for example, on various surfaces and substrates, such as damp walls and on spoiled food, where they are commonly called molds. Mycelia grown on solid agar media in laboratory petri dishes are usually referred to as colonies. These colonies can exhibit growth shapes and colours (due to spores or pigmentation) that can be used as diagnostic features in the identification of species or groups. Some individual fungal colonies can reach extraordinary dimensions and ages as in the case of a clonal colony of *Armillaria solidipes*, which extends over an area of more than 900 ha (3.5 square miles), with an estimated age of nearly 9,000 years.

The apothecium—a specialized structure important in sexual reproduction in the ascomycetes—is a cup-shaped fruiting body that holds the hymenium, a layer of tissue containing the spore-bearing cells. The fruiting bodies of the basidiomycetes (basidiocarps) and some ascomycetes can sometimes grow very large, and many are well-known as mushrooms.

The growth of fungi as hyphae on or in solid substrates or as single cells in aquatic environments is adapted for the efficient extraction of nutrients, because these growth forms have high surface area to volume ratios. Hyphae are specifically adapted for growth on solid surfaces, and to invade substrates and tissues. They can exert large penetrative mechanical forces; for example, the plant pathogen *Magnaporthe grisea* forms a structure called an appressorium which evolved to puncture plant tissues. The pressure generated by the appressorium, directed against the plant epidermis, can exceed 8 megapascals (1200 psi). The filamentous fungus *Paecilomyces lilacinus* uses a similar structure to penetrate the eggs of nematodes.

The mechanical pressure exerted by the appressorium is generated from physiological processes that increase intracellular turgor by producing osmolytes such as glycerol. Morphological adaptations such as these are complemented by hydrolytic enzymes secreted into the environment to digest large organic molecules—such as polysaccharides, proteins, lipids, and other organic substrates—into smaller molecules that may then be absorbed as nutrients. The vast majority of filamentous fungi grow in a polar fashion—i.e., by extension into one direction—by elongation at the tip (apex) of the hypha. Alternative forms of fungal growth include intercalary extension (i.e., by longitudinal expansion of hyphal compartments that are below the apex) as in the case of some endophytic fungi, or growth by volume expansion during the development of mushroom stipes and other large organs. Growth of fungi as multicellular structures consisting of somatic and reproductive cells—a feature independently evolved in animals and plants—has several functions, including the development of fruiting bodies for dissemination of sexual spores (see above) and biofilms for substrate colonization and intercellular communication.

Traditionally, the fungi are considered heterotrophs, organisms that rely solely on carbon fixed by other organisms for metabolism. Fungi have evolved a high degree of metabolic versatility that allows them to use a diverse range of organic substrates for growth, including simple compounds such as nitrate, ammonia, acetate, or ethanol. For some species it has been shown that the pigment melanin may play a role in extracting energy from ionizing radiation, such as gamma radiation; however, this form of "radiotrophic" growth has only been described for a few species, the effects on growth rates are small, and the underlying biophysical and biochemical processes are not known. The authors speculate that this process might bear similarity to CO_2 fixation via visible light, but instead utilizing ionizing radiation as a source of energy.

Reproduction

Fungal reproduction is complex, reflecting the differences in lifestyles and genetic makeup within this kingdom of organisms. It is estimated that a third of all fungi reproduce by different modes of propagation; for example, reproduction may occur in two well-differentiated stages within the life cycle of a species, the teleomorph and the anamorph. Environmental conditions trigger genetically determined developmental states that lead to the creation of specialized structures for sexual or asexual reproduction. These structures aid reproduction by efficiently dispersing spores or spore-containing propagules.

Asexual Reproduction

Asexual reproduction via vegetative spores (conidia) or through mycelial fragmentation is common; it maintains clonal populations adapted to a specific niche, and allows more rapid dispersal than sexual reproduction. The "Fungi imperfecti" (fungi lacking the perfect or sexual stage) or Deuteromycota comprise all the species which lack an observable sexual cycle.

Sexual Reproduction

Sexual reproduction with meiosis exists in all fungal phyla (with the exception of the Glomeromycota). It differs in many aspects from sexual reproduction in animals or plants. Differences also exist between fungal groups and can be used to discriminate species by morphological differences in sexual structures and reproductive strategies. Mating experiments between fungal isolates may identify species on the basis of biological species concepts. The major fungal groupings have initially been delineated based on the morphology of their sexual structures and spores; for example, the spore-containing structures, asci and basidia, can be used in the identification of ascomycetes and basidiomycetes, respectively. Some species may allow mating only between individuals of opposite mating type, while others can mate and sexually reproduce with any other individual or itself. Species of the former mating system are called heterothallic, and of the latter homothallic.

Most fungi have both an haploid and diploid stage in their life cycles. In sexually reproducing fungi, compatible individuals may combine by fusing their hyphae together into an interconnected network; this process, anastomosis, is required for the initiation of the sexual cycle. Ascomycetes and basidiomycetes go through a dikaryotic stage, in which the nuclei inherited from the two parents do not combine immediately after cell fusion, but remain separate in the hyphal cells.

In ascomycetes, dikaryotic hyphae of the hymenium (the spore-bearing tissue layer) form a characteristic *hook* at the hyphal septum. During cell division, formation of the hook ensures proper distribution of the newly divided nuclei into the apical and basal hyphal compartments. An ascus (plural *asci*) is then formed, in which karyogamy (nuclear fusion) occurs. Asci are embedded in an ascocarp, or fruiting body. Karyogamy in the asci is followed immediately by meiosis and the production of ascospores. After dispersal, the ascospores may germinate and form a new haploid mycelium.

Sexual reproduction in basidiomycetes is similar to that of the ascomycetes. Compatible haploid hyphae fuse to produce a dikaryotic mycelium. However, the dikaryotic phase is more extensive in the basidiomycetes, often also present in the vegetatively growing mycelium. A specialized anatomical structure, called a clamp connection, is formed at each hyphal septum. As with the structurally similar hook in the ascomycetes, the clamp connection in the basidiomycetes is required for controlled transfer of nuclei during cell division, to maintain the dikaryotic stage with two genetically different nuclei in each hyphal compartment. A basidiocarp is formed in which club-like structures known as basidia generate haploid basidiospores after karyogamy and meiosis. The most commonly known basidiocarps are mushrooms, but they may also take other forms.

In glomeromycetes (formerly zygomycetes), haploid hyphae of two individuals fuse, forming a gametangium, a specialized cell structure that becomes a fertile gamete-producing cell. The gametangium develops into a zygospore, a thick-walled spore formed by the union of gametes. When the zygospore germinates, it undergoes meiosis, generating new haploid hyphae, which may then form asexual sporangiospores. These sporangiospores allow the fungus to rapidly disperse and germinate into new genetically identical haploid fungal mycelia.

Both asexual and sexual spores or sporangiospores are often actively dispersed by forcible ejection from their reproductive structures. This ejection ensures exit of the spores from the reproductive structures as well as travelling through the air over long distances.

Specialized mechanical and physiological mechanisms, as well as spore surface structures (such as hydrophobins), enable efficient spore ejection. For example, the structure of the spore-bearing cells in some ascomycete species is such that the buildup of substances affecting cell volume and fluid balance enables the explosive discharge of spores into the air. The forcible discharge of single spores termed *ballistospores* involves formation of a small drop of water (Buller's drop), which upon contact with the spore leads to its projectile release with an initial acceleration of more than 10,000 g; the net result is that the spore is ejected 0.01-0.02 cm, sufficient distance for it to fall through the gills or pores into the air below. Other fungi, like the puffballs, rely on alternative mechanisms for spore release, such as external mechanical forces. The bird's nest fungi use the force of falling water drops to liberate the spores from cup-shaped fruiting bodies. Another strategy is seen in the stinkhorns, a group of fungi with lively colours and putrid odor that attract insects to disperse their spores.

Other Sexual Processes

Besides regular sexual reproduction with meiosis, certain fungi, such as those in the genera *Penicillium* and *Aspergillus*, may exchange genetic material via parasexual processes, initiated by anastomosis between hyphae and plasmogamy of fungal cells. The frequency and relative importance of parasexual events is unclear and may be lower than other sexual processes. It is known to play a role in intraspecific hybridization and is likely required for hybridization between species, which has been associated with major events in fungal evolution.

Evolution

In contrast to plants and animals, the early fossil record of the fungi is meager. Factors that likely contribute to the under-representation of fungal species among fossils include the nature of fungal fruiting bodies, which are soft, fleshy, and easily degradable tissues and the microscopic dimensions of most fungal structures, which therefore are not readily evident. Fungal fossils are difficult to distinguish from those of other microbes, and are most easily identified when they resemble extant fungi. Often recovered from a permineralized plant or animal host, these samples are typically studied by making thin-section preparations that can be examined with light microscopy or transmission electron microscopy. Compression fossils are studied by dissolving the surrounding matrix with acid and then using light or scanning electron microscopy to examine surface details.

The earliest fossils possessing features typical of fungi date to the Proterozoic eon, some 1430 million years ago (Ma); these multicellular benthic organisms had filamentous structures with septa, and were capable of anastomosis. Studies estimate the arrival of fungal organisms at about 760-1060 Ma on the basis of comparisons of the rate of evolution in closely related groups. For much of the Paleozoic Era (542-251 Ma), the fungi appear to have been aquatic and consisted of organisms similar to the extant Chytrids in having flagellum-bearing spores. The evolutionary adaptation from an aquatic to a terrestrial lifestyle necessitated a diversification of ecological strategies for obtaining nutrients, including parasitism, saprobism, and the development of mutualistic relationships such as mycorrhiza and lichenization. Studies suggest that the ancestral ecological state of the Ascomycota was saprobism, and that independent lichenization events have occurred multiple times.

The fungi probably colonized the land during the Cambrian (542-488.3 Ma), long before land plants. Fossilized hyphae and spores recovered from the Ordovician of Wisconsin (460 Ma) resemble modern-day Glomerales, and existed at a time when the land flora likely consisted of only non-vascular bryophyte-like plants. Prototaxites, which was probably a fungus or lichen, would have been the tallest organism of the late Silurian. Fungal fossils do not become common and uncontroversial until the early Devonian (416-359.2 Ma), when they are abundant in the Rhynie chert, mostly as Zygomycota and Chytridiomycota. At about this same time, approximately 400 Ma, the Ascomycota and Basidiomycota diverged, and all modern classes of fungi were present by the Late Carboniferous (Pennsylvanian, 318.1-299 Ma).

Lichen-like fossils have been found in the Doushantuo Formation in southern China dating back to 635-551 Ma. Lichens were a component of the early terrestrial ecosystems, and the estimated age of the oldest terrestrial lichen fossil is 400 Ma; this date corresponds to the age of the oldest known sporocarp fossil, a *Paleopyrenomycites* species found in the Rhynie Chert. The oldest fossil with microscopic features resembling modern-day basidiomycetes is *Palaeoancistrus*, found permineralized with a fern from the Pennsylvanian. Rare in the fossil record are the homobasidiomycetes (a taxon roughly equivalent to the mushroom-producing species of the agaricomycetes). Two amber-preserved specimens provide evidence that the earliest known mushroom-forming fungi (the extinct species *Archaeomarasmius legletti*) appeared during the mid-Cretaceous, 90 Ma.

Some time after the Permian-Triassic extinction event (251.4 Ma), a fungal spike (originally thought to be an extraordinary abundance of fungal spores in sediments) formed, suggesting that fungi were the dominant life form at this time, representing nearly 100% of the available fossil record for this period. However, the relative proportion of fungal spores relative to spores formed by algal species is difficult to assess, the spike did not appear worldwide, and in many places it did not fall on the Permian-Triassic boundary.

Although commonly included in botany curricula and textbooks, fungi are more closely related to animals than to plants and are placed with the animals in the monophyletic group of opisthokonts. Analyses using molecular phylogenetics support a monophyletic origin of the Fungi. The taxonomy of the Fungi is in a state of constant flux, especially due to recent research based on DNA comparisons. These current phylogenetic analyses often overturn classifications based on older and sometimes less discriminative methods based on morphological features and biological species concepts obtained from experimental matings.

There is no unique generally accepted system at the higher taxonomic levels and there are frequent name changes at every level, from species upwards. Efforts among researchers are now underway to establish and encourage usage of a unified and more consistent nomenclature. Fungal species can also have multiple scientific names depending on their life cycle and mode (sexual or asexual) of reproduction.

The 2007 classification of Kingdom Fungi is the result of a large-scale collaborative research effort involving dozens of mycologists and other scientists working on fungal taxonomy. It recognizes seven phyla, two of which—the Ascomycota and the Basidiomycota—are contained within a branch representing subkingdom Dikarya. The below cladogram depicts the major fungal taxa and their relationship to opisthokont and unikont organisms. The lengths of the branches in this tree are not proportional to evolutionary distances.

Taxonomic Groups

The major phyla (sometimes called divisions) of fungi have been classified mainly on the basis of characteristics of their sexual reproductive structures. Currently, seven phyla are proposed: Microsporidia, Chytridiomycota, Blastocladiomycota, Neocallimastigomycota, Glomeromycota, Ascomycota, and Basidiomycota.

Phylogenetic analysis has demonstrated that the Microsporidia, unicellular parasites of animals and protists, are fairly recent and highly derived endobiotic fungi (living within the tissue of another species). One 2006 study concludes that the Microsporidia are a sister group to the true fungi, that is, they are each other's closest evolutionary relative. Hibbett and colleagues suggest that this analysis does not clash with their classification of the Fungi, and although the

Microsporidia are elevated to phylum status, it is acknowledged that further analysis is required to clarify evolutionary relationships within this group.

The Chytridiomycota are commonly known as chytrids. These fungi are distributed worldwide. Chytrids produce zoospores that are capable of active movement through aqueous phases with a single flagellum, leading early taxonomists to classify them as protists. Molecular phylogenies, inferred from rRNA sequences in ribosomes, suggest that the Chytrids are a basal group divergent from the other fungal phyla, consisting of four major clades with suggestive evidence for paraphyly or possibly polyphyly.

The Blastocladiomycota were previously considered a taxonomic clade within the Chytridiomycota. Recent molecular data and ultrastructural characteristics, however, place the Blastocladiomycota as a sister clade to the Zygomycota, Glomeromycota, and Dikarya (Ascomycota and Basidiomycota). The blastocladiomycetes are saprotrophs, feeding on decomposing organic matter, and they are parasites of all eukaryotic groups. Unlike their close relatives, the chytrids, which mostly exhibit zygotic meiosis, the blastocladiomycetes undergo sporic meiosis.

The Neocallimastigomycota were earlier placed in the phylum Chytridomycota. Members of this small phylum are anaerobic organisms, living in the digestive system of larger herbivorous mammals and possibly in other terrestrial and aquatic environments. They lack mitochondria but contain hydrogenosomes of mitochondrial origin. As the related chrytrids, neocallimastigomycetes form zoospores that are posteriorly uniflagellate or polyflagellate.

Members of the Glomeromycota form arbuscular mycorrhizae, a form of symbiosis where fungal hyphae invade plant root cells and both species benefit from the resulting increased supply of nutrients. All known Glomeromycota species reproduce asexually. The symbiotic association between the Glomeromycota and plants is ancient, with evidence dating to 400 million years ago. Formerly part of the Zygomycota (commonly known as 'sugar' and 'pin' molds), the Glomeromycota were elevated to phylum status in 2001 and now replace the older phylum Zygomycota. Fungi that were placed in the Zygomycota are now being reassigned to the Glomeromycota, or the subphyla incertae sedis Mucoromycotina, Kickxellomycotina, the Zoopagomycotina and the Entomophthoromycotina. Some well-known examples of fungi formerly in the Zygomycota include black bread mold (*Rhizopus stolonifer*), and *Pilobolus* species, capable of ejecting spores several meters through the air. Medically relevant genera include *Mucor*, *Rhizomucor*, and *Rhizopus*.

The Ascomycota, commonly known as sac fungi or ascomycetes, constitute the largest taxonomic group within the Eumycota. These fungi form meiotic spores called ascospores, which are enclosed in a special sac-like structure called an ascus. This phylum includes morels, a few mushrooms and truffles, single-celled yeasts (e.g., of the genera *Saccharomyces*, *Kluyveromyces*, *Pichia*, and *Candida*), and many filamentous fungi living as saprotrophs, parasites, and mutualistic symbionts. Prominent and important genera of filamentous ascomycetes include *Aspergillus*, *Penicillium*, *Fusarium*, and *Claviceps*. Many ascomycete species have only been observed undergoing asexual reproduction (called anamorphic species), but analysis of molecular data has often been able to identify their closest teleomorphs in the Ascomycota. Because the products of meiosis are retained within the sac-like ascus, ascomycetes have been used for elucidating principles of genetics and heredity (e.g. *Neurospora crassa*).

Members of the Basidiomycota, commonly known as the club fungi or basidiomycetes, produce meiospores called basidiospores on club-like stalks called basidia. Most common mushrooms belong to this group, as well as rust and smut fungi, which are major pathogens of grains. Other important basidiomycetes include the maize pathogen *Ustilago maydis*, human commensal species of the genus *Malassezia*, and the opportunistic human pathogen, *Cryptococcus neoformans*.

Because of similarities in morphology and lifestyle, the slime molds (myxomycetes) and water molds (oomycetes) were formerly classified in the kingdom Fungi. Unlike true fungi the cell walls of these organisms contain cellulose and lack chitin. Myxomycetes are unikonts like fungi, but are grouped in the Amoebozoa. Oomycetes are diploid bikonts, grouped in the Chromalveolate kingdom. Neither water molds nor slime molds are closely related to the true fungi, and, therefore, taxonomists no longer group them in the kingdom Fungi. Nonetheless, studies of the oomycetes and myxomycetes are still often included in mycology textbooks and primary research literature.

The nucleariids, currently grouped in the Choanozoa, may be a sister group to the eumycete clade, and as such could be included in an expanded fungal kingdom.

Although often inconspicuous, fungi occur in every environment on Earth and play very important roles in most ecosystems. Along with bacteria, fungi are the major decomposers in most terrestrial (and some aquatic) ecosystems, and therefore play a critical role in biogeochemical cycles and in many food webs. As decomposers, they play an essential role in nutrient cycling, especially as saprotrophs and symbionts, degrading organic matter to inorganic molecules, which can then re-enter anabolic metabolic pathways in plants or other organisms.

Symbiosis

Many fungi have important symbiotic relationships with organisms from most if not all Kingdoms. These interactions can be mutualistic or antagonistic in nature, or in the case of commensal fungi are of no apparent benefit or detriment to the host.

With Plants

Mycorrhizal symbiosis between plants and fungi is one of the most well-known plant–fungus associations and is of significant importance for plant growth and persistence in many ecosystems; over 90 per cent of all plant species engage in mycorrhizal relationships with fungi and are dependent upon this relationship for survival.

The dark filaments are hyphae of the endophytic fungus *Neotyphodium coenophialum* in the intercellular spaces of tall fescue leaf sheath tissue.

The mycorrhizal symbiosis is ancient, dating to at least 400 million years ago. It often increases the plant's uptake of inorganic compounds, such as nitrate and phosphate from soils having low concentrations of these key plant nutrients. The fungal partners may also mediate plant-to-plant transfer of carbohydrates and other nutrients. Such mycorrhizal communities are called "common mycorrhizal networks".

A special case of mycorrhiza is myco-heterotrophy, whereby the plant parasitizes the fungus, obtaining all of its nutrients from its fungal symbiont. Some fungal species inhabit the tissues inside roots, stems, and leaves, in which case they are called endophytes. Similar to mycorrhiza, endophytic colonization by fungi may benefit both symbionts; for example, endophytes of grasses impart to their host increased resistance to herbivores and other environmental stresses and receive food and shelter from the plant in return. With algae and cyanobacteria.

Lichens are formed by a symbiotic relationship between algae or cyanobacteria (referred to in lichen terminology as "photobionts") and fungi (mostly various species of ascomycetes and a few basidiomycetes), in which individual photobiont cells are embedded in a tissue formed by the fungus.

Lichens occur in every ecosystem on all continents, play a key role in soil formation and the initiation of biological succession, and are the dominating life forms in extreme environments, including polar, alpine, and semiarid desert regions. They are able to grow on inhospitable surfaces, including bare soil, rocks, tree bark, wood, shells, barnacles and leaves. As in mycorrhizas, the photobiont provides sugars and other carbohydrates via photosynthesis, while the fungus provides minerals and water. The functions of both symbiotic organisms are so closely intertwined that they function almost as a single organism; in most cases the resulting organism differs greatly from the individual components. Lichenization is a common mode of nutrition; around 20 per cent of fungi—between 17,500 and 20,000 described species—are lichenized. Characteristics common to most lichens include obtaining organic carbon by photosynthesis, slow growth, small size, long life, long-lasting (seasonal) vegetative reproductive structures, mineral nutrition obtained largely from airborne sources, and greater tolerance of desiccation than most other photosynthetic organisms in the same habitat.

Many insects also engage in mutualistic relationships with fungi. Several groups of ants cultivate fungi in the order Agaricales as their primary food source, while ambrosia beetles cultivate various species of fungi in the bark of trees that they infest.

Similarly, females of several wood wasp species (genus *Sirex*) inject their eggs together with spores of the wood-rotting fungus *Amylostereum areolatum* into the sapwood of pine trees; the growth of the fungus provides ideal nutritional conditions for the development of the wasp larvae. Termites on the African savannah are also known to cultivate fungi, and yeasts of the genera *Candida* and *Lachancea* inhabit the gut of a wide range of insects, including neuropterans, beetles, and cockroaches; it is not known whether these fungi benefit their hosts.

Many fungi are parasites on plants, animals (including humans), and other fungi. Serious pathogens of many cultivated plants causing extensive damage and losses to agriculture and forestry include the rice blast fungus *Magnaporthe oryzae*, tree pathogens such as *Ophiostoma ulmi* and *Ophiostoma novo-ulmi* causing Dutch elm disease, and *Cryphonectria parasitica* responsible for chestnut blight, and plant pathogens in the genera *Fusarium, Ustilago, Alternaria,* and *Cochliobolus*. Some carnivorous fungi, like *Paecilomyces lilacinus*, are predators of nematodes, which they capture using an array of specialized structures such as constricting rings or adhesive nets.

Some fungi can cause serious diseases in humans, several of which may be fatal if untreated. These include aspergilloses, candidoses, coccidioidomycosis, cryptococcosis, histoplasmosis, mycetomas, and paracoccidioidomycosis. Furthermore, persons with immuno-deficiencies are particularly susceptible to disease by genera such as *Aspergillus*, *Candida*, *Cryptoccocus*, *Histoplasma*, and *Pneumocystis*. Other fungi can attack eyes, nails, hair, and especially skin, the so-called dermatophytic and keratinophilic fungi, and cause local infections such as ringworm and athlete's foot. Fungal spores are also a cause of allergies, and fungi from different taxonomic groups can evoke allergic reactions.

The human use of fungi for food preparation or preservation and other purposes is extensive and has a long history. Mushroom farming and mushroom gathering are large industries in many countries. The study of the historical uses and sociological impact of fungi is known as ethnomycology. Because of the capacity of this group to produce an enormous range of natural products with antimicrobial or other biological activities, many species have long been used or are being developed for industrial production of antibiotics, vitamins, and anti-cancer and cholesterol-lowering drugs.

More recently, methods have been developed for genetic engineering of fungi, enabling metabolic engineering of fungal species. For example, genetic modification of yeast species — which are easy to grow at fast rates in large fermentation vessels—has opened up ways of pharmaceutical production that are potentially more efficient than production by the original source organisms.

Drugs

Many species produce metabolites that are major sources of pharmacologically active drugs. Particularly important are the antibiotics, including the penicillins, a structurally related group of ß-lactam antibiotics that are synthesized from small peptides. Although naturally occurring penicillins such as penicillin G (produced by *Penicillium chrysogenum*) have a relatively narrow spectrum of biological activity, a wide range of other penicillins can be produced by chemical modification of the natural penicillins. Modern penicillins are semisynthetic compounds, obtained initially from fermentation cultures, but then structurally altered for specific desirable properties. Other antibiotics produced by fungi include: ciclosporin, commonly used as an immunosuppressant during transplant surgery; and fusidic acid, used to help control infection from methicillin-resistant *Staphylococcus aureus* bacteria.

Widespread use of these antibiotics for the treatment of bacterial diseases, such as tuberculosis, syphilis, leprosy, and many others began in the early 20th century and continues to play a major part in anti-bacterial chemotherapy. In nature, antibiotics of fungal or bacterial origin appear to play a dual role: at high concentrations they act as chemical defense against competition with other microorganisms in species-rich environments, such as the rhizosphere, and at low concentrations as quorum-sensing molecules for intra- or interspecies signaling.

Other drugs produced by fungi include griseofulvin isolated from *Penicillium griseofulvum*, used to treat fungal infections, and statins (HMG-CoA reductase inhibitors), used to inhibit cholesterol synthesis. Examples of statins found in fungi include mevastatin from *Penicillium citrinum* and lovastatin from *Aspergillus terreus* and the oyster mushroom.

Cultured Foods

Baker's yeast or *Saccharomyces cerevisiae*, a single-celled fungus, is used to make bread and other wheat-based products, such as pizza dough and dumplings. Yeast species of the genus *Saccharomyces* are also used to produce alcoholic beverages through fermentation. Shoyu koji mold (*Aspergillus oryzae*) is an essential ingredient in brewing Shoyu (soy sauce) and sake, and the preparation of miso, while *Rhizopus* species are used for making tempeh.

Several of these fungi are domesticated species that were bred or selected according to their capacity to ferment food without producing harmful mycotoxins (see below), which are produced by very closely related *Aspergilli*. Quorn, a meat substitute, is made from *Fusarium venenatum*.

Certain mushrooms enjoy usage as therapeutics in folk medicines, such as Traditional Chinese medicine. Notable medicinal mushrooms with a well-documented history of use include *Agaricus subrufescens*, *Ganoderma lucidum*, and *Cordyceps sinensis*. Research has identified compounds produced by these and other fungi that have inhibitory biological effects against viruses and cancer cells. Specific metabolites, such as polysaccharide-K, ergotamine, and ß-lactam antibiotics, are routinely used in clinical medicine.

The shiitake mushroom is a source of lentinan, a clinical drug approved for use in cancer treatments in several countries, including Japan. In Europe and Japan, polysaccharide-K (brand name Krestin), a chemical derived from *Trametes versicolour*, is an approved adjuvant for cancer therapy.

Edible and Poisonous Species

Edible mushrooms are well-known examples of fungi. Many are commercially raised, but others must be harvested from the wild. *Agaricus bisporus*, sold as button mushrooms when small or Portobello mushrooms when larger, is a commonly eaten species, used in salads, soups, and many other dishes. Many Asian fungi are commercially grown and have increased in popularity in the West.

They are often available fresh in grocery stores and markets, including straw mushrooms (*Volvariella volvacea*), oyster mushrooms (*Pleurotus ostreatus*), shiitakes (*Lentinula edodes*), and enokitake (*Flammulina* spp.).

There are many more mushroom species that are harvested from the wild for personal consumption or commercial sale. Milk mushrooms, morels, chanterelles, truffles, black trumpets, and *porcini* mushrooms (*Boletus edulis*) (also known as king boletes) demand a high price on the market. They are often used in gourmet dishes.

Certain types of cheeses require inoculation of milk curds with fungal species that impart a unique flavor and texture to the cheese. Examples include the blue colour in cheeses such as Stilton or Roquefort, which are made by inoculation with *Penicillium roqueforti*.

Molds used in cheese production are non-toxic and are thus safe for human consumption; however, mycotoxins (e.g., aflatoxins, roquefortine C, patulin, or others) may accumulate because of growth of other fungi during cheese ripening or storage. Many mushroom species are poisonous to humans, with toxicities ranging from slight digestive problems or allergic reactions as well as hallucinations to severe organ failures and death. Genera with mushrooms containing deadly toxins include *Conocybe*, *Galerina*, *Lepiota*, and most infamously, *Amanita*. The latter genus includes the destroying angel *(A. virosa)* and the death cap *(A. phalloides)*, the most common cause of deadly mushroom poisoning. The false morel (*Gyromitra esculenta*) is occasionally considered a delicacy when cooked, yet can be highly toxic when eaten raw. *Tricholoma equestre* was considered edible until being implicated in serious poisonings causing rhabdomyolysis.

Fly agaric mushrooms (*Amanita muscaria*) also cause occasional non-fatal poisonings, mostly as a result of ingestion for use as a recreational drug for its hallucinogenic properties. Historically, fly agaric was used by different peoples in Europe and Asia and its present usage for religious or shamanic purposes is reported from some ethnic groups such as the Koryak people of north-eastern Siberia.

As it is difficult to accurately identify a safe mushroom without proper training and knowledge, it is often advised to assume that a wild mushroom is poisonous and not to consume it.

Pest Control

In agriculture, fungi may be useful if they actively compete for nutrients and space with pathogenic microorganisms such as bacteria or other fungi via the competitive exclusion principle, or if they are parasites of these pathogens. For example, certain species may be used to eliminate or suppress the growth of harmful plant pathogens, such as insects, mites, weeds, nematodes and other fungi that cause diseases of important crop plants. This has generated strong interest in practical applications that use these fungi in the biological control of these agricultural pests. Entomopathogenic fungi can be used as biopesticides, as they actively kill insects. Examples that have been used as biological insecticides are *Beauveria bassiana*, *Metarhizium* spp, *Hirsutella* spp, *Paecilomyces* (*Isaria*) spp, and *Lecanicillium lecanii*. Endophytic fungi of grasses of the genus *Neotyphodium*, such as *N. coenophialum*, produce alkaloids that are toxic to a range of invertebrate and vertebrate herbivores.

These alkaloids protect grass plants from herbivory, but several endophyte alkaloids can poison grazing animals, such as cattle and sheep. Infecting cultivars of pasture or forage grasses with *Neotyphodium* endophytes is one approach being used in grass breeding programmes; the fungal strains are selected for producing only alkaloids that increase resistance to herbivores such as insects, while being non-toxic to livestock.

Certain fungi, in particular "white rot" fungi, can degrade insecticides, herbicides, pentachlorophenol, creosote, coal tars, and heavy fuels and turn them into carbon dioxide, water, and basic elements. Fungi have been shown to biomineralize uranium oxides, suggesting they may have application in the bioremediation of radioactively polluted sites.

Model Organisms

Several pivotal discoveries in biology were made by researchers using fungi as model organisms, that is, fungi that grow and sexually reproduce rapidly in the laboratory. For example, the one gene-one enzyme hypothesis was formulated by scientists who used the bread mold *Neurospora crassa* to test their biochemical theories. Other important model fungi are *Aspergillus nidulans* and the yeasts, *Saccaromyces cerevisiae* and *Schizosaccharomyces pombe*, each of which has a long history of use to investigate issues in eukaryotic cell biology and genetics, such as cell cycle regulation, chromatin structure, and gene regulation. Other fungal models have more recently emerged that each address specific biological questions relevant to medicine, plant pathology, and industrial uses; examples include *Candida albicans*, a dimorphic, opportunistic human pathogen, *Magnaporthe grisea*, a plant pathogen, and *Pichia pastoris*, a yeast widely used for eukaryotic protein expression.

Others

Fungi are used extensively to produce industrial chemicals like citric, gluconic, lactic, and malic acids, and industrial enzymes, such as lipases used in biological detergents, cellulases used in making cellulosic ethanol and stonewashed jeans, and amylases, invertases, proteases and xylanases. Several species, most notably *Psilocybin mushrooms* (colloquially known as *magic mushrooms*), are ingested for their psychedelic properties, both recreationally and religiously.

Mycotoxins

Many fungi produce biologically active compounds, several of which are toxic to animals or plants and are therefore called mycotoxins. Of particular relevance to humans are mycotoxins produced by molds causing food spoilage, and poisonous mushrooms. Particularly infamous are the lethal amatoxins in some *Amanita* mushrooms, and ergot alkaloids, which have a long history of causing serious epidemics of ergotism (St Anthony's Fire) in people consuming rye or related cereals contaminated with sclerotia of the ergot fungus, *Claviceps purpurea*. Other notable mycotoxins include the aflatoxins, which are insidious liver toxins and highly carcinogenic metabolites produced by certain *Aspergillus* species often growing in or on grains and nuts consumed by humans, ochratoxins, patulin, and trichothecenes (e.g., T-2 mycotoxin) and fumonisins, which have significant impact on human food supplies or animal livestock.

Mycotoxins are secondary metabolites (or natural products), and research has established the existence of biochemical pathways solely for the purpose of producing mycotoxins and other natural products in fungi. Mycotoxins may provide fitness benefits in terms of physiological adaptation, competition with other microbes and fungi, and protection from consumption (fungivory).

Mycology

Mycology is the branch of biology concerned with the systematic study of fungi, including their genetic and biochemical properties, their taxonomy, and their use to humans as a source of medicine, food, and psychotropic substances consumed for religious purposes, as well as their dangers, such as poisoning or infection. The field of phytopathology, the study of plant diseases, is closely related because many plant pathogens are fungi.

Use of fungi by humans dates back to prehistory; Ötzi the Iceman, a well-preserved mummy of a 5,300 year old Neolithic man found frozen in the Austrian Alps, carried two species of polypore mushrooms that may have been used as tinder (*Fomes fomentarius*), or for medicinal purposes (*Piptoporus betulinus*). Ancient peoples have used fungi as food sources–often unknowingly–for millennia, in the preparation of leavened bread and fermented juices. Some of the oldest written records contain references to the destruction of crops that were probably caused by pathogenic fungi.

History

Mycology is a relatively new science that became systematic after the development of the microscope in the 16th century. Although fungal spores were first observed by Giambattista della Porta in 1588, the seminal work in the development of mycology is considered to be the publication of Pier Antonio Micheli's 1729 work *Nova plantarum genera.*

Micheli not only observed spores, but showed that under the proper conditions, they could be induced into growing into the same species of fungi from which they originated.

Extending the use of the binomial system of nomenclature introduced by Carl Linnaeus in his *Species plantarum* (1753), the Dutch Christian Hendrik Persoon (1761-1836) established the first classification of mushrooms with such skill so as to be considered a founder of modern mycology. Later, Elias Magnus Fries (1794–1878) further elaborated the classification of fungi, using spore colour and various microscopic characteristics, methods still used by taxonomists today. Other notable early contributors to mycology in the 17th–19th and early 20th centuries include Miles Joseph Berkeley, August Carl Joseph Corda, Anton de Bary, the brothers Louis René and Charles Tulasne, Arthur H. R. Buller, Curtis G. Lloyd, and Pier Andrea Saccardo.

The 20th century has seen a modernization of mycology that has come from advances in biochemistry, genetics, molecular biology, and biotechnology. The use of DNA sequencing technologies and phylogenetic analysis has provided new insights into fungal relationships and biodiversity, and has challenged traditional morphology-based groupings in fungal taxonomy.

Yeast

Yeasts are eukaryotic micro-organisms classified in the kingdom Fungi, with 1,500 species currently described estimated to be only one per cent of all fungal species. Most reproduce asexually by budding, although a few do so by mitosis. Yeasts are unicellular, although some species with yeast forms may become multicellular through the formation of a string of connected budding cells known as pseudohyphae, or false hyphae, as seen in most molds. Yeast size can vary greatly depending on the species, typically measuring 3-4 μm in diameter, although some yeasts can reach over 40 μm.

The yeast species *Saccharomyces cerevisiae* has been used in baking and in fermenting alcoholic beverages for thousands of years. It is also extremely important as a model organism in modern cell biology research, and is one of the most thoroughly researched eukaryotic microorganisms. Researchers have used it to gather information about the biology of the eukaryotic cell and ultimately human biology. Other species of yeast, such as *Candida albicans*, are opportunistic pathogens and can cause infections in humans. Yeasts have recently been used to generate electricity in microbial fuel cells, and produce ethanol for the biofuel industry.

Yeasts do not form a single taxonomic or phylogenetic grouping. The term "yeast" is often taken as a synonym for *Saccharomyces cerevisiae*, but the phylogenetic diversity of yeasts is shown by their placement in two separate phyla, the Ascomycota and the Basidiomycota. The budding yeasts ("true yeasts") are classified in the order Saccharomycetales.

The word "yeast" comes to us from Old English *gist*, *gyst*, and from the Indo-European root *yes-*, meaning *boil*, *foam*, or *bubble*. Yeast microbes are probably one of the earliest domesticated organisms. People have used yeast for fermentation and baking throughout history. Archaeologists digging in Egyptian ruins found early grinding stones and baking chambers for yeasted bread, as well as drawings of 4,000-year-old bakeries and breweries. In 1680, the Dutch naturalist Anton van Leeuwenhoek first microscopically observed yeast, but at the time did not consider them to be living organisms, but rather globular structures. In 1857, French microbiologist Louis Pasteur proved in the paper "*Mémoire sur la fermentation alcoolique*" that alcoholic fermentation was conducted by living yeasts and not by a chemical catalyst. Pasteur showed that by bubbling oxygen into the yeast broth, cell growth could be increased, but fermentation was inhibited – an observation later called the "Pasteur effect".

By the late 18th century, two yeast strains used in brewing had been identified: *Saccharomyces cerevisiae*, so called top fermenting yeast, and *S. carlsbergensis*, bottom fermenting yeast. *S. cerevisiae* has been sold commercially by the Dutch for bread making since 1780; while around 1800, the Germans started producing *S. cerevisiae* in the form of cream. In 1825 a method was developed to remove the liquid so the yeast could be prepared as solid blocks. The industrial production of yeast blocks was enhanced by the introduction of the filter press in 1867. In 1872, Baron Max de Springer developed a manufacturing process to create granulated yeast, a technique that was used until the first World War. In the United States, naturally occurring airborne yeasts were used almost exclusively until commercial yeast was marketed at the Centennial Exposition in 1876 in Philadelphia, where Charles L. Fleischmann exhibited the product and a process to use it, as well as serving the resultant baked bread.

Yeasts are chemoorganotrophs, as they use organic compounds as a source of energy and do not require sunlight to grow. Carbon is obtained mostly from hexose sugars, such as glucose and fructose, or disaccharides such as sucrose and maltose. Some species can metabolize pentose sugars like ribose, alcohols, and organic acids. Yeast species either require oxygen for aerobic cellular respiration (obligate aerobes), or are anaerobic, but also have aerobic methods of energy production (facultative anaerobes). Unlike bacteria, there are no known yeast species that grow only anaerobically (obligate anaerobes). Yeasts grow best in a neutral or slightly acidic pH environment.

Yeasts vary in what temperature range they grow best. For example, *Leucosporidium frigidum* grows at -2 to 20 °C (28 to 68 °F), *Saccharomyces telluris* at 5 to 35 °C (41 to 95 °F) and *Candida slooffi* at 28 to 45 °C (82 to 113 °F). The cells can survive freezing under certain conditions, with viability decreasing over time.

Yeasts are generally grown in the laboratory on solid growth media or in liquid broths. Common media used for the cultivation of yeasts include potato dextrose agar (PDA) or potato dextrose broth, Wallerstein Laboratories nutrient (WLN) agar, yeast peptone dextrose agar (YPD), and yeast mould agar or broth (YM). Home brewers who cultivate yeast frequently use dried malt extract (DME) and agar as a solid growth medium. The antibiotic cycloheximide is sometimes added to yeast growth media to inhibit the growth of *Saccharomyces* yeasts and select for wild/indigenous yeast species. This will change the yeast process.

The appearance of a white, thready yeast, commonly known as kahm yeast, is often a byproduct of the lactofermentation (or pickling) of certain vegetables, usually the result of exposure to air. Although harmless, it can give pickled vegetables a bad flavour and so must be removed regularly during fermentation.

Yeasts are very common in the environment, but are usually isolated from sugar-rich material. Examples include naturally occurring yeasts on the skins of fruits and berries (such as grapes, apples or peaches), and exudates from plants (such as plant saps or cacti). Some yeasts are found in association with soil and insects. The ecological function and biodiversity of yeasts are relatively unknown compared to those of other microorganisms. Yeasts, including *Candida albicans, Rhodotorula rubra, Torulopsis* and *Trichosporon cutaneum,* have been found living in between people's toes as part of their skin flora. Yeasts are also present in the gut flora of mammals and some insects and even deep-sea environments host an array of yeasts.

An Indian study of seven bee species and nine plant species found 45 species from 16 genera colonise the nectaries of flowers and honey stomachs of bees. Most were members of the *Candida* genus; the most common species in honey stomachs was *Dekkera intermedia* and in flower nectaries, *Candida blankii*. Yeast colonising nectaries of the stinking hellebore have been found to raise the temperature of the flower, which may aid in attracting pollinators by increasing the evaporation of volatile organic compounds. A black yeast has been recorded as a partner in a complex relationship between ants, their mutualistic fungus, a fungal parasite of the fungus and a bacterium that kills the parasite. The yeast have a negative effect on the bacteria that normally produce antibiotics to kill the parasite and so may affect the ants' health by allowing the parasite to spread.

Yeasts have asexual and sexual reproductive cycles. The most common mode of vegetative growth in yeast is asexual reproduction by budding. Here a small bud, or daughter cell, is formed on the parent cell. The nucleus of the parent cell splits into a daughter nucleus and migrates into the daughter cell. The bud continues to grow until it separates from the parent cell, forming a new cell. Some yeasts, including *Schizosaccharomyces pombe*, reproduce by mitosis instead of budding.

Under high stress conditions, haploid cells will generally die; under the same conditions, however, diploid cells can undergo sporulation, entering sexual reproduction (meiosis) and producing a variety of haploid spores, which can go on to mate (conjugate), reforming the diploid.

The useful physiological properties of yeast have led to their use in the field of biotechnology. Fermentation of sugars by yeast is the oldest and largest application of this technology. Many types of yeasts are used for making many foods: baker's yeast in bread production; brewer's yeast in beer fermentation; yeast in wine fermentation and for xylitol production. So-called red rice yeast is actually a mold, *Monascus purpureus*. Yeasts include some of the most widely used model organisms for genetics and cell biology.

Alcoholic Beverages

Alcoholic beverages are defined as beverages that contain ethanol (C_2H_5OH). This ethanol is almost always produced by fermentation – the metabolism of carbohydrates by certain species of yeast under anaerobic or low-oxygen conditions. Beverages such as wine, beer, or distilled spirits all use yeast at some stage of their production. A distilled beverage is a beverage containing ethanol that has been purified by distillation. Carbohydrate-containing plant material is fermented by yeast, producing a dilute solution of ethanol in the process. Spirits such as whiskey and rum are prepared by distilling these dilute solutions of ethanol. Components other than ethanol are collected in the condensate, including water, esters, and other alcohols, which account for the flavour of the beverage.

Brewing yeasts may be classed as "top cropping" (or "top fermenting") and "bottom cropping" (or "bottom-fermenting"). Top cropping yeasts are so called because they form a foam at the top of the wort during fermentation. An example of a top cropping yeast is *Saccharomyces cerevisiae*, sometimes called an "ale yeast". Bottom cropping yeasts are typically used to produce lager-type beers, though they can also produce ale-type beers. These yeasts ferment more sugars, creating a dryer beer, and grow well at low temperatures. An example of bottom cropping yeast is *Saccharomyces pastorianus*, formerly known as *S. carlsbergensis*.

The most common top cropping brewer's yeast, *S. cerevisiae*, is the same species as the common baking yeast. However, baking and brewing yeasts typically belong to different strains, cultivated to favour different characteristics: baking yeast strains are more aggressive, to carbonate dough in the shortest amount of time possible; brewing yeast strains act slower, but tend to produce fewer off-flavours and tolerate higher alcohol concentrations (with some strains, up to 22%).

Brettanomyces is a genus of wild yeast important in brewing lambic, a beer produced not by the deliberate addition of brewer's yeasts, but by spontaneous fermentation by wild yeasts and bacteria. *Brettanomyces lambicus, B. bruxellensis* and *B. claussenii* are native to the Senne Valley region of Belgium, where lambic beer is produced.

Yeast is used in winemaking, where it converts the sugars present in grape juice (must) into ethanol. Yeast is normally already present on grape skins (the white powder called "the bloom"). Fermentation can be done with this endogenous "wild yeast," but this procedure gives unpredictable results, which depend upon the exact types of yeast species present. For this reason, a pure yeast culture is usually added to the must; this yeast quickly dominates the fermentation. The wild yeasts are repressed, which ensures a reliable and predictable fermentation.

Most added wine yeasts are strains of *S. cerevisiae*, though not all strains of the species are suitable. Different *S. cerevisiae* yeast strains have differing physiological and fermentative properties, therefore the actual strain of yeast selected can have a direct impact on the finished wine. Significant research has been undertaken into the development of novel wine yeast strains that produce atypical flavour profiles or increased complexity in wines.

The growth of some yeasts, such as *Zygosaccharomyces* and *Brettanomyces*, in wine can result in wine faults and subsequent spoilage. *Brettanomyces* produces an array of metabolites when growing in wine, some of which are volatile phenolic compounds. Together, these compounds are often referred to as "*Brettanomyces* character", and are often described as "antiseptic" or "barnyard" type aromas. *Brettanomyces* is a significant contributor to wine faults within the wine industry.

Researchers from University of British Columbia, Canada, have found a new strain of yeast that has reduced amines. The amines in red wine and Chardonnay produce off-flavors and cause headaches and hypertension in some people. About 30 per cent of people are sensitive to biogenic amines, such as histamines.

Yeast, most commonly *S. cerevisiae*, is used in baking as a leavening agent, where it converts the fermentable sugars present in dough into the gas carbon dioxide. This causes the dough to expand or rise as gas forms pockets or bubbles. When the dough is baked, the yeast dies and the air pockets "set", giving the baked product a soft and spongy texture. The use of potatoes, water from potato boiling, eggs, or sugar in a bread dough accelerates the growth of yeasts. Most yeasts used in baking are of the same species common in alcoholic fermentation. Additionally, *Saccharomyces exiguus* (also known as *S. minor*), a wild yeast found on plants, fruits, and grains, is occasionally used for baking. Sugar and vinegar provide the best conditions for yeast to ferment. In bread making, the yeast initially respires aerobically, producing carbon dioxide and water. When the oxygen is depleted, anaerobic respiration begins, producing ethanol as a waste product; however, this evaporates during baking.

It is not known when yeast was first used to bake bread. The first records that show this use came from Ancient Egypt.

Researchers speculate a mixture of flour meal and water was left longer than usual on a warm day and the yeasts that occur in natural contaminants of the flour caused it to ferment before baking. The resulting bread would have been lighter and tastier than the normal flat, hard cake.

Today, there are several retailers of baker's yeast; one of the best-known in North America is Fleischmann's Yeast, which was developed in 1868. During World War II, Fleischmann's developed a granulated active dry yeast, which did not require refrigeration and had a longer shelf life than fresh yeast. The company created yeast that would rise twice as fast, reducing baking time. Baker's yeast is also sold as a fresh yeast compressed into a square "cake". This form perishes quickly, and must therefore be used soon after production. A weak solution of water and sugar can be used to determine if yeast is expired. In the solution, active yeast will foam and bubble as it ferments the sugar into ethanol and carbon dioxide. Some recipes refer to this as proofing the yeast as it "proves" (tests) the viability of the yeast before the other ingredients are added. When using a sourdough starter, flour and water are added instead of sugar; this is referred to as proofing the sponge.

When yeast is used for making bread, it is mixed with flour, salt, and warm water or milk. The dough is kneaded until it is smooth, and then left to rise, sometimes until it has doubled in size. Some bread doughs are knocked back after one rising and left to rise again. A longer rising time gives a better flavour, but the yeast can fail to raise the bread in the final stages if it is left for too long initially. The dough is then shaped into loaves, left to rise until it is the correct size, and then baked. Dried yeast is usually specified for use in a bread machine; however, a (wet) sourdough starter can also work.

Bioremediation

Some yeasts can find potential application in the field of bioremediation. One such yeast, *Yarrowia lipolytica,* is known to degrade palm oil mill effluent, TNT (an explosive material), and other hydrocarbons, such as alkanes, fatty acids, fats and oils. It can also tolerate high concentrations of salt and heavy metals, and is being investigated for its potential as a heavy metal biosorbent.

The ability of yeast to convert sugar into ethanol has been harnessed by the biotechnology industry to produce ethanol fuel. The process starts by milling a feedstock, such as sugar cane, field corn, or other cereal grains, and then adding dilute sulfuric acid, or fungal alpha amylase enzymes, to break down the starches into complex sugars. A glucoamylase is then added to break the complex sugars down into simple sugars. After this, yeasts are added to convert the simple sugars to ethanol, which is then distilled off to obtain ethanol up to 96 per cent in concentration.

Saccharomyces yeasts have been genetically engineered to ferment xylose, one of the major fermentable sugars present in cellulosic biomasses, such as agriculture residues, paper wastes, and wood chips. Such a development means ethanol can be efficiently produced from more inexpensive feedstocks, making cellulosic ethanol fuel a more competitively priced alternative to gasoline fuels.

Root beer and other sweet carbonated beverages can be produced using the same methods as beer, except the fermentation is stopped sooner, producing carbon dioxide, but only trace amounts of alcohol, and a significant amount of sugar is left in the drink. *Kvass*, a fermented drink made from rye, is popular in Eastern Europe; it has a recognizable, but low alcoholic content. Yeast in symbiosis with acetic acid bacteria is used in the preparation of *kombucha*, a fermented sweetened tea. Species of yeast found in the tea can vary, and may include: *Brettanomyces bruxellensis*, *Candida stellata*, *Schizosaccharomyces pombe*, *Torulaspora delbrueckii* and *Zygosaccharomyces bailii*. *Kombucha* is a popular beverage in Eastern Europe and some former Soviet republics under the name *chajnyj grib* , which means "tea mushroom". *Kefir* and *kumis* are made by fermenting milk with yeast and bacteria.

Yeast is used in nutritional supplements popular with vegans and the health conscious, where it is often referred to as "nutritional yeast". It is a deactivated yeast, usually *S. cerevisiae*. It is an excellent source of protein and vitamins, especially the B-complex vitamins, whose functions are related to metabolism, as well as other minerals and cofactors required for growth. It is also naturally low in fat and sodium. Some brands of nutritional yeast, though not all, are fortified with vitamin B_{12}, which is produced separately by bacteria. Nutritional yeast, though it has a similar appearance to brewer's yeast, is very different and has a very different taste. Brewer's yeast is a good source of B-complex vitamins but, contrary to some claims, it contains little or no vitamin B_{12}.

Nutritional yeast has a nutty, cheesy flavor which makes it popular as an ingredient in cheese substitutes. It is often used by vegans in place of Parmesan cheese. Another popular use is as a topping for popcorn. It can also be used in mashed and fried potatoes, as well as in scrambled eggs. It comes in the form of flakes, or as a yellow powder similar in texture to cornmeal, and can be found in the bulk aisle of most natural food stores. In Australia, it is sometimes sold as "savory yeast flakes". Though "nutritional yeast" usually refers to commercial products, inadequately fed prisoners have used "home-grown" yeast to prevent vitamin deficiency.

Probiotics

Some probiotic supplements use the yeast *S. boulardii* to maintain and restore the natural flora in the gastrointestinal tract. *S. boulardii* has been shown to reduce the symptoms of acute diarrhea in children, prevent reinfection of *Clostridium difficile*, reduce bowel movements in diarrhea-predominant IBS patients, and reduce the incidence of antibiotic, traveller's, and HIV/AIDS associated diarrheas.

Aquarium Hobby

Yeast is often used by aquarium hobbyists to generate carbon dioxide (CO_2) to nourish plants in planted aquariums. A homemade setup is widely used as a cheap and simple alternative to pressurized CO_2 systems. While not as effective as these, the homemade setup is considerably cheaper for less demanding hobbyists.

There are several recipes for homemade CO_2, but they are variations of the basic recipe: Baker's yeast, with sugar, baking soda and water, are added to a plastic bottle. A few drops of vegetable oil at the start reduces surface tension and speeds the release of CO_2. This will produce CO_2 for about 2 or 3 weeks; the use of a bubble counter determines production. The CO_2 is injected in the aquarium via a narrow hose and released through a diffuser that helps dissolve the gas in the water. The CO_2 is used by plants in the photosynthesis process.

Several yeasts, particularly *S. cerevisiae,* have been widely used in genetics and cell biology. This is largely because *S. cerevisiae* is a simple eukaryotic cell, serving as a model for all eukaryotes, including humans for the study of fundamental cellular processes such as the cell cycle, DNA replication, recombination, cell division and metabolism. Also, yeasts are easily manipulated and cultured in the laboratory, which has allowed for the development of powerful standard techniques, such as yeast two-hybrid, synthetic genetic array analysis and tetrad analysis. Many proteins important in human biology were first discovered by studying their homologues in yeast; these proteins include cell cycle proteins, signaling proteins, and protein-processing enzymes.

On 24 April 1996 *S. cerevisiae* was announced to be the first eukaryote to have its genome, consisting of 12 million base pairs, fully sequenced as part of the Genome project. At the time, it was the most complex organism to have its full genome sequenced, and took seven years and the involvement of more than 100 laboratories to accomplish. The second yeast species to have its genome sequenced was *Schizosaccharomyces pombe,* which was completed in 2002. It was the sixth eukaryotic genome sequenced and consists of 13.8 million base pairs.

Yeast extract is the common name for various forms of processed yeast products that are used as food additives or flavours. They are often used in the same way that monosodium glutamate (MSG) is used, and like MSG, often contain free glutamic acid. The general method for making yeast extract for food products such as Vegemite and Marmite on a commercial scale is to add salt to a suspension of yeast making the solution hypertonic, which leads to the cells shrivelling up. This triggers *autolysis*, where the yeast's digestive enzymes break their own proteins down into simpler compounds, a process of self-destruction. The dying yeast cells are then heated to complete their breakdown, after which the husks (yeast with thick cell walls which would give poor texture) are separated. Yeast autolysates are used in Vegemite and Promite (Australia); Marmite, Bovril and Oxo (the United Kingdom, Republic of Ireland and South Africa); and Cenovis (Switzerland).

Some species of yeast are opportunistic pathogens where they can cause infection in people with compromised immune systems.

Cryptococcus neoformans is a significant pathogen of immunocompromised people causing the disease termed cryptococcosis. This disease occurs in about 7-9 per cent of AIDS patients in the USA, and a slightly smaller percentage (3-6%) in western Europe. The cells of the yeast are surrounded by a rigid polysaccharide capsule, which helps to prevent them from being recognised and engulfed by white blood cells in the human body.

Yeasts of the *Candida* genus are another group of opportunistic pathogens which causes oral and vaginal infections in humans, known as candidiasis. *Candida* is commonly found as a commensal yeast in the mucus membranes of humans and other warm-blooded animals. However, sometimes these same strains can become pathogenic. Here the yeast cells sprout a hyphal outgrowth, which locally penetrates the mucosal membrane, causing irritation and shedding of the tissues. The pathogenic yeasts of candidiasis in probable descending order of virulence for humans are: *C. albicans, C. tropicalis, C. stellatoidea, C. glabrata, C. krusei, C. parapsilosis, C. guilliermondii, C. viswanathii, C. lusitaniae* and *Rhodotorula mucilaginosa. Candida glabrata* is the second most common *Candida* pathogen after *C. albicans,* causing infections of the urogenital tract, and of the bloodstream (candidemia).

Food Spoilage

Yeasts are able to grow in foods with a low pH, (5.0 or lower) and in the presence of sugars, organic acids and other easily metabolized carbon sources. During their growth, yeasts metabolize some food components and produce metabolic end products. This causes the physical, chemical, and sensible properties of a food to change, and the food is spoiled. The growth of yeast within food products is often seen on their surface, as in cheeses or meats, or by the fermentation of sugars in beverages, such as juices, and semi-liquid products, such as syrups and jams. The yeast of the *Zygosaccharomyces* genus have had a long history as a spoilage yeast within the food industry. This is mainly due to the fact that these species can grow in the presence of high sucrose, ethanol, acetic acid, sorbic acid, benzoic acid, and sulfur dioxide concentrations, representing some of the commonly used food preservation methods. Methylene blue is used to test for the presence of live yeast cells.

Chapter 4: Ascocarp

An ascocarp, or ascoma (plural: ascomata), is the fruiting body (sporocarp) of an ascomycete fungus. It consists of very tightly interwoven hyphae and may contain millions of asci, each of which typically contains eight ascospores. Ascocarps are most commonly bowl-shaped, but may take on a number of other forms.

Classification of Ascocarps

The ascocarp is classified according to its placement (in ways not fundamental to the basic taxonomy). It is called epigeous if it grows above ground, as with the morels, whilst underground ascocarps, such as truffles are hypogeous.

The form of the hymenium is divided into the following types (which *are* important for classification). Apothecia can be relatively large and fleshy, whereas the others are microscopic — about the size of flecks of ground pepper.

Apothecium: here the ascocarp is open above like a cup. The fertile layer is free, so that many spores can be dispersed simultaneously. The morel, *Morchella*, an edible ascocarp, not a mushroom, favored by gourmets, is a mass of apothecia fused together in a single large structure or cap. The genera *Helvella* and *Gyromitra* are similar.

Cleistothecium: in this case the ascocarp is round with the hymenium enclosed, so the spores do not automatically get released, and fungi with cleistothecia have had to develop new strategies to disseminate their spores. The truffles, for instance, have solved this problem by attracting animals such as wild boars, which break open the tasty ascocarps and spread the spores over a wide area. Cleistothecia are found mostly in fungi that have little room available for their ascocarps, for instance those that live under tree bark, or underground like truffles. Also, the dermatophyte *Arthroderma* forms cleistothecia.

Perithecium: this has the shape of a skittle or a ball. Its distinguishing feature is that on top it has a small pore, the ostiole, through which the spores are released one by one when ripe (in contrast to apothecia where they are released together). Perithecia are found for example on *Xylaria* (Dead Man's Fingers, Candle Snuff) and *Nectria*.

Pseudothecium: this is similar to a perithecium, but the asci are not regularly organised into a hymenium and they are bitunicate, having a double wall that expands when it takes up water and shoots the enclosed spores out suddenly to disperse them. Example species are Apple scab (*Venturia inaequalis*) and the horse chestnut disease *Guignardia aesculi*.

Basidiocarp

In fungi, a basidiocarp, basidiome or basidioma (plural: basidiomata), is the sporocarp of a basidiomycete, the multicellular structure on which the spore-producing hymenium is borne. Basidiocarps are characteristic of the hymenomycetes; rusts and smuts do not produce such structures. As with other sporocarps, epigeous (above-ground) basidiocarps that are visible to the naked eye (especially those with a more or less agaricoid morphology) are commonly referred to as mushrooms, while hypogeous (underground) basidiocarps are usually called false truffles.

All basidiocarps serve as the structure on which the hymenium is produced. Basidia are found on the surface of the hymenium, and the basidia ultimately produce spores. In its simplest form, a basidiocarp consists of an undifferentiated fruiting structure with a hymenium on the surface; such a structure is characteristic of many simple jelly and club fungi. In more complex basidiocarps, there is differentiation into a stipe, a pileus, and/or various types of hymenophores.

Basidiocarps are classified into various types of growth forms based on the degree of differentiation into a stipe, pileus, and hymenophore, as well as the type of hymenophore, if present.

Growth forms include:

- *Jelly fungus* – fruiting body is an undifferentiated mass of jelly-like tissue.
- *Club fungus* and *coral fungus* – erect fruiting body without a distinct stipe and pileus, either unbranched (club fungus) or profusely branched (coral fungus).
- *Polypore* – fruiting body is hard, woody, and perennial, and often grows shelf-like on the side of a tree or log. Polypores have a pileus, and usually (but not always) tubes and no stipe.
- *Cantharelloid fungus* – fruiting body with shallow fold-like lamellae running over most of the lower surface of the fruiting body and not much differentiation between the stipe and pileus.
- *Tooth fungus* or *"hydnoid fungus"* – fruiting body with tooth-like hymenophores.
- *Gasteromycete* or *"gastroid fungus"* – fruiting body has a ball-like shape and in which the hymenophore has become entirely enclosed on the inside of the fruiting body.
- *False truffle* – like a gasteromycete, however, but with a hypogeous (underground) fruiting body.
- *Secotioid fungus* – like a gasteromycete, but with stipe. Though to be an evolutionarily intermediate stage between a gasteromycete and an agaric.
- *Agaric* or *"agaricoid fungus"* – fruiting body with a pileus, lamellae, and (usually) a stipe.

- *Bolete* – fruiting body with a pileus, a stipe, and tubes.

Basic divisions of Agaricomycotina were formerly based entirely upon the growth form of the mushroom. Molecular phylogenetic investigation (as well as supporting evidence from micromorphology and chemotaxonomy) has since demonstrated that similar types of basidiomycete growth form are often examples of convergent evolution and do not always reflect a close relationship between different groups of fungi. For example, agarics have arisen independently in the Agaricales, the Boletales, the Russulales, and other groups, while secotioid fungi and false truffles have arisen independently many times just within the Agaricales.

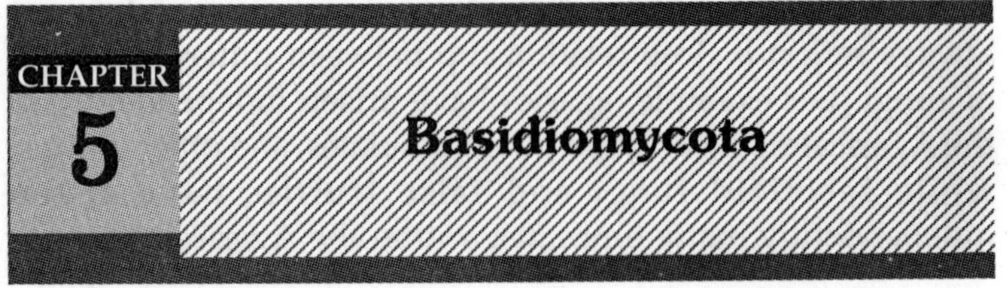

CHAPTER 5 Basidiomycota

Basidiomycota is one of two large phyla that, together with the Ascomycota, comprise the subkingdom Dikarya (often referred to as the "higher fungi") within the Kingdom Fungi. More specifically the Basidiomycota include mushrooms, puffballs, stinkhorns, bracket fungi, other polypores, jelly fungi, boletes, chanterelles, earth stars, smuts, bunts, rusts, mirror yeasts, and the human pathogenic yeast *Cryptococcus*. Basically, Basidiomycota are filamentous fungi composed of hyphae (except for those forming yeasts), and reproducing sexually via the formation of specialized club-shaped end cells called basidia that normally bear external meiospores (usually four). These specialized spores are called basidiospores. However, some Basidiomycota reproduce asexually, and may or may not also reproduce sexually. Asexually reproducing Basidiomycota can be recognized as members of this phylum by gross similarity to others, by the formation of a distinctive anatomical feature, cell wall components, and definitively by phylogenetic molecular analysis of DNA sequence data.

The most recent classification adopted by a coalition of 67 mycologists recognizes three subphyla (Pucciniomycotina, Ustilaginomycotina, Agaricomycotina) and two other class level taxa (Wallemiomycetes, Entorrhizomycetes) outside of these, among the Basidiomycota. As now classified, the subphyla join and also cut across various obsolete taxonomic groups (see below) previously commonly used to describe various Basidiomycota. According to a 2008 estimate, Basidiomycota comprises three subphyla (including six unassigned classes) 16 classes, 52 orders, 177 families, 1,589 genera, and 31,515 species.

The Basidiomycota had traditionally been divided into two obsolete classes, the Homobasidiomycetes (including true mushrooms); and the Heterobasidiomycetes (the jelly, rust and smut fungi). Previously the entire Basidiomycota were called Basidiomycetes, an invalid class level name coined in 1959 as a counterpart to the Ascomycetes, when neither of these taxa were recognized as phyla. The terms basidiomycetes and ascomycetes are frequently used loosely to refer to Basidiomycota and Ascomycota. They are often abbreviated to "basidios" and "ascos" as mycological slang.

Agaricomycotina

The Agaricomycotina include what had previously been called the Hymenomycetes (an obsolete morphological based class of Basidiomycota that formed hymenial layers on their fruitbodies), the Gasteromycetes (another obsolete class that included species mostly lacking hymenia and mostly forming spores in enclosed fruitbodies), as well as most of the jelly fungi. The three classes in the Agaricomycotina are the Agaricomycetes, the Dacrymycetes, and the Tremellomycetes.

Pucciniomycotina

The Pucciniomycotina includes the rust fungi, the insect parasitic/symbiotic genus *Septobasidium,* a former group of smut fungi (in the Microbotryomycetes, which includes mirror yeasts), and a mixture of odd, infrequently seen or seldom recognized fungi, often parasitic on plants. The eight classes in the Pucciniomycotina are Agaricostilbomycetes, Atractiellomycetes, Classiculomycetes, Cryptomycocolacomycetes, Cystobasidiomycetes, Microbotryomycetes, Mixiomycetes, and Pucciniomycetes.

Ustilaginomycotina

The Ustilaginomycotina are most (but not all) of the former smut fungi and along with the Exobasidiales. The classes of the Ustilaginomycotina are the Exobasidiomycetes, the Entorrhizomycetes, and the Ustilaginomycetes.

The class Wallemiomycetes is not yet placed in a subphylum.

Typical life-cycle

Unlike higher animals and plants which have readily recognizable male and female counterparts, Basidiomycota (except for the Rust (Pucciniales)) tend to have mutually indistinguishable, compatible haploids which are usually mycelia being composed of filamentous hyphae. Typically haploid Basidiomycota mycelia fuse via plasmogamy and then the compatible nuclei migrate into each other's mycelia and pair up with the resident nuclei. Karyogamy is delayed, so that the compatible nuclei remain in pairs, called a dikaryon. The hyphae are then said to be dikaryotic. Conversely, the haploid mycelia are called monokaryons. Often, the dikaryotic mycelium is more vigorous than the individual monokaryotic mycelia, and proceeds to take over the substrate in which they are growing. The dikaryons can be long-lived, lasting years, decades, or centuries. *The monokaryons are neither male nor female.* They have either a bipolar (unifactorial) or a tetrapolar (bifactorial) mating system. This results in the fact that following meiosis, the resulting haploid basidiospores and resultant monokaryons, have nuclei that are compatible with 50 per cent (if bipolar) or 25 per cent (if tetrapolar) of their sister basidiospores (and their resultant monokaryons) because the mating genes must differ for them to be compatible. However, there are many variations of these genes in the population, and therefore, over 90 per cent of monokaryons are compatible with each other. It is as if there were multiple sexes.

The maintenance of the dikaryotic status in dikaryons in many Basidiomycota is facilitated by the formation of clamp connections that physically appear to help coordinate and re-establish pairs of compatible nuclei following synchronous mitotic nuclear divisions. Variations are frequent and multiple. In a typical Basidiomycota lifecycle the long lasting dikaryons periodically (seasonally or occasionally) produce basidia, the specialized usually club-shaped end cells, in which a pair of compatible nuclei fuse (karyogamy) to form a diploid cell. Meiosis follows shortly with the production of four haploid nuclei that migrate into four external, usually apical basidiospores. Variations occur, however. Typically the basidiospores are ballistic, hence they are sometimes also called ballistospores. In most species, the basidiospores disperse and each can start a new haploid mycelium, continuing the lifecycle. Basidia are microscopic but they are often produced on or in multicelled large fructifications called basidiocarps or basidiomes, or fruitbodies), variously called mushrooms, puffballs, etc. Ballistic basidiospores are formed on sterigmata which are tapered spine-like projections on basidia, and are typically curved, like the horns of a bull. In some Basidiomycota the spores are not ballistic, and the sterigmata may be straight, reduced to stubbs, or absent. The basidiospores of these non-ballistosporic basidia may either bud off, or be released via dissolution or disintegration of the basidia.

Schematic of a typical basidiocarp, the dipoid reproductive structure of a basidiomycete, showing fruiting body, hymenium and basidia.

In summary, meiosis takes place in a diploid basidium. Each one of the four haploid nuclei migrates into its own basidiospore. The basidiospores are ballistically discharged and start new haploid mycelia called monokaryons. There are no males or females, rather there are compatible thalli with multiple compatibility factors. Plasmogamy between compatible individuals leads to delayed karyogamy leading to establishment of a dikaryon. The dikaryon is long lasting but ultimately gives rise to either fruitbodies with basidia or directly to basidia without fruitbodies. The paired dikaryon in the basidium fuse (i.e. karyogamy takes place). The diploid basidium begins the cycle again.

Variations in Life-cycles

Many variations occur. Some are self compatible and spontaneously form dikaryons without a separate compatible thallus being involved. These fungi are said to be *homothallic*, versus the normal *heterothallic* species with mating types. Others are secondarily homothallic, in that two compatible nuclei following meiosis migrate into each basidiospore, which is then dispersed as a pre-existing dikaryon. Often such species form only two spores per basidium, but that too varies. Following meiosis, mitotic divisions can occur in the basidium. Multiple numbers of basidiospores can result, including odd numbers via degeneration of nuclei, or pairing up of nuclei, or lack of migration of nuclei.

For example, the chanterelle genus *Craterellus* often has 6-spored basidia, while some corticioid *Sistotrema* species can have 2-, 4-, 6-, or 8-spored basidia, and the cultivated button mushroom, *Agaricus bisporus*. can have 1-, 2-, 3- or 4-spored basidia under some circumstances. Occasionally monokaryons of some taxa can form morphologically fully formed basidiomes and anatomically correct basidia and ballistic basidiospores in the absence of dikaryon formation, diploid nuclei, and meiosis. A rare few number of taxa have extended diploid life-cycles, but can be common species. Examples exist in the mushroom genera *Armillaria* and *Xerula*, both in the Physalacriaceae.

Occasionally basidiospores are not formed and parts of the "basidia" act as the dispersal agents, e.g. the peculiar mycoparasitic jelly fungus, *Tetragoniomyces* or the entire "basidium" acts as a "spore", e.g. in some false puffballs (*Scleroderma*). In the human pathogenic genus *Cryptococcus*, 4 nuclei following meiosis remain in the basidium but continually divide mitotically, each nucleus migrating into synchronously forming nonballistic basidiospores that are then pushed upwards by another set forming below them, resulting in 4 parallel chains of dry "basidiospores".

Other variations occur, some as standard life-cycles (that themselves have variations within variations) within specific orders.

Rusts

Rusts (Pucciniales, previously known as Uredinales) at their greatest complexity produce five different types of spores on two different hosts in two unrelated host families. Such rusts are heteroecious (requiring 2 hosts) and macrocyclic (producing all 5 spores types). Wheat stem rust is an example. By convention the stages and spore states are numbered by Roman numerals. Typically, basidiospores infect host one, the mycelium forms pycnidia, called spermagonia, which are miniature, flask-shaped, hollow, submicroscopic bodies embedded in host tissue (such as a leaf).

This stage, numbered "0", produces single-celled, minute spores that ooze out in a sweet liquid and that act as nonmotile spermatia, and also protruding receptive hyphae. Insects and probably other vectors such as rain carry the spermatia from spermagonia to spermagonia, cross inoculating the mating types. Neither thallus is male or female. Once crossed, the dikaryons are established and a second spore stage is formed, numbered "I" and called aecia, which form dikaryotic aeciospores in dry chains in inverted cup-shaped bodies embedded in host tissue. These aeciospores then infect the second host genus and cannot infect the host on which they are formed (in macrocyclic rusts). On the second host a repeating spore stage is formed, numbered "II", the urediospores in dry pustules called uredinia. Urediospores are dikaryotic and can infect the same host that produced them.

They repeatedly infect this host over the growing season. At the end of the season, a fourth spore type, the teliospore, is formed. It is thicker-walled and serves to overwinter or to survive other harsh conditions. It does not continue the infection process, rather it remains dormant for a period and then germinates to form basidia (stage "IV"), sometimes called a promycelium. In the Pucciniales, the basidia are cylindrical and become 3-septate after meiosis, with each of the 4 cells bearing one basidiospore each. The basidospores disperse and start the infection process on host 1 again. Autoecious rusts complete their life-cycles on one host instead of two, and microcyclic rusts cut out one or more stages.

Smuts

The characteristic part of the life-cycle of smuts is the thick-walled, often darkly pigmented, ornate, teliospore that serves to survive harsh conditions such as overwintering and also serves to help disperse the fungus as dry diaspores. The teliospores are initially dikaryotic but become diploid via karyogamy. Meiosis takes place at the time of germination. A promycelim is formed that consists to a short hypha (equated to a basidium). In some smuts such as *Ustilago maydis* the nuclei migrate into the promycelium that becomes septate, and haploid yeast-like conidia/basidiospores sometimes called sporidia, bud off laterally from each cell. In various smuts, the yeast phase may proliferate, or they may fuse, or they may infect plant tissue and become hyphal. In other smuts, such as *Tilletia caries*, the elongated haploid basidiospores form apically, often in compatible pairs that fuse centrally resulting in "H"-shaped diaspores which are by then dikaryotic. Dikaryotic conidia may then form. Eventually the host is infected by infectious hyphae. Teliospores form in host tissue. Many variations on these general themes occur.

Smuts with both a yeast phase and an infectious hyphal state are examples of dimorphic Basidiomycota. In plant parasitic taxa, the saprotrophic phase is normally the yeast while the infectious stage is hyphal. However, there are examples of animal and human parasites where the species are dimorphic but it is the yeast-like state that is infectious. The genus *Filobasidiella* forms basidia on hyphae but the main infectious stage is more commonly known by the anamorphic yeast name *Cryptococcus*, e.g. *Cryptococcus neoformans* and *Cryptococcus gattii*.

The dimorphic Basidiomycota with yeast stages and the pleiomorphic rusts are examples of fungi with anamorphs, which are the asexual stages. Some Basidiomycota are only known as anamorphs. Many are yeasts, collectively called basidiomycetous yeasts to differentiate them from ascomycetous yeasts in the Ascomycota. Aside from yeast anamorphs, and uredinia, aecia and pycnidia, some Basidiomycota form other distinctive anamorphs as parts of their life-cycles. Examples are *Collybia tuberosa* with its apple-seed-shaped and coloured sclerotium, *Dendrocollybia racemosa* with its sclerotium and its *Tilachlidiopsis racemosa* conidia, *Armillaria* with their rhizomorphs, *Hohenbuehelia* with their *Nematoctonus* nematode infectious, state and the coffee leaf parasite, *Mycena citricolour* and its *Decapitatus flavidus* propagules called gemmae.

Agaricomycetes is a class of fungi. The taxon is roughly identical to that defined for the Homobasidiomycetes by Hibbett & Thorn, with the inclusion of Auriculariales and Sebacinales. It includes not only mushrooms but also most species placed in the deprecated taxa Gasteromycetes and Homobasidiomycetes. Within the subclass Agaricomycotina, which already excludes the smut and rust fungi, the Agaricomycetes can be further defined by the exclusion of the classes Tremellomycetes and Dacrymycetes which are generally considered to be jelly fungi. However, a few former "jelly fungi", such as *Auricularia*, are classified in the Agaricomycetes. Agaricomycetes include 17 orders, 100 families, 1147 genera, and 20951 species.

Although morphology of the mushroom or fruiting body was the basis of early classification of the Agaricomycetes, this is no longer the case. As an example, the distinction between the *Gasteromycetes* (puffballs) and *Agaricomycetes* (most other mushrooms) is no longer recognized as a natural one—various puffball species have apparently evolved independently from agaricomycete fungi. However, most mushroom guide books still group the puffballs or gasteroid forms separate from other mushrooms because the older Friesian classification is still convenient for categorizing fruiting body forms. Similarly, modern classifications divide the gasteroid order Lycoperdales between Agaricales and Phallales.

All members of the class produce basidiocarps and these range in size from tiny cups a few millimeters across to giant polypores greater than a meter across and weighing up to 130 kg (286 lb). The group also includes what are arguably the largest and oldest individual organisms on earth: the mycelium of *Armillaria gallica* have been estimated to extend over 150,000 square metres (37 acres) with a mass of 10,000 kg (22,000 lb) and an age of 1500 years.

Nearly all species are terrestrial (a few are aquatic), occurring in a wide range of environments where most function as decayers, especially of wood. However, some species are pathogenic or parasitic, and yet others are symbiotic, these including the important ectomycorrhizal symbionts of forest trees. General discussions on the forms and life cycles of these fungi are developed in the article on mushrooms, in the treatments of the various orders (links in table at right), and in individual species accounts.

CHAPTER 6

Puffball

A puffball is a member of any of a number of groups of fungus in the division Basidiomycota. The puffballs were previously treated as a taxonomic group called the Gasteromycetes or Gasteromycetidae, but they are now known to be a polyphyletic assemblage. Their distinguishing feature is that they have *gasterothecia* (gasteroid basidiocarps) in which the spores are produced internally; that is, the basidiocarp remains closed, or opens only after the spores have been released from the basidia. The spores of puffballs are *statismospores* rather than ballistospores, meaning they are not actively shot off the basidium. They are called puffballs because a cloud of brown dust-like spores is emitted when the mature fruiting body bursts. Puffballs and similar forms are thought to have evolved repeatedly (that is, in numerous independent events) from hymenomycetes by *gasteromycetation*, through secotioid stages. Thus Gasteromycetes or Gasteromycetidae are now considered descriptive terms (more properly *gasteroid* or *gasteromycetes*) and not valid cladistic terms.

Puffballs encompass the genera Calvatia, Calbovista, Lycoperdon. The true puffballs, of the Lycoperdales, do not consist of a visible stalk (stem). Avoid the genus Scleroderma which have a young purple gleba. The stalked puffballs, of the lycoperdales, do have a stalk which supports the gleba. None of the stalked puffballs are edible as they are tough and woody mushrooms. The Hymenogastrales are the *false puffballs*. A gleba which is powdery on maturity is a feature of true puffballs, stalked puffballs and earthstars. False puffballs are hard like rock or brittle. All false puffballs are inedible, as they are tough and bitter to taste.

Puffballs were traditionally used in Tibet for making ink by burning them vigorously, grinding them, then putting them in water and adding glue liquid and "a *nye shing ma* decoction", which, when pressed for a long time, made a very black dark substance which was used as ink.

While most puffballs are not poisonous, some often look similar to young agarics, especially the deadly Amanitas, such as the Death Cap mushroom. It is for this reason that all puffballs gathered in mushroom hunting should be cut in half lengthwise. Young puffballs in the edible stage have undifferentiated white flesh within; whereas the gills of immature Amanita mushrooms can be seen if they are closely examined.

The giant puffball, *Calvatia gigantea* (earlier classified as *Lycoperdon giganteum*), reaches a foot (30 cm) or more in diameter, and is difficult to mistake for any other fungus. It has been estimated that a large specimen of this fungus when mature will produce around 7×10^{12} spores. If collected before spores have formed, while the flesh is still white, it may be cooked as slices fried in butter, with a strong earthy, mushroom flavor. It can often be used in recipes that would ordinarily call for eggplant. It does not store well in a freezer - the entire freezer rapidly acquires a strong mushroom smell.

Not all true puffball mushrooms are without stalk. Some may also be stalked like the *Podaxis pistillaris* which is also called the False Shaggy Mane. On the other hand, there are a number of false puffballs that look similar to the true ones.

Stalked Puffballs

- *Battarrea phalloides*
- *Calostoma cinnabarina* (Stalked Puffball-in-Aspic)
- *Pisolithus tinctorius*
- *Tulostoma simulans*

True Puffballs

- *Bovista pila*
- *Calvatia cyathiformis*
- *Calvatia gigantea*
- *Calvatia utriformis*
- *Calvatia booniana*
- *Calvatia fumosa*
- *Calvatia lepidophora*
- *Calvatia sculpta*
- *Calvatia subcretacea*
- *Calbovista subsculpta*
- *Handkea utriformis*
- *Lycoperdon candidum*
- *Lycoperdon echinatum*
- *Lycoperdon fusillum*
- *Lycoperdon umbrinum*
- *Scleroderma auratium*
- *Scleroderma geaster*

False Puffballs

- *Endoptychum agaricoides*
- *Nivatogastrium nubigenum*
- *Podaxis pistillaris*
- *Rhizopogon rubescens*
- *Truncocolumella citrina*

Classification

- *Lycoperdon pyriforme*

Major orders:

- Lycoperdales, Tulostomatales, Nidulariales (related to Agaricales)
- Basidiomycetes: Agaricales: Lycoperdaceae: *Calvatia*
- *Calvatia booniana*
- *Calvatia bovista* (*Handkea utriformis*)
- *Calvatia craniiformis*
- *Calvatia cyathiformis*
- *Calvatia fumosa* (Handkea fumosa)
- *Calvatia gigantea*
- *Calvatia lepidophora*
- *Calvatia rubroflava*
- *Calvatia sculpta*
- *Calvatia subcretacea* (*Handkea subcretacea*)
- Basidiomycetes: Agaricales: Lycoperdaceae: *Lycoperdon*
- *Lycoperdon foetidum* (*Lycoperdon nigrescens*)
- *Lycoperdon perlatum*
- *Lycoperdon pulcherrimum*
- *Lycoperdon pusillum*
- *Lycoperdon pyriforme*
- Basidiomycetes: Agaricales: Lycoperdaceae: *Vascellum*
- *Vascellum curtisii*
- *Vascellum pratense*
- Geastrales and Phallales (related to Cantharellales)
- Basidiomycetes: Phallales: Geastraceae: *Geastrum*
- *Geastrum coronatum*
- *Geastrum fornicatum*
- *Geastrum saccatum*
- Sclerodermatales (related to Boletales)
- Basidiomycetes: Boletales: Sclerodermataceae: *Scleroderma*
- *Scleroderma areolatum*
- *Scleroderma bovista*

- *Scleroderma cepa*
- *Scleroderma citrinum*
- *Scleroderma meridionale*
- *Scleroderma michiganense*
- *Scleroderma polyrhizum*
- *Scleroderma septentrionale*

Various false-truffles (hypogaeic gasteromycetes) related to different hymenomycete orders.

Similarly, the true truffles (Tuberales) are gasteroid Ascomycota. Their ascocarps are called tuberothecia.

Agaricus

Agaricus is a large and important genus of mushrooms containing both edible and poisonous species, with possibly over 300 members worldwide. The genus includes the common ("button") mushroom (*Agaricus bisporus*) and the field mushroom (*Agaricus campestris*), the dominant cultivated mushrooms of the West.

Members of *Agaricus* are characterized by having a fleshy cap or *pileus*, from the underside of which grow a number of radiating plates or gills on which are produced the naked spores. They are distinguished from other members of their family, Agaricaceae, by their chocolate-brown spores. Members of *Agaricus* also have a stem or *stipe*, which elevates the pileus above the object on which the mushroom grows, or substrate, and a partial veil, which protects the developing gills and later forms a ring or annulus on the stalk.

For many years members of the genus *Agaricus* were given the generic name *Psalliota*, and this can still be seen in older books on mushrooms. All proposals to conserve *Agaricus* against *Psalliota* or vice versa have so far been considered superfluous.

Several origins of *Agaricus* have been proposed; It possibly derives "from Agarica of Sarmatica, a district of Russia" (!). Note also Greek "a sort of tree fungus" (There's been an *Agaricon* Adans. genus, treated by Donk in *Persoonia* 1:180).

Donk reports Linnaeus' name is devalidated (so that the proper author citation apparently is "L. *per* Fr., 1821") because *Agaricus* was not linked to Tournefort's name (Linnaeus places both *Agaricus* Dill. and *Amanita* Dill. in synonymy), but truly a replacement for *Amanita* Dill., which would require that *A. quercinus*, not *A. campestris* be the type. This question compounded by the fact that Fries himself used *Agaricus* roughly in Linnaeus' sense (which leads to issues with *Amanita*), and that *A. campestris* was eventually excluded from *Agaricus* by Karsten and was apparently in *Lepiota* at the time Donk wrote this, commenting that a type conservation might become necessary.

The alternate name for the genus, *Psalliota*, derived from the Greek *psalion/ "ring"*, was first published by Fries (1821) as trib. *Psalliota*. The type is *Agaricus campestris* (widely accepted, except by Earle, who proposed *A. cretaceus*).

Phylogenetics

The use of phylogenetic analysis to determine evolutionary relationships amongst *Agaricus* species has increased our understanding of this taxonomically difficult genus, although there remains much work to be done to fully delineate infrageneric relationships. Prior to these analyses, the genus *Agaricus*, as circumscribed by Rolf Singer (1986), was divided into 42 species grouped into five sections based on reactions of mushroom tissue to air or various chemical reagents, as well as subtle differences in mushroom morphology. Restriction fragment length polymorphism analysis demonstrated that this classification scheme needed revision.

Sections

This genus is divided into several sections:

- Section *Agaricus*
- Section *Arvense* Konrad & Maubl

Contains 19 species in six subgroups similar to the horse mushroom, *A. arvensis*, and with versatile heterothallic life cycles.

- Section *Xanthodermatei*

Outlined by Singer in 1948, this section includes species with various characteristics similar to the type species *A. xanthodermus*. The section forms a single clade based on analysis of ITS1+2.

- Section *Chitonioides*
- Section *Sanguinoletti*
- Section *Spissicaules* (Hainem.) Kerrigan
- Section *Duploannulatae*

Based on DNA analysis of ITS1, ITS2, and 5.8S sequences, the section *Duploannulatae* (also known as section *Hortenses*) may be divided into six distinct clades, five of which correspond to well-known species from the temperate Northern Hemisphere: *A. bisporus, A. subfloccosus, A. bitorquis, A. vaporarius* and *A. cupressicola*. The sixth clade comprises the species complex *A. devoniensis*.

Edibility

The genus contains the most widely consumed and best known mushroom today, *Agaricus bisporus*, with *A. campestris* also well known. The most notable inedible species is the yellow-staining mushroom *A. xanthodermus*. All three are found worldwide.

One species reported from Africa, *A. aurantioviolaceus*, is reportedly deadly poisonous.

CHAPTER 7 Mycelium

Mycelium (pl. mycelia) is the vegetative part of a fungus, consisting of a mass of branching, thread-like hyphae. The mass of hyphae is sometimes called shiro, especially within the fairy ring fungi. Fungal colonies composed of mycelia are found in soil and on or within many other substrates. A typical single spore germinates into a homokaryotic mycelium, which cannot reproduce sexually; when two compatible homokaryotic mycelia join and form a dikaryotic mycelium, that mycelium may form fruiting bodies such as mushrooms. A mycelium may be minute, forming a colony that is too small to see, or it may be extensive.

Mycelium is vital in terrestrial and aquatic ecosystems for its role in the decomposition of plant material. It contributes to the organic fraction of soil, and its growth releases carbon dioxide back into the atmosphere.

Is this the largest organism in the world? This 2400-acre (9.7 km^2) site in eastern Oregon had a contiguous growth of mycelium before logging roads cut through it. Estimated at 1665 football fields in size and 2200 years old, this one fungus has killed the forest above it several times over, and in so doing has built deeper soil layers that allow the growth of ever-larger stands of trees. Mushroom-forming forest fungi are unique in that their mycelial mats can achieve such massive proportions.

It is through the mycelium that a fungus absorbs nutrients from its environment. It does this in a two-stage process. First, the hyphae secrete enzymes onto or into the food source, which break down biological polymers into smaller units such as monomers. These monomers are then absorbed into the mycelium by facilitated diffusion and active transport.

Mycelium is vital in terrestrial and aquatic ecosystems for its role in the decomposition of plant material. It contributes to the organic fraction of soil, and its growth releases carbon dioxide back into the atmosphere. The mycelium of mycorrhizal fungi increases the efficiency of water and nutrient absorption of most plants and confers resistance to some plant pathogens. Mycelium is an important food source for many soil invertebrates.

One of the primary roles of fungi in an ecosystem is to decompose organic compounds. Petroleum products and pesticides that can be contaminants of soil are organic molecules. Therefore, fungi should have potential to remove such pollutants from the soil environment, a process known as bioremediation.

Mycelium is currently being employed by the company Ecovative Design LLC to make biodegradable packaging, a direct replacement for the petroleum based styrofoam.

Mycelial mats have been suggested as having potential as biological filters, removing chemicals and microorganisms from soil and water. The use of fungal mycelia to accomplish this has been termed "mycofiltration".

Knowledge of the relationship between mycorrhizal fungi and plants suggests new ways to improve crop yields.

When spread on logging roads, mycelium can act as a binder, holding new soil in place and preventing washouts until woody plants can be established.

Mycelium has been used to bind agricultural by-products to form products dubbed Greensulate and Ecocradle, which are alternatives to plastic styrofoam for packaging and insulation. Two inventors, Eben Bayer and Gavin McIntyre, and their company Ecovative Design, developed the method to manipulate a network of mycelia into desirable shapes, with properties comparable to its plastic counterpart. The invention has won two awards and is now in use commercially by Steelcase as packaging for furniture.

Phallaceae

The Phallaceae are a family of fungi, commonly known as stinkhorn mushrooms. Belonging to the fungal order Phallales, the Phallaceae have a worldwide distribution, but are especially prevalent in tropical regions. They are known for their foul smelling sticky spore masses, or gleba, borne on the end of stalks called the *receptaculum*. The characteristic fruiting body structure—a single, unbranched receptaculum with an externally attached gleba on the upper part—distinguish the Phallaceae from other families in the Phalalles. The spore mass typically smells of carrion or dung, and attracts flies and other insects to help disperse the spores. Although there is a great diversity of body structure shape amongst the various genera, all species in the Phallaceae begin their development as oval or round structures known as "eggs". According to a 2008 estimate, the family contains 21 genera and 77 species.

Species in the Phallaceae are gasteroid—having spores that are produced internally. Fruit bodies originate as a gelatinous, spherical or egg-shaped structure that may be completely or partially buried underground. The peridium, the outer layer of the egg, is white, or purple/red, with two or three layers. The outer layer is thin, membranous and elastic, while the inner layer is thicker, gelatinous and continuous. At maturity the peridium opens up and remains as a volva at the base of the receptaculum.

The fertile portion of the fruiting body is often borne on the end of a wide fleshy or spongy stalk (as in the *Phallales*), which may be cylindrical, star-shaped, or reticulate (forming a network). They may be brightly colored, sometimes with a lattice- or veil-like membrane enclosing and protecting the spores. The spore-containing substance, the gleba, is typically gelatinous, often foetid-smelling, and deliquescent (becoming liquid from the absorption of water). The gleba is formed on the exterior face of the cap or the upper part of the receptacle.

The basidia are small and narrowly club-shaped or fusiform, short-lived (*evanescent*), with 4 to 8 sterigmata. The spores are usually ellipsoid or cylindrical in shape, hyaline or pale brown, smooth, more or less smooth-walled, and truncate at the base.

Anthurus Kalchbr. & MacOwan (1880)

Fruiting bodies have a short stalk from which arises a spore-bearing structure (the receptaculum) of 5–8 arched arms. These arms, initially joined at the top, disconnect and curve irregularly to expose the inner surface of each arm, which is covered with green spore-containing gleba. Spores are 3–4 × 1–1.5 µm.

Aporophallus Möller (1895)

Mature fruiting bodies contain a roughly cylindrical white or pinkish stalk approximately 6 × 2 cm, with a volva at the base. At the top is a bright red disc with a variable number of arms, typically 3-7 cm long. The gleba that is found on the disc and inner side of the arms is slimy, foetid, and green colored. Spores are hyaline, with dimensions of 4-6 1.5-2 µm. *Aseroë rubra*, an Australian and Pacific species which has spread to Europe and North America.

Blumenavia Möller (1895)

Clathrus P. Micheli ex L.

Colus Cavalier & Séchier (1835)

A genus of four species with fruit bodies that are a short stalk from which six columns arise, joining at the top to form a red, arching, clathrate receptaculum. The gleba is smeared on the inside surface of the receptaculum.

Echinophalus Henn. (1898)

Endophallus Zang. & Petersen (1989)

Contains a single species, *E. yunnanensis* found in China, that resembles *Phallus* expect for a peridium that is separated from the base of the stem and which does not persist as a volva.

Ileodictyon Tul. ex M. Raoul (1844)

Fruiting bodies are latticed (clathrate), and have gelatinous arms that lie sessile within the volva. Spores are elliptical, and have dimensions of 4-6 1.5-2.5 μm. The New Zealand native, *Ileodictyon cibarium*, known as the basket fungus, has a fruiting body shaped somewhat like a round or oval ball with interlaced or latticed branches.

Itajahya Möller (1895)

Characters in this genus include a white calyptra (tissue which covers the top of the fruiting body to which the gleba is attached), lamellate plates covered with gleba. The gleba has a white mottled surface, and the pileus appears wig-like when removed of the gleba. The thick, stout stalk has many chambered walls.

Kobayasia (Kobayasi) S. Imai & A. Kawam. (1958)

This genus circumscribes the single species *Kobayasia nipponica*, found in Japan in 1958.

Laternea Turpin (1822)

Ligiella J.A. Sáenz (1980)

Fruiting bodies are 4.5-6.5 cm long, 2.2-5 cm in diameter, and have four or five thick white chambered arms that are joined at the top, but free at the base. This monotypic genus, containing the single species *L. rodrigueziana*, is known only from Costa Rica.

Lysurus Fr. (1823)

*Lysurus mokusin*Fruiting bodies consist of a long stalk with 3 or 4 short, thick arms. These arms, initially joined together, but usually separate in maturity, are covered with the brownish-olivaceous gleba. Spores are ellipsoidal, with dimensions of 4-5 × 1.5-2 μm.

Mutinus (Huds.) Fr. (1849)

The mature fruiting body has a spongy, cylindrical hollow stalk which ends in a slender, tapered, sometimes curved head covered with the dark olivaceous, slimy gleba. In older specimens, the gleba may be washed or worn off to show the orange or red color of the head itself. Notable species include the dog stinkhorn *Mutinus caninus.*

Neolysurus O.K. Mill., Ovrebo & Burk (1991)

This genus contains the single species *Neolysurus arcipulvinus,* described from Costa Rica. The stipe and arms have a tubular construction, similar to species from *Lysurus. Neolysurus* is unique in having a long stipe, ending in arms or columns that branch and interconnect to support a cushion-shaped, olive green gleba. The glebal cushion is divided into polygonal compartments by a fine pinkish white, solid mesh. The hymenium is continuous between the mesh.

Phallus Junius ex L. (1753)

Phallus ravenelii

In species of *Phallus,* the receptaculum is a tall unbranched stalk that ends in a cap-like structure that bears the gleba. Notable species include *Phallus impudicus,* the common stinkhorn, *Phallus hadriani, Phallus ravenelii,* and *Phallus indusiatus* (syn. *Dictyophora indusiata*), the Chinese "bamboo fungus", eaten as a food in southwestern China after the foul smelling cap is removed.

Protubera Möller (1895)

Fruiting bodies are egg-shaped, 2.2-3.5 cm in diameter by 3-4 cm high, with a dull white, soft exoperidium (roughly 1 mm thick) and a grayish exoperidium (3-4 mm thick). The gleba is contained within internal chambers that are separated by whitich, gelatinous tissue that originates from a columella-like, gelatinous central core. Spores are elliptical, smooth, nearly hyaline, and 3.5-4.5 1.5-2 µm.

Pseudoclathrus B. Liu & Y.S. Bau (1980)

Pseudocolus Lloyd (1907)

Protuberella (S. Imai) S. Imai & Kawam. (1958)

This genus resembles the *Protubera*, except that the tissue is "gelatinous fleshy in the peridium and not so distincly gelatinous as in *Protubera maracuja*, they are less gelatinous in the nature of the sterile strands than those of *P. maracuja*". Spores are clylindric, thin-walled, and 3.7-5 2-2.5 µm. This monotypic genus contains the single species *Protuberella borealis*, known only from Asia.

Simblum Klotzsch ex Hook. (1831)

Fruiting bodies have a long stalk that has an oval, chambered head larger in diameter than the stalk. The green gleba develops within the chambers of the chambered head. Spores are narrowly elliptical, and 3.5-4.4 × 1.4-2 µm.

Staheliomyces E. Fisch. (1921)

Clathrus columnatus Fruiting bodies are latticed (clathrate), and made of hollow tubular arms that originate from the basal tissue within the volva. Spores are elliptical, smooth, hyaline, with dimensions of 4-6 ×1.5-2.5 µm. Examples include *Clathrus ruber*, the lattice stinkhorn, *Clathrus archeri*, the octopus stinkhorn, and *Clathrus columnatus*, the columned stinkhorn.

CHAPTER 8

Edible Mushrooms

Edible mushrooms are the fleshy and edible fruiting bodies of several species of fungi. They belong to the macrofungi, because their fruiting structures are large enough to be seen with the naked eye. They can appear either below ground (hypogeous) or above ground (epigous) where they may be picked by hand. Edibility may be defined by criteria that include absence of poisonous effects on humans and desirable taste and aroma. By some accounts, less than 10 per cent of all mushrooms may be edible. Of the estimated 1.5 million species of fungi, only about 150 are considered toxic.

Edible mushrooms are consumed by humans for their nutritional and occasionally medicinal value as comestibles. Mushrooms consumed for health reasons are known as medicinal mushrooms. While hallucinogenic mushrooms (e.g. Psilocybin mushrooms) are occasionally consumed for recreational or religious purposes, they can produce severe nausea and disorientation, and are therefore not commonly considered edible mushrooms.

Edible mushrooms include many fungal species that are either harvested wild or cultivated. Easily cultivatable and common wild mushrooms are often available in markets, and those that are more difficult to obtain (such as the prized truffle and matsutake) may be collected on a smaller scale by private gatherers. Some preparations may render certain poisonous mushrooms fit for consumption.

Before assuming that any wild mushroom is edible, it should be identified. Proper identification of a species is the only safe way to ensure edibility. Some mushrooms that are edible for most people can cause allergic reactions in some individuals, and old or improperly stored specimens can cause food poisoning. Deadly poisonous mushrooms that are frequently confused with edible mushrooms and responsible for many fatal poisonings include several species of the *Amanita* genus, in particular, *Amanita phalloides*, the *death cap*.

Mycophagy , the act of consuming mushrooms, dates to ancient times. Edible mushroom species have been found in association with 13,000 year old ruins in Chile, but the first reliable evidence of mushroom consumption dates to several hundred years BC in China. The Chinese value mushrooms for medicinal properties as well as for food. Ancient Romans and Greeks ate mushrooms, particularly the upper class. The Roman Caesars would have a food taster taste the mushrooms before the Caesar to make sure they were safe.

Mushrooms are also easily preserved, and historically have provided additional nutrition over winter.

Many cultures around the world have either used or continue to use psilocybin mushrooms for spiritual purposes as well as medicinal mushrooms in folk medicine. Mushroom cultivation reached the United States in the late 1800s with imported spores from Mexico.

Current Culinary Use

A fraction of the many fungi consumed by humans are currently cultivated and sold commercially. Commercial cultivation is important ecologically, as there have been concerns of depletion of larger fungi such as chanterelles in Europe, possibly because the group has grown so popular yet remains a challenge to cultivate.

Commercially Cultivated

Commercial cultivated Japanese edible mushroom species. Clockwise from left, enokitake, buna-shimeji, bunapi-shimeji, king oyster mushroom and shiitake.

Mushroom cultivation has a long history, with over twenty species commercially cultivated. Mushrooms are cultivated in at least 60 countries with China, the United States, Netherlands, France and Poland being the top five producers in 2000.

Some species are difficult to cultivate; others (particularly mycorrhizal species) have not yet been successfully cultivated. Some of these species are harvested from the wild, and can be found in markets. When in season they can be purchased fresh, and many species are sold dried as well. The following species are commonly harvested from the wild:

- *Boletus edulis* or edible Boletus, native to Europe, known in Italian as Fungo Porcino (plural 'porcini') (Pig mushroom), in German as Steinpilz (Stone mushroom), in Russian as "white mushroom", in Albanian as (Wolf mushroom) and in French the *cep*. It also known as the king bolete, and is renowned for its delicious flavor. It is sought after worldwide, and can be found in a variety of culinary dishes.
- *Cantharellus cibarius* (The chanterelle), The yellow chanterelle is one of the best and most easily recognizable mushrooms, and can be found in Asia, Europe, North America and Australia. There are poisonous mushrooms which resemble it, though these can be confidently distinguished if one is familiar with the chanterelle's identifying features.
- *Cantharellus tubaeformis*, the tube chanterelle or yellow-leg
- *Clitocybe nuda* - Blewit (or Blewitt)
- *Cortinarius caperatus* the Gypsy mushroom (recently moved from genus *Rozites*)

- *Craterellus cornucopioides* - Trompette du Mort or Horn of Plenty

Grifola frondosa, known in Japan as *maitake* (also "hen of the woods" or "sheep's head"); a large, hearty mushroom commonly found on or near stumps and bases of oak trees, and believed to have Macrolepiota procera properties.

Gyromitra esculenta this " False morel" is prized by the Finns. This mushroom is deadly poisonous if eaten raw, but highly regarded when parboiled.

Hericium erinaceus, a tooth fungus; also called "lion's mane mushroom".

Hydnum repandum Sweet tooth fungus, hedgehog mushroom, urchin of the woods.

Lactarius deliciosus Saffron milk cap - Consumed around the world and prized in Russia.

Morchella species, (morel family), morels belong to the ascomycete grouping of fungi. They are usually found in open scrub, woodland or open ground in late spring. When collecting this fungus, care must be taken to distinguish it from the poisonous false morels, including *Gyromitra esculenta.*

- *Morchella conica* var *deliciosa*
- *Morchella esculenta* var *rotunda*
- *Tricholoma matsutake* the Matsutake, a mushroom highly prized in Japanese cuisine.

Tuber species, (the truffle), Truffles have long eluded the modern techniques of domestication known as *trufficulture.* Although the field of trufficulture has greatly expanded since its inception in 1808, several species still remain uncultivated. Domesticated truffles include:

- *Tuber borchii*
- *Tuber brumale*
- *Tuber indicum* - Chinese black truffle
- *Tuber macrosporum* - White truffle
- *Tuber mesentericum* - The Bagnoli truffle
- *Tuber uncinatum* - Black summer truffle

Other Edible Wild Species

Many wild species are consumed around the world. The species which can be identified "in the field" (without use of special chemistry or a microscope) and therefore safely eaten vary widely from country to country, even from region to region. This list is a sampling of lesser-known species that are reportedly edible.

- *Amanita caesarea* (Caesar's Mushroom)
- *Armillaria mellea*
- *Boletus badius*
- *Boletus elegans*
- *Chroogomphus rutilus* (pine-spikes or spike-caps)
- *Calvatia gigantea* (Giant Puffball)
- *Clavariaceae* species (coral fungus family)
- *Clavulinaceae* species (coral fungus family)
- *Coprinus comatus*, the Shaggy mane. Must be cooked as soon as possible after harvesting or the caps will first turn dark and unappetizing, then deliquesce and turn to ink. Not found in markets for this reason.
- *Cortinarius variecolor*
- *Fistulina hepatica* (beefsteak polypore or the ox tongue)
- *Hygrophorus chrysodon*
- *Lactarius salmonicolor*
- *Lactarius subdulcis* (mild milkcap)
- *Lactarius volemus*
- *Laetiporous sulphureus* (Sulphur shelf). Also known by names such as the "chicken mushroom", "chicken fungus", sulphur shelf is a distinct bracket fungus popular among mushroom hunters.
- *Leccinum aurantiacum* (Red-capped scaber stalk)
- *Leccinum scabrum* (Birch bolete)
- *Lepiota procera*
- *Macrolepiota procera* Parasol Mushroom - Globally, it is widespread in temperate regions

- *Polyporus squamosus* (Dryad's saddle and Pheasant's back mushroom)
- *Polyporus sulphureus*
- *Polyporus mylittae*
- *Ramariaceae* species (coral fungus family)
- *Rhizopogon luteolus*
- *Russula,* some members of this genus are edible.
- *Sparassis crispa.* Also known as "cauliflower mushroom".
- *Suillus bovinus*
- *Suillus luteus*
- *Suillus tomentosus*
- *Tricholoma terreum*

Conditionally Edible Species

There are a number of fungi that are considered choice by some and toxic by others. In some cases, proper preparation can remove some or all of the toxins:

- *Amanita muscaria* is edible if parboiled to leach out toxins. Fresh mushrooms cause vomiting, twitching, drowsiness, and hallucinations due to the presence of muscimol. Although present in *A. muscaria,* Ibotenic acid is not in high enough concentration to produce any physical or psychological effects unless massive amounts are ingested.
- *Coprinopsis atramentaria* is edible without special preparation. However, consumption with alcohol is toxic due to the presence of coprine. Some other *Coprinus* spp. share this property.
- *Gyromitra esculenta* is eaten by some after it has been parboiled; however, mycologists do not recommend it. Raw *Gyromitra* are toxic due to the presence of gyromitrin, and it is not known if all of the toxin can be removed by parboiling.
- *Lactarius* spp. - Apart from *Lactarius deliciosus* which is universally considered edible, other *Lactarius spp.* that are considered toxic elsewhere in the world are eaten in Russia after pickling or parboiling.

- *Verpa bohemica* - Considered choice by some, it even can be found for sale as a "morel", but cases of toxicity have been reported. Verpas contain toxins similar to gyromitrin and similar precautions apply.

Current Medical Use

Medicinal mushrooms are mushrooms or extracts from mushrooms that are used or studied as possible treatments for diseases. Research has shown some medicinal mushroom isolates that have promising cardiovascular, anticancer, antiviral, antibacterial, antiparasitic, anti-inflammatory, and antidiabetic properties. Currently, several extracts (polysaccharide-K, polysaccharide peptide, lentinan have widespread use in Japan, Korea and China, as adjuvants to radiation treatments and chemotherapy.

The concept of a medicinal mushroom has a history spanning millennia in parts of Asia. Only a few mushroom extracts have been extensively tested for efficacy. The available results for most other extracts, are on isolated cell lines, animal research with rodents, or underpowered clinical human trials. Although medicinal molds do not produce mushrooms, these fungi were the original source of penicillin, the first statins, and griseofulvin.

Preparing Wild Edibles

Some wild species are toxic, or at least indigestible, when raw. As a rule all wild mushroom species should be cooked thoroughly before eating. Many species can be dried and rehydrated by pouring boiling water over the dried mushrooms and letting them steep for approximately 30 minutes. The soaking liquid can be used for cooking as well, provided that any dirt at the bottom of the container is discarded.

One recipe for Auricularia auricula-judae is to collect it while still soft, wash it thoroughly and cut it into thin slices. The prepared slices should be stewed in stock or milk for around three-quarters of an hour, and then served with plenty of pepper. The result is crispy and not unlike seaweed.

The difficult task of identifying mushrooms in the wild, for culinary or recreational purposes, can produce severe poisoning.

Mushrooms that have been exposed to ultraviolet (UV) light contain large amounts of vitamin D_2. Mushrooms, when exposed to UV light, convert ergosterol, a chemical found in large concentrations in many mushrooms, to vitamin D_2. This is similar to the reaction in humans, where Vitamin D_3 is synthesized after exposure to UV light.

Testing conducted by the Pennsylvania State University showed an hour of UV light exposure made a serving of mushrooms contain twice the U.S. Food and Drug Administration's daily recommendation of vitamin D. Testing by the Monterey Mushrooms Company demonstrated 5 minutes of UV light exposure made a serving of mushrooms contain four times the FDA's daily recommendation of vitamin D. High performance liquid chromatography analysis has also demonstrated the effect sunlight has on mushroom vitamin D_2 content.

The ergocalciferol, vitamin D_2, in UV-irradiated mushrooms is not the same form of vitamin D as is produced by UV-irradiation of human skin or animal skin, fur, or feathers (cholecalciferol, vitamin D_3). Although vitamin D_2 clearly has vitamin D activity in humans and formerly was widely used in milk fortification and in nutritional supplements, vitamin D_3, cholecalciferol is the preferred form.

CHAPTER 9

Mushrooming

Mushrooming, mushroom picking, and similar terms describe the activity of gathering mushrooms in the wild, typically for eating. This is popular in most of Europe, including the Nordic, Baltic, and Slavic countries and the Mediterranean Basin, as well as in Australia, Japan, Korea, Canada, and the northwestern, Midwestern and Appalachian United States.

A large number of mushroom species are favoured for eating by mushroom hunters. The king bolete is a popular delicacy. Sulphur shelf (also known as Chicken Mushroom or Chicken of the Woods) is often gathered because it occurs in bulk, recurs year after year, is easily identified, and has a wide variety of culinary uses. Lactarius deliciosus (Pine Mushrooms), Chanterelles, Morels, Oyster Mushrooms, Puffballs and Polypores are among the most popular types of mushrooms to gather, most of these being relatively hard to misidentify by anyone with practice. Only experts, however, collect from dangerous groups, such as *Amanita*, which include some of the most toxic mushrooms in existence.

Naturally, there are abundant mushroom guides, i.e. field guides on mushrooms available, but especially in the Slavic countries the ability to identify and prepare edible mushrooms is usually passed down through generations.

Identification is not the only element of mushroom hunting that takes practice—knowing where and when to search does as well. Most mushroom species require very specific conditions—some only grow at the base of a certain type of tree, for example. Finding a desired species that is known to grow in a certain region can be a challenge.

Some mushrooms are deadly or extremely hazardous when consumed; see List of deadly fungi. Others, while not deadly, can nevertheless cause permanent organ damage. The literature strongly advises that you:

- Only eat mushrooms you have positively identified yourself.
- Identify mushrooms a second time during preparation and cook them properly (only a few species can be eaten raw).
- Don't combine mushrooms types.
- Inform yourself about deadly mushrooms that are look-alikes of edible ones. "Deadly twins" differ regionally, so take into account regional variation.
- Don't gather mushrooms that are difficult to identify, unless you have expert knowledge. This applies especially to the mushrooms of the genus *Amanita* or *Cortinarius* and "little brown mushrooms".
- Consume only a small amount the first time you try a certain species. People react differently to different mushrooms, and all mushroom species cause adverse reaction in a few individuals, even the common champignon.

"Little brown mushrooms"

Inocybe lacera is a typical little brown mushroom, and is easily identifiable only by distinctive microscopic features.

"Little brown mushroom," or LBM refers to any of a large number of small, dull-coloured agaric species, with few macromorphological uniquely distinguishing characteristics. As a result, LBMs typically range from difficult to impossible for mushroom hunters to identify. Experienced mushroomers may discern more subtle identifying traits that help narrow the mushroom down to a particular genus or group of species, but exact identification of LBMs often requires close examination of microscopic characteristics plus a certain degree of familiarity or specialization in that particular group.

For mycologists, LBMs are the equivalent of LGBs ("little grey birds") and DYCs ("damned yellow composite") that are the bane of ornithologists and botanists, respectively.

"Big white mushroom" (BWM) is also sometimes used to describe groups of difficult to identify larger and paler agarics, many of which are in the genus *Clitocybe.*

Psychotropics

The *Amanita muscaria*'s psychotropic properties have been traditionally used by shamans in Siberia in their rituals. However, its use for such purposes today is very rare, despite the mushroom's abundance. Instead, the *Psilocybe semilanceata,* being the only psilocybin-containing mushroom common in Slavic countries, is sought after for its hallucinogenic properties, the latter being more desirable with fewer side effects than those of *A. muscaria.* The use of *P. semilanceata* is however significantly hindered by its small size, requiring larger quantities and being hard to spot. Other Psilocybe species are abundant in the American south and west, as well as Mexico, where they have been used by traditional shamans for centuries. In the west, one can often find mushroom pickers in cow pastures in a stereotypical stoop looking in the grass for Psilocybes. This can be quite dangerous, as many species grow in pastures and amateurs often misidentify Psilocybes.

In the United States mushroom picking is particularly popular in the Appalachian areas of the United States and on the west coast from the San Francisco Bay Area northward along the Pacific Coast, in northern California, Oregon and Washington, and in many other regions. British enthusiasts today enjoy an extended average picking season of 75 days compared to just 33 in the 1950s. In Slavic countries, such as Russia, Poland, Ukraine, Croatia, Slovenia, Slovakia and the Czech Republic also in Lithuania, mushroom picking is a common family activity. After a heavy rain during mushroom season whole families often venture into the nearest forest, picking bucketfuls of mushrooms, which are cooked and eaten for dinner upon return or alternatively dried or marinated for later consumption. Commercial exploitation of wild mushrooms in Canada has become a multi-million dollar industry.

In the Iberian Peninsula mushroom hunting is a popular activity in many regions including Castile and Leon, the Basque Country, and Catalonia, where a mushroom hunter is called *boletaire*. Spanish mushroom hunters often keep picking location secret to prevent others from pillaging the area for monetary gain. Pickers can be competitive, with some listening in on unknowing subjects ("incautos") to glean information about picking areas. Such behaviour is not considered inappropriate among Spaniards, since it is part of the innate sense of competition that permeates Spanish society.

The social dynamic of mushroom picking can be particularly complex and more dedicated pickers have established unspoken rules and etiquette to the activity. Much like secret fishing spots, mushroom picking areas (which vary from season to season) may only be shared with close friends, and informed pickers are expected to remain discreet. Becoming the first successful picker of the season is a goal of any social picker and successful pickers can gain a high standing within their social group. In rural Spain, mushroom picking is a common conversation point in local bars. Families or friends choose mushroom hunting as the focus for weekend trips, which (as well as providing part of a meal) often serves as a bonding activity.

Occasionally, mushroom gatherers may devise an elaborate prank on a novice gatherer. The joke played on the unknowing subject (another "incauto") may vary from getting them lost in the woods to making them believe a wolf or other dangerous animal is stalking them. Like any other anecdote-rich story, the prank is retold countless times in the local bars, providing Spaniards with even more enjoyment.

Eventually, as Winter sets in and mushrooms cease to sprout, Spaniards forget about mushroom picking until the next season.

The popularity of mushroom picking in some parts of the world has led to mushroom festivals. The festivals are usually between September and October, depending on the mushrooms available in a particular region. Festivals in North America include:

- Aerie Resort on Vancouver Island—Great Fall Mushroom Hunt
- Bamfield, Vancouver Island—Bamfield Mushroom festival
- Boyne City, Michigan—Annual National Morel Mushroom Festival
- Washington's Long Beach Peninsula—Wild Mushroom Celebration
- Lake Quinault Lodge in Washington's Olympic National Forest—Quinault Rain Forest Mushroom Festival
- Mendocino County (North of San Francisco)—Mushroom Festival
- Madisonville, Texas—Mushroom Festival
- Telluride, Colorado—Fungifest
- Kennett Square, Pennsylvania—Mushroom Festival
- Girdwood, Alaska—Fungus Fair
- Muscoda, Wisconsin-Morel Mushroom Festival

Radiation

Nuclear fallout from the Chernobyl disaster is an important issue concerning mushroom picking in Europe. Due to the wide spread of their mycelium, mushrooms tend to accumulate more radioactive caesium-137 than surrounding soil and other organisms. Special state agencies (in Belarus it is Bellesrad) monitor and analyze the degree of radionuclide accumulation in various wild species of plants and animals.

This is not only an issue in Poland, Belarus, Ukraine and Russia; the fallout also reached western Europe, and until recently the German government discouraged people gathering certain mushrooms.

Guidelines for Mushroom Picking

Good mushroom guidebooks call attention to similarities between species, especially if an edible species is similar to or commonly confused with one that is potentially harmful.
Examples:

False chanterelles (*Hygrophoropsis aurantiaca*) can look like real chanterelles (*Cantharellus cibarius*) to the inexperienced eye. The latter do not have sharp gills, but rather blunt veins on the underside. A mistake here would, however, not be very serious, since false chanterelles are considered edible, just not tasty. Mild symptoms have reported from consuming them. The Jack O'Lantern Mushroom, on the other hand, is often mistaken for a chanterelle, and it is potently toxic.

True morels are distinguished from false morels (*Gyromitra spp.* and *Verpa* spp.). The impostors have caps attached at the top of the stalk, while true morels have a honeycombed cap and a single, continuous hollow chamber within.

Immature *Chlorophyllum molybdites* can be confused with edible *Agaricus* mushrooms.

Immature puffballs are generally edible, but care must be taken to avoid species such as *Scleroderma citrinum* and immature *Amanitas*. These can be identified by cutting a puffball in half and looking for a dark reticulated gleba or the articulated, nonhomogenous structures of a gilled mushroom, respectively.

Conocybe filaris, and some *Galerina* species can look like, and grow next to, *Psilocybe*. Psilocybe is not deadly but contains the alkaloids psilocybin and psilocin, hence it is often sought for use as a recreational psychedelic drug. Galerina and Conocybe Filaris on the other hand are highly poisonous.

Eating Poisonous Species

There are treatments to reduce or eliminate the toxicity of certain (but not all) poisonous species to the point where they may be edible. For instance, false morels are deadly poisonous when eaten raw or incorrectly prepared, but their toxins can be reduced by a proper method of parboiling. Prepared in this way, this mushroom is widely used and considered a delicacy in the Scandinavian countries, although recent research suggests that there may still be long-term health consequences from eating it.

Commonly Gathered Mushrooms

The commonly gathered species, grouped by their order taxa, are as follows: Mushroom species mentioned in each group are listed at the end of the paragraph using the following convention: Latin name (Russian name [transliteration of Russian name] - literal translation of name; *common English names, if any*).

Agaricaceae

While the family of Amanitas should be approached with extreme caution, as it contains the lethal *Amanita phalloides* and *Amanita virosa,* those confident in their skills often pick the *Amanita rubescens,* which is highly prized in Europe and to a much lesser extent in Russia, accounted by some not to superior taste, but to its relation to the *Amanita caesarea,* which is not found in Russia, but was considered a delicacy worthy of the emperor in Ancient Rome.

- *Amanita rubescens* [Mukhomor Sero-Rozoviy] - Grey-Pink Fly-Killer; *European blusher*)
- *Amanita caesarea* [Tsezarskiy Grib] - Caesar's Mushroom)
- *Coprinus comatus* is a unique mushroom that decomposes into ink, and hence must be prepared soon after picking and only young specimens should be collected. While being a general mushroom hunting guideline, the avoidance of specimens growing in areas with high pollution is especially important with this family, as it is a very effective pollutant absorber.
- *Agaricus bisporus* also known as the table or button mushroom. Sales of this mushroom in 1996 reached $209

million in Canada. Another well known mushroom known as the *portobello* is a large brown strain of this fungus.

Boletaceae

This order is often viewed as the order of "noble" mushrooms, containing few poisonous species, identifiable with relative ease, and having superior palatability. The most notable species is the *Boletus edulis*, the "mushroom king", a beautiful, almost legendary, relatively rare mushroom, edible in almost any (even raw) form, and commonly considered *the* best-tasting mushroom. (Note: Do not confuse the Russian name, literally "white mushroom", with Champignons, often known in English as "white mushrooms".)

The *Leccinum* family includes two well-known mushroom species named after the trees they can usually be found next to. The *Leccinum aurantiacum* (as well as the *L. versipelle*), found under aspen trees, and the *Leccinum scabrum* (as well as the *L. holopus*), found under birch trees. The secondary mentioned species, are significantly different in cap colour only. Both types are very sought after, being highly palatable and beautiful, while more common than the B. edulis.

The *Suillus* family, characterised by its slimy cap, is another prized mushroom, the *Suillus luteus* and *Suillus granulatus* being its most common varieties, and while abundant in some parts of Eurasia, is a rare occurrence in others. It is easy to identify and very palatable.

The *Xerocomus* genus is generally considered a less desirable (though mostly edible) mushroom group, due to common abundant mould growth on their caps, which can make them poisonous. The *Xerocomus badius*, however is an exception, being moderately sought after, especially in Europe. Note that some scientific classifications now consider species in the *Xerocomus* genus as members of *Boletus*.

Cantharellus cibarius

The *Cantharellus cibarius*, a common and popular mushroom, especially in Europe, is a choice edible and unique mushroom. It is very rarely infested by worms or larvae, has a unique appearance, and when rotting, the decomposed parts are easily distinguishable and separable from those that are edible.

Helvellaceae

The *Gyromitra esculenta* is considered poisonous, but can be consumed if dried and stored for over a year, according to Slavic literature, and can be used to supplement or replace morel mushrooms, while Western literature claims that even the fumes of the mushroom are dangerous. It is similar to morels both in appearance and palatability.

Lepiotaceae

The *Macrolepiota* genus, usually the *Macrolepiota procera*, and, to a lesser extent, the *M. rhacodes* are highly regarded, especially in Europe, being very palatable and very large, with specimens of *M. procera* as high as 1 metre being reported. Morchellaceae

A Basket of Morels

The Morel, *Morchella esculenta* is highly prized in Western Europe, India and North America. It is significantly less prized in Slavic countries where, like the *Gyromitra esculenta*, is considered marginally edible with mediocre palatability. Boiling the mushroom and discarding the water is often recommended.

Lactarius

Members of the genus *Lactarius*, as the name suggests, lactate a milky liquid when wounded and are often scoffed upon by Western literature. The *Lactarius deliciosus* is however regarded as one of the most palatable mushrooms in Slavic culture, comparable to the *Boletus edulis*. Also considered as similarly palatable are the species *Lactarius necator* and particularly *Lactarius resimus*. Thermal treatment may however be necessary in some cases. Slightly less appealing due to its bitter taste is the Lactarius pubescens.

There is a Russian proverb: "If you call yourself gruzd, then get into the basket," which encourages people who boast about themselves too much to actually do some work. Gruzd means a valuable mushroom.

Russulaceae

The Russula family includes over 750 species and is one of the most common and abundant mushrooms in Eurasia. Their cap colours include red, brown, yellow, blue and green and can be easily spotted. The *Russula vesca* species, one of the many red-capped varieties, is one of the most common, is reasonably palatable and can be eaten raw. The edible Russulas have a mild taste, compared to many inedible/poisonous species that have an strong hot or bitter taste. The *Russula emetica* (The Sickener) is known to cause gastrointestinal upset and has a very hot taste when a small bit is placed on the tongue. Due to their abundance they are however often regarded as an inferior mushroom for hunting. Note that mushrooms should not be eaten raw without proper cleaning and removal of all insects and decay.

Tricholomataceae

Armillaria [Opyonok Osenniy] - Autumn Stump-Grower; *The Honey Mushroom, Shoestring Rot*). The genus *Armillaria*, with the popular species *A. gallica* and *A. mellea*, being so similar that they are rarely differentiated, are palatable, highly abundant mushrooms. Generally found on decaying tree stumps, they grow in very large quantities and are easy to spot and identify, arguably reducing the fun and challenge in mushroom hunting.

Pleurotus ostreatus [Veshenka Ustrichnaya] - Oyster-Like Hanging Mushroom; *The Oyster Mushroom*). It is the most commonly picked tree-dwelling mushroom and is often also artificially cultivated for sale in grocery stores. This sturdy mushroom can be quite palatable when young. Growing these mushrooms at home can be a profitable enterprise and some Russians engage in the activity.

Matsutake, the highly-sought-after pine mushroom, found in coniferous forests in Hiroshima in autumn.

Tricholoma matsutake - = syn. *T. nauseosum*, the rare red pine mushroom that has a very fine aroma. Its undeniable fragrance is both sweet and spicy. They grow under trees and are usually concealed under fallen leaves and/or the duff layer. It forms a symbiotic relationship with the roots of a limited number of tree species. In Japan it is most commonly associated with Japanese Red Pine. However in the Pacific Northwest it is found in coniferous forests of Douglas fir, Noble fir, sugar pine, and Ponderosa pine.

Further south, it is also associated with hardwoods, namely Tanoak and Madrone forests. The Pacific Northwest and other similar temperate regions along the Pacific Rim also hold great habitat producing these and other quality wild mushrooms. In 1999, N. Bergius and E. Danell reported that Swedish (*Tricholoma nauseosum*) and Japanese matsutake (*T. matsutake*) are the same species. The report aroused the import from Northern Europe to Japan because of the comparable flavor and taste. Matsutake are difficult to find and are therefore very expensive.

Moreover, domestic productions of Matsutake in Japan have been sharply reduced over the last fifty years due to a pine nematode Bursaphelenchus xylophilus, and it has influenced the price a great deal. The annual harvest of Matsutake in Japan has since further decreased. The price for Matsutake in the Japanese market is highly dependent on quality, availability and origin. The Japanese Matsutake at the beginning of the season, which is the highest grade, can go up to $2000 per kilogram, while the average value for imported Matsutake from China, Europe, and the United States is only about $90 per kilogram.

The *Tricholoma magnivelare* is a very popular and commonly cultivated mushroom in North America. British Columbia exports large quantities of this mushroom overseas to Asia where it is in high demand.

CHAPTER 10

Mushroom Poisoning

Mushroom poisoning (also known as mycetism) refers to harmful effects from ingestion of toxic substances present in a mushroom. These symptoms can vary from slight gastrointestinal discomfort to death. The toxins present are secondary metabolites produced in specific biochemical pathways in the fungal cells. Mushroom poisoning is usually the result of ingestion of wild mushrooms after misidentification of a toxic mushroom as an edible species. The most common reason for this misidentification is close resemblance in terms of colour and general morphology of the toxic mushrooms species with edible species. Even very experienced wild mushroom gatherers are upon rare occasion poisoned by eating toxic species, despite being well aware of the risks, through carelessness.

To prevent mushroom poisoning, mushroom gatherers need to be very familiar with the mushrooms they intend to collect as well as with any similar-looking toxic species. In addition, edibility of mushrooms may depend on methods of preparation for cooking. Collectors also need to be well aware that edibility or toxicity of some species varies with geographic location.

Lepista nuda

The Fruiting Body of the Fungus Pilobolus

Ascocarp of *Sarcoscypha Austriaca*

Omphalotus Nidiformis, a bioluminescent mushroom

Armillaria solidipes

The Ascocarp of a Morel Contains Numerous Apothecia

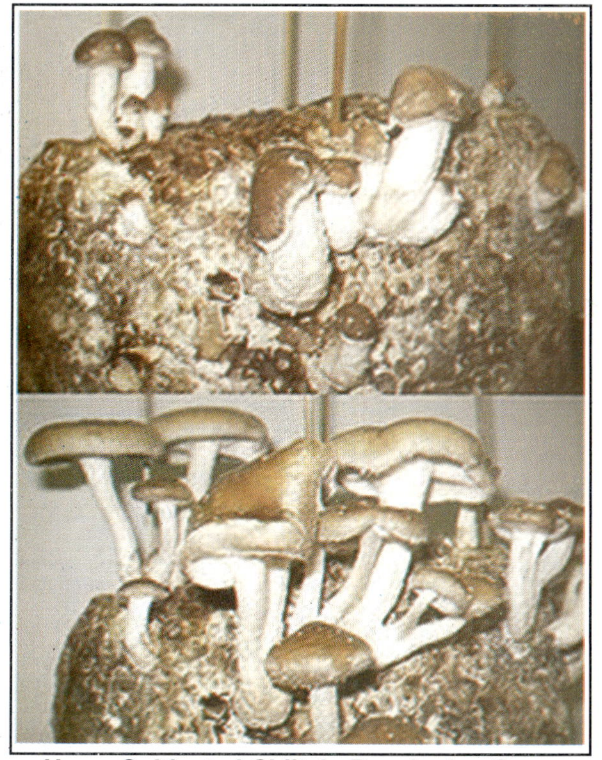

Home Cultivated *Shiitake* Developing Over Approximately 24 Hours

Psilocybe villarrealiae, which is Only Known to a Small Area of Mexico

Fomes Fomentarius

Fomitopsis Pinicola is a Lookalike Species

A. Campestris

A bisected Stinkhorn Egg (*Phallus impudicus*)

Phallus ravenelii

White Mushrooms Ready for Cooking.
While Common, They are just One of the Many Types of Mushrooms Cultivated and Eaten

Sarcoscypha Coccinea

Honey Fungus

Folk Traditions

There are many folk traditions concerning the defining features of poisonous mushrooms. Unfortunately there are no general identifiers for poisonous mushrooms, and so such traditions are unreliable guides. Use of folk traditions to try to identify edible mushrooms is a frequent cause of mushroom poisoning. Examples of erroneous folklore "rules" include:

- *"Poisonous mushrooms are brightly coloured"*—While the toxic/hallucinogenic fly agaric is usually bright red or yellow, the deadly destroying angel is an unremarkable white, and the deadly *Galerinas* are brown. Some choice edible species (chanterelles, *Amanita caesarea, Laetiporus sulphureus*, etc.) are brightly coloured, while most poisonous species are brown or white.
- *"Insects/animals will avoid toxic mushrooms"*—Fungi that are harmless to invertebrates can still be toxic to humans; the death cap, for instance, is often infested by insect larvae.
- *"Poisonous mushrooms blacken silver"*—None of the known mushroom toxins have a reaction with silver.
- *"Poisonous mushrooms taste bad"*—People who have eaten the deadly *Amanitas* reported that the mushrooms tasted quite good.
- *"All mushrooms are safe if cooked/parboiled/dried/pickled/etc."*—While it is true that some otherwise inedible species can be rendered safe by special preparation, many toxic species cannot be made toxin-free. Many fungal toxins are not particularly sensitive to heat and so are not broken down during cooking; particularly a-amanitin, the poison produced by the death cap (*Amanita phalloides*) and others of the genus, is not denatured by heat.
- *"Poisonous mushrooms will turn rice red when boiled"* —A number of Laotian refugees were hospitalized after eating mushrooms (probably toxic *Russula* species) deemed safe by this folklore rule and this misconception cost at least one person her life.

- *"Poisonous mushrooms have a pointed cap.* Edible ones have a flat, rounded cap."—The shape of the mushroom cap does not correlate with presence or absence of mushroom toxins, so this is not a reliable method to distinguish between edible and poisonous species. Death cap, for instance, has a rounded cap when mature.
- *"Boletes are generally safe to eat"* — It is true that unlike a number of *Amanita* species in particular, in most parts of the world, there are no known deadly varieties of the Boletus genus, which reduces the risks associated with misidentification. However, mushrooms like the Devil's Bolete are poisonous both raw and cooked and can lead to strong gastrointestinal symptoms, and other species like the *Lurid Bolete* require thorough cooking to break down toxins. As with other mushroom *genera,* proper caution is therefore advised in determining the correct species.

Causes of Poisonings

Of the many thousands of mushroom species in the world, only 32 have been associated with fatalities, and an additional 52 have been identified as containing significant toxins. By far the majority of mushroom poisonings are not fatal, but the majority of fatal poisonings are attributable to the *Amanita phalloides* mushroom.

A majority of these cases are due to "mistaken identity." One way this can happen is that the victim attempts to apply folk knowledge from one geographic area to another. This is a common occurrence with *A. phalloides* in particular, due to its resemblance to the Asian "paddy-straw" mushroom, *Volvariella volvacea.* Both are light-coloured and covered with a universal veil when young.

Amanitas can be mistaken for other species, as well, particularly when immature. On at least one occasion they have been mistaken for *Coprinus comatus.* In this case the victim had some (obviously limited) experience in identifying mushrooms, but did not take the time to correctly identify these particular mushrooms until after he began to experience symptoms of mushroom poisoning.

The author of "Mushrooms Demystified", David Arora cautions puffball-hunters to beware of Amanita "eggs", which are Amanitas still entirely encased in their universal veil. Amanitas at this stage are difficult to distinguish from puffballs.

A majority of mushroom poisonings in general are the result of small children, especially toddlers in the "grazing" stage, ingesting mushrooms found in the lawn. While this can happen with any mushroom, *Chlorophyllum molybdites* is often implicated due to its preference for growing in lawns. *C. molybdites* causes severe gastrointestinal upset but is not considered deadly poisonous.

A few poisonings are the result of misidentification while attempting to collect hallucinogenic mushrooms for recreational use. In 1981, one fatality and two hospitalizations occurred following consumption of *Galerina autumnalis,* mistaken for a *Psilocybe* species. *Galerina* and *Psilocybe* species are both small, brown, and sticky, and can be found growing together. However, *Galerina* contains amatoxins, the same poison found in the deadly Amanita species. Another case reports kidney failure following ingestion of *Cortinarius orellanus,* a mushroom containing orellanine.

Naturally, accidental ingestion of hallucinogenic species also occurs, but is rarely harmful when ingested in small quantities. Cases of serious toxicity have been reported in small children. *Amanita pantherina,* while it contains the same hallucinogens as *Amanita muscaria* (e.g., ibotenic acid and muscimol), has been more commonly associated with severe gastrointestinal upset than its better-known counterpart.

Although usually not fatal, *Omphalotus* ssp., "Jack-o-lantern mushrooms," are another cause of sometimes significant toxicity. They are sometimes mistaken for chanterelles. Both are bright orange and fruit at the same time of year, although *Omphalotus* grows on wood and has true gills rather than the veins of a *Cantharellus*. They contain muscarine, which causes vomiting, diarrhea, salivation, perspiration, and tears. In high doses it can cause respiratory failure. The same toxin occurs in *Clitocybe dealbata*, which is occasionally mistaken for an oyster mushroom or other edible species.

Toxicities can also occur with collection of morels. Even true morels, if eaten raw, will cause gastrointestinal upset. Therefore morels should always be thoroughly cooked before eating. *Verpa bohemica*, although referred to as "thimble morels" or "early morels" by some, have caused toxic effects in some individuals. "False morels" or *Gyromitra* spp., are deadly poisonous if eaten raw. They contain a toxin called gyromitrin, which can cause neurotoxicity, gastrointestinal toxicity, and destruction of the blood cells. The Finns consume the mushroom after parboiling, but it is not known if this renders the mushroom entirely safe, resulting in its being called the "fugu of the Finnish cuisine."

A more unusual toxin is coprine, a disulfiram-like compound which is harmless unless ingested within a few days of ingesting alcohol. It inhibits aldehyde dehydrogenase, an enzyme required for breaking down alcohol. Thus the symptoms of toxicity are similar to being "hung over" — flushing, headache, nausea, palpitations, and in severe cases, trouble breathing. *Coprinus* species, including *Coprinopsis atramentaria*, contain coprine. Notably, *Coprinus comatus* does not, but it is best to avoid mixing alcohol with other members of this genus.

Recently, poisonings have also been associated with *Amanita smithii*. These poisonings may be due to orellanine, but the onset of symptoms occurs in 4 to 11 hours, which is much quicker than the 3 to 20 days normally associated with orellanine.

In some cases, toxicity can occur even with mushrooms that are widely considered edible.

Paxillus involutus is also indigestible when raw, but is eaten in Europe after pickling or parboiling. However, after the death of the German mycologist Dr. Julius Schäffer, it was discovered that the mushroom contains a toxin which can stimulate the immune system to attack its own red blood cells. This reaction is rare, but can occur even after safely eating the mushroom for many years. Similarly, *Tricholoma equestre* was widely considered edible and good, until it was connected with rare cases of rhabdomyolysis.

In the fall of 2004, thirteen deaths were associated with consumption of *Pleurocybella porrigens* or "angel's wings." These mushrooms are generally considered edible. All the victims died of an acute brain disorder, and all had pre-existing kidney disease. The exact cause of the toxicity was not known at this time and the deaths cannot be definitively attributed to mushroom consumption.

However, mushroom poisoning is not always due to mistaken identity. For example, the highly toxic ergot (*Claviceps purpurea*), which grows on rye, is sometimes ground up with rye, unnoticed, and later consumed. This can cause devastating, even fatal effects, which is called Ergotism.

Cases of idiosyncratic or "unusual" reactions to fungi can also occur. Some are probably due to allergy, others to some other kind of sensitivity. It is not uncommon for an individual person to experience gastrointestinal upset associated with one particular mushroom species or genus. Eating small portions when trying a new mushroom may be used as a precaution to identify individual problems with the new species.

Toxins and Their Symptoms

Poisonous mushrooms contain a variety of different toxins that can differ markedly in toxicity. Symptoms of mushroom poisoning may vary from gastric upset to life-threatening organ failure resulting in death. Serious symptoms do not always occur immediately after eating; often not until the toxin attacks the kidney or liver, sometimes days or weeks later.

The most common consequence of mushroom poisoning is simply gastrointestinal upset. Most "poisonous" mushrooms contain gastrointestinal irritants which cause vomiting and diarrhea (sometimes requiring hospitalization), but usually no long-term damage. However, there are a number of recognized mushroom toxins with specific, and sometimes deadly, effects:

- *Alpha-amanitin* (deadly: causes liver damage 1–3 days after ingestion)–principal toxin in genus *Amanita*.
- *Phallotoxin* (causes gastrointestinal upset)–also found in poisonous *Amanitas*
- *Orellanine* (deadly: causes kidney failure within 3 weeks after ingestion)–principal toxin in genus *Cortinarius*.
- *Muscarine* (sometimes deadly: can cause respiratory failure)–found in genus *Omphalotus*.
- *Gyromitrin* (deadly: causes neurotoxicity, gastrointestinal upset, and destruction of blood cells)–principal toxin in genus *Gyromitra*.
- *Coprine* (causes illness when consumed with alcohol)–principal toxin in genus *Coprinus*.
- *Ibotenic acid* and muscimol (hallucinogenic)–principal toxin in *A. muscaria*, *A. pantherina*, and *A. gemmata*.
- *Psilocybin* and *psilocin* (hallucinogenic)–principal 'toxin' in genus *Psilocybe*.
- *Arabitol* (causes gastrointestinal irritation in some people).
- *Bolesatine* a toxin found in *Boletus satanas*
- *Ergotamine* (deadly: affects the vascular system and can lead to loss of limbs and death): An alkaloid found in genus *Claviceps*.

Symptoms of mushroom poisoning vary depending on the toxins involved.

- *Alpha-amanitin:* For 6–12 hours, there are no symptoms. This is followed by a period of gastrointestinal upset (vomiting and profuse, watery diarrhea). This stage is caused primarily by the phallotoxins and typically lasts

24 hours. At the end of this second stage is when severe liver damage begins. The damage may continue for another 2–3 days. Kidney damage can also occur. Some patients will require a liver transplant. Amatoxins are found in some mushrooms in the genus *Amanita,* but are also found in some species of *Galerina* and *Lepiota*. Overall, mortality is between 10 and 15 percent. Recently, *Silybum marianum* or blessed milk thistle has been shown to protect the liver from amanita toxins and promote regrowth of damaged cells, including a study in which 60 patients exposed to death cap poison were given 20 mg/kg of milk thistle seeds per day within 48 hours of consuming the deadly mushrooms. None of the patients died.

- *Orellanine:* This toxin causes no symptoms for 3-20 days after ingestion. Typically around day 11, the process of kidney failure begins, and is usually symptomatic by day 20. These symptoms can include pain in the area of the kidneys, thirst, vomiting, headache, and fatigue. A few species in the very large genus *Cortinarius* contain this toxin. People who have eaten mushrooms containing orellanine may experience early symptoms as well, because the mushrooms often contain other toxins in addition to orellanine. A related toxin that causes similar symptoms but within 3-6 days has been isolated from *Amanita smithiana* and some other related toxic *Amanita*s.
- *Muscarine:* Muscarine stimulates the muscarinic receptors of the nerves and muscles. Symptoms include sweating, salivation, tears, blurred vision, palpitations, and, in high doses, respiratory failure. Muscarine is found in mushrooms of the genus *Omphalotus,* notably the Jack o' Lantern mushrooms. It is also found in *A. muscaria,* although it is now known that the main effect of this mushroom is caused by ibotenic acid. Muscarine can also be found in some *Inocybe* species and *Clitocybe* species, particularly *Clitocybe dealbata,* and some red-pored *Boletes.*
- *Gyromitrin:* Stomach acids convert gyromitrin to monomethylhydrazine (MMH), a compound employed

in rocket fuel. It affects multiple body systems. It blocks the important neurotransmitter GABA, leading to stupor, delirium, muscle cramps, loss of coordination, tremors, and/or seizures. It causes severe gastrointestinal irritation, leading to vomiting and diarrhea. In some cases, liver failure has been reported. It can also cause red blood cells to break down, leading to jaundice, kidney failure, and signs of anemia. It is found in mushrooms of the genus *Gyromitra*. A gyromitrin-like compound has also been identified in mushrooms of the genus *Verpa*.

- *Coprine:* Coprine is metabolized to a chemical that resembles disulfiram. It inhibits aldehyde dehydrogenase (ALDH), which generally causes no harm, unless the person has alcohol in their bloodstream while ALDH is inhibited. This can happen if alcohol is ingested shortly before or up to a few days after eating the mushrooms. In that case the alcohol cannot be completely metabolized, and the person will experience flushed skin, vomiting, headache, dizziness, weakness, apprehension, confusion, palpitations, and sometimes trouble breathing. Coprine is found mainly in mushrooms of the genus *Coprinus*, although similar effects have been noted after ingestion of *Clitocybe clavipes*.
- *Ibotenic acid:* This organic acid is metabolized to muscimol. The effects of muscimol vary, but nausea and vomiting are common. Confusion, euphoria, or sleepiness are possible. Loss of muscular coordination, sweating, and chills are likely. Some people experience visual distortions, a feeling of strength, or delusions. Symptoms normally appear after 30 minutes to 2 hours and last for several hours. *A. muscaria*, the "Alice in Wonderland" mushroom, is known for the toxic/hallucinogenic properties caused by ibotenic acid, but *A. pantherina* and *A. gemmata* also contain the same compound. While normally self-limiting, fatalities have been associated with *A. pantherina*, and consumption of a large number of any of these mushrooms is likely to be dangerous.

- *Psilocybin:* This compound is converted into psilocin when ingested. Symptoms begin shortly after ingestion. The effects can include euphoria, visual and religious hallucinations, and heightened perception. However, some persons experience fear, agitation, confusion, and schizophrenialike symptoms. All symptoms generally pass after several hours. Some (though not all) members of the genus *Psilocybe* contain psilocybin, as do some *Panaeolus, Copelandia, Conocybe, Gymnopilus,* and others. Some of these mushrooms also contain baeocystin, which has effects similar to psilocin.
- *Arabitol:* A sugar alcohol, similar to mannitol, which causes no harm in most people but causes gastrointestinal irritation in some. It is found in small amounts in oyster mushrooms, and considerable amounts in *Suillus* species and *Hygrophoropsis aurantiaca* (the " false chanterelle").

Some mushrooms contain less toxic compounds and, therefore, are not severely poisonous. Poisonings by these mushrooms may respond well to treatment. However, certain types of mushrooms, such as the Amanitas, contain very potent toxins and are very poisonous; so even if symptoms are treated promptly mortality is high. With some toxins, death can occur in a week or a few days. Although a liver or kidney transplant may save some patients with complete organ failure, in many cases there are no organs available. Patients who are hospitalized and given aggressive support therapy almost immediately after ingestion of amanitin-containing mushrooms have a mortality rate of only 10 per cent, whereas those admitted 60 or more hours after ingestion have a 50-90 per cent mortality rate.

Poisonous Mushrooms

Three of the most lethal mushrooms belong to the genus *Amanita*: the death cap (*A. phalloides*) and destroying angels (*A. virosa,* and *A. bisporigera*); the fool's mushroom (*A. verna*) and two are from the genus *Cortinarius*: the deadly webcap (*C. rubellus*), and the fool's webcap (*C. orellanus*). Several species of Galerina, Lepiota, and Conocybe also contain lethal amounts of amatoxins. Deadly species are listed in the List of deadly fungi.

The following species may cause great discomfort, sometimes requiring hospitalization, but are not considered deadly.

- *Amanita muscaria* (fly agaric)–known for its use as an entheogen, and it is now known that the toxins convert to psychoactives upon drying.
- *Amanita muscaria var. regalis*–symptoms generally mild.
- *Amanita pantherina* (panther mushroom)–contains similar toxins as *A. muscaria,* but is associated with more fatalities than *A. muscaria.*
- *Chlorophyllum molybdites* (greengills)–causes intense gastrointestinal upset.
- *Entoloma* (pinkgills)–some species are highly poisonous, such as livid entoloma (*Entoloma sinuatum*), *Entoloma rhodopolium*, and *Entoloma nidorosum*. Symptoms of intense gastrointestinal upset appear after 20 minutes to 4 hours, caused by an unidentified gastrointestinal irritant.
- Many *Inocybe* species such as *Inocybe fastigiata* and *Inocybe geophylla* contain muscarine, while *Inocybe erubescens* is the only one known to have caused death.
- Some white *Clitocybe* species, including *C. rivulosa* and *C. dealbata*–contain muscarine.
- *Tricholoma pardinum, Tricholoma tigrinum* (Tiger Tricholoma)–gastrointestinal upset due to an unidentified toxin, begins in 15 minutes to 2 hours and lasts 4 to 6 days.
- *Tricholoma equestre* Man-on-horseback–until recently thought edible and good, can lead to rhabdomyolysis after repeated consumption.
- *Hypholoma fasciculare / Naematoloma fasciculare* (Sulfur tuft)–usually causes gastrointestinal upset but the toxins fasciculol E and F could lead to paralysis and death.

- *Paxillus involutus* (Brown roll-rim)–once thought edible, but now found to destroy red blood cells with regular or long-term consumption.
- *Boletus satanas* (Devil's bolete), *Boletus luridus, Boletus legaliae, Boletus piperatus, Boletus erythropus, Boletus pulcherrimus*–gastrointestinal irritation. Of these, only *B. pulcherrimus* has been implicated in a death. Many books list *B. erythropus* as edible, but Arora lists it as "to be avoided."
- *Hebeloma crustuliniforme* (known as Poison pie or Fairy cakes)–causes gastrointestinal symptoms such as nausea and vomiting.
- *Russula emetica* (the Sickener)– as its name implies, causes rapid vomiting. Other Russulas with a peppery taste (*Russula silvicola, Russula mairei*) will likely do the same.
- *Agaricus hondensis, Agaricus californicus, Agaricus praeclaresquamosus, Agaricus xanthodermus*–cause vomiting and diarrhea in most people, although some people seem to be immune.
- *Lactarius piperatus, Lactarius torminosus, Lactarius rufus*–these and other peppery-tasting *Lactarius* are pickled and eaten in Scandinavia, but are indigestible or poisonous unless correctly prepared.
- *Lactarius vinaceorufescens, Lactarius uvidus*–reportedly poisonous. Arora reports that all yellow- or purple-staining *Lactarius* are "best avoided."
- *Ramaria gelatinosa*–causes indigestion in many people, although some seem immune.
- *Gomphus floccosus* (the scaly chanterelle)–causes gastric upset in many people, although some eat it without problems. *G. floccosus* is related to the chanterelle and sometimes confused with it.

Other Causes of Poisoning

Mushrooms may be rendered poisonous by insecticides or herbicides sprayed on lawns or reserves. At least one author recommends never picking them in non-natural landscapes for this reason.

Also, mushrooms are sometimes contaminated by concentrating pollutants, such as heavy metals or radioactive material.

Rotten mushrooms may cause food poisoning. Mushrooms which are mushy, bad-smelling, or moldy (even of a choice edible species) may be toxic due to bacterial decay or mold.

Many mushrooms are high in fiber. Excessive consumption of mushrooms may lead to indigestion, which may be diagnosed as mushroom "poisoning."

CHAPTER 11 Medicinal Mushrooms

Medicinal mushrooms are mushrooms, or mushroom extracts, that are used or studied as possible treatments for diseases. Research has shown some medicinal mushroom isolates that have promising cardiovascular, anticancer, antiviral, antibacterial, antiparasitic, anti-inflammatory, and antidiabetic properties. Currently, several extracts (polysaccharide-K, polysaccharide peptide, lentinan) have widespread use in Japan, Korea and China, as adjuvants to radiation treatments and chemotherapy.

The concept of a medicinal mushroom has a history spanning millennia in parts of Asia. Only a few mushroom extracts have been extensively tested for efficacy. The available results for most other extracts, are on isolated cell lines, animal research with rodents, or underpowered/small clinical human trials. Although medicinal molds do not produce mushrooms, these fungi were the original source of penicillin, the first statins, and griseofulvin.

Mushrooms have long been valued as highly tasty and nutritional foods by many societies throughout the world. Early civilizations, by trial and error built up a practical knowledge of those suitable to eat and those to be avoided, e.g. poisonous or even psychotropic. However, in the Orient several thousand years ago, there was the recognition that many edible and certain non-edible mushrooms could have valuable health benefits. In addition, research with some non-mushroom forming fungi, or "medicinal molds", led to the discovery of many new medicines.

Mushrooms with a long record of medicinal use include the edibles *Grifola frondosa* (maitake) and *Lentinula edodes* (shiitake). *Ganoderma lucidum*, used as tea, is known in Chinese as língzhi ("spirit plant") and in Japanese mannentake ("10,000 year mushroom"). In ancient Japan, *Grifola frondosa* was considered medicinal, and was worth it's weight in silver. The prophet Muhammad said, "Truffles are 'manna' which Allah, sent to the people of Israel through Moses, and its juice is a medicine for the eyes". The ancient Egyptians considered mushrooms food for royalty.

Ötzi the Iceman, a mummified human from 3300 BC, was found carrying *Fomes fomentarius* (ice man fungus) and *Piptoporus betulinus* wrapped in a leather string. Hippocrates wrote that *Fomes fomentarius* was used as an ointment for the skin. *Fomes fomentarius* was used topically in Europe during the 18th and 19th centuries to treat wounds. Genetic testing has shown animals are much more closely related to mushrooms than plants.

Immune System and Cancer

A diverse group of polysaccharides found in mushrooms, has been a subject of research since the 1960s. Studies show that mushroom extracts may alter the immune response, acting as biological response modifiers. Although the mechanism of action is not fully understood, mushroom beta-glucans are known to interact with the immune system receptors complement receptor 3, scavenger receptors, lactosylceramide, and dectin-1.

"While the mechanism of their antitumor actions is still not completely understood, stimulation and modulation of key host immune responses by these mushroom polymers appears central. Particularly and most importantly for modern medicine are polysaccharides with antitumor and immunostimulating properties. Several of the mushroom polysaccharide compounds have proceeded through phases I, II, and III clinical trials and are used extensively and successfully in Asia to treat various cancers and other diseases."

The fungus *nodulisporium sylviforme* is able to create small amounts of the anticancer drug paclitaxel.

Statins

Pleurotus ostreatus (oyster mushroom) naturally contains the statin lovastatin up to 2.8% based on dry weight). Statins, are a class of drugs used for high cholesterol, they are some of the best-selling pharmaceuticals. Statins were first discovered in medicinal molds.

Effect on Cholesterol

Some mushrooms have shown potential to reduce cholesterol levels *Tremella fuciformis, Auricularia auricula-judae, Agaricus subrufescens* (agaricus blazei), *Grifola frondosa* (maitake), and *Ganoderma lucidum* (reishi). Some fungi produce cholesterol inhibitors known as zaragozic acids. *Lentinula edodes* (shiitake) contains the anticholesterol compound eritadenine.

Effect on Cognition

In vitro experiments with *Hericium erinaceus* (lion's mane) have demonstrated ability to stimulate rat nerve cells, stimulate nerve growth factor, and stimulate myelination. In 2009, a double-blind, parallel-group, placebo-controlled trial showed that supplementation with *Hericium erinaceus* improved cognitive ability. *Hericium erinaceus* was reported to be able to enhance mental well being.

The following cognitive drugs were created using *Claviceps purpurea* (ergot) extracts; cafergot, pergolide and cabergoline, ergoloid and lysergic acid diethylamide (LSD).

Over 200 species of mushrooms, distributed amongst the following genera: *Psilocybe* (magic mushrooms), *Gymnopilus*,

Panaeolus, Copelandia, Hypholoma, Pluteus, Inocybe, Conocybe, Panaeolina, Gerronema, and *Agrocybe, Galerina*, and *Mycena* contain the entheogens psilocybin, psilocin, and baeocystin.

Boletus badius (bay bolete) contains L-theanine, an amino acid with mild psychoactive properties. *Polyozellus multiplex* (blue chanterelle) contains the compound polyozellin.

The following non-edible/poisonous mushrooms, *Amanita muscaria* (fly agaric), *Amanita pantherina*, and *Amanita gemmata* contain muscimol and the neurotoxin ibotenic acid.

In vitro Antiviral, Antibacterial, Antifungal, and Antimicrobial Activities

Mushrooms and medicinal molds create and secrete antiviral, antibacterial, antifungal, and antimicrobial compounds to survive in the wild against competing or pathogenic agents.

"Of an evaluation of over 200 mushroom species, more than 75 per cent of screened polypores showed strong antimicrobial activity."

Agaricus subrufescens (agaricus blazei) - Activity against poliovirus and the western equine encephalitis virus. *Agrocybe aegerita* (pioppino) - Activity against the tobacco mosaic virus. *Boletus edulis* (porcini) - Activity against HIV and the tobacco mosaic virus. *Cantharellus cibarius* (chanterelle) - Activity against certain microbes, bacteria, and fungi. *Cordyceps* (cordyceps)- Activity against *Bipolaris maydis, Mycosphaerella arachidicola, Rhizoctonia solani, Candida albicans* and HIV. *Fistulina hepatica* (beefsteak fungus) - Antibacterial activity. *Ganoderma applanatum* (artist's conk) - Activity against the vaccinia virus, *Bacillus subtilis, Escherichia coli,* and *Pseudomonas syringae. Ganoderma lucidum* (reishi) - Activity against malaria virus, *Physalospora piricola, Botrytis cinerea, Fusarium oxysporum,* HSV-1, HSV-2, influenza virus, and *vesicular stomatitis. Grifola frondosa* (maitake) - Activity against HSV-1, and hepatitis B virus. *Hypsizygus tessellatus* (beech mushroom) - Activity against the Epstein-Barr virus. *Kuehneromyces mutabilis* (sheathed woodtuft) - Activity against the influenza virus.

Laetiporus sulphureus (chicken of the woods) - Activity against methicillin-resistant *Staphylococcus aureus* and glycopeptide-resistant *Leuconostoc mesenteroides*. *Lepista nuda* (blewit) - Antimicrobial activity. *Lentinula edodes* (shiitake) - Contains a proteinase inhibitor and has shown activity against HSV-1 and HIV. *Piptoporus betulinus* (birch polypore) - Activity against the vaccinia virus, *staphylococcus aureus, enterococcus faecalis, bacillus subtilis, escherichia coli, rhodotorula rubra, kluyveromyces marxianus, candida albicans, sporobolomyces salmonicolor*, and *penicillium notatum*. *Pleurotus eryngii* (king oyster mushroom)- Activity against the tobacco mosaic virus. *Pleurotus ostreatus* (oyster mushroom) - activity against hepatitis C virus. *Pleurotus pulmonarius* (indian oyster) - Nematicidal activity. *Polyporus umbellatus* (zhu-ling) - Activity against *Chlamydia trachomatis*. *Poria cocos* (fu-ling) - Activity against *Chlamydia trachomatis*. *Sparassis crispa* (cauliflower mushroom) - Antifungal activity and activity against HIV. *Terfezia* (desert truffle) - Activity against *Bacillus subtilis* and *Staphylococcus aureus*. *Ustilago maydis* (huitlacoche) - Contains the antibiotic ustilagic acid.

The following mushrooms inhibited the HIV virus *in vitro*, *Hericium erinaceum* (lion's mane mushroom), *Flammulina velutipes* (enokitake), *Lactarius camphoratus* (candy cap), *Inonotus obliquus* (chaga), *Pleurotus ostreatus* (oyster mushroom), *Pleurotus pulmonarius* (indian oyster), *Trametes versicolor* (turkey tail mushroom), *Poria cocos* (hoelen), *Umbilicaria esculenta* (iwatake) *Boletus edulis* (porcini), *Cordyceps* (cordyceps), *Lentinula edodes* (shiitake), *Sparassis crispa* (cauliflower mushroom), and *Russula delica* (milk-white brittlegill).

In vitro Antihormone Activity

Mushrooms were shown *in vitro*, to alter the production of certain human hormones. *Agaricus bisporus* (portobello) is able to partially inhibit the activity of aromatase. *Ganoderma lucidum* (reishi) is able to partially inhibit the activity of 5-alpha reductase.

Anti-inflammatory Activity

Animals studies noted extracts of *Fomes fomentarius* (ice man fungus), *Phellinus linteus, Ganoderma lucidum* (reishi), and the *Inonotus obliquus* (chaga) could reduce inflammation. *In vitro*, extracts of *Geastrum saccatum*, *Agrocybe aegerita*, and *Grifola frondosa* (maitake), inhibited the pro-inflammatory enzyme cyclooxygenase. *Piptoporus betulinus* demonstrated *in vitro* anti-inflammatory properties. A small clinical study noted an extract of *Agaricus subrufescens* (agaricus blazei) has anti-inflammatory activity.

Effect on Blood Sugar

Animal research and limited clinical data have shown that some mushrooms have potential to lower elevated blood sugar *Tremella fuciformis* (white jelly fungus), *Poria cocos*, *Ganoderma lucidum* (reishi), *Auricularia auricula-judae* (jelly ear), *Agaricus campestris* (meadow mushroom), *Agaricus subrufescens* (agaricus blazei), *Inonotus obliquus* (chaga), *Hericium erinaceus* (lion's mane), *Agrocybe aegerita* (pioppino), *Coprinus comatus* (shaggy mane), and *cordyceps*.

Grifola frondosa (maitake); may be able to lower blood sugar levels and has been reported to contain compounds that act as alpha-glucosidase inhibitors.

Vitamin D_2 and Conjugated Linoleic Acid (CLA)

Mushrooms are rare vegan sources of vitamin D and conjugated linoleic acid (CLA). *Agaricus bisporus* (portobello) and *Lentinula edodes* (shiitake) contain significant levels of vitamin D_2 after UV light exposure. *Agaricus bisporus* and *Agaricus subrufescens* (agaricus blazei) contain CLA.

Antioxidant Activity

Mushrooms contain various antioxidant compounds. Ergothioneine is present in *Flammulina velutipes* (enokitake) and *Agaricus bisporus* (portobello).

Epidemiological Research

A study noted *Flammulina velutipes* (enokitake) producers had statistically lower cancer rates. A case-control study showed a strong correlation between mushroom consumption and reduced risk of breast cancer. A similar case-control study involving women with breast cancer, found a strong correlation between mushroom consumption and decreased risk of breast cancer (only in postmenopausal woman). A case-control study with 136 subjects and 136 controls showed a correlation between mushroom consumption and decreased risk of gastric cancer.

Edible Species

Agaricus bisporus (Portobello, crimini, white button, champignon mushroom)

Agaricus bisporus is the world's most popular edible mushroom. Research *in vitro* demonstrated this mushroom is most potent in inhibiting the enzyme aromatase among various mushrooms screened. The FDA and National Cancer Institute have shown interest in researching *Agaricus bisporus* and its possible effects on breast cancer. Mouse studies have reported potential immune system regulation, while an *in vitro* study reported activity against various cancer cell lines.

Agaricus subrufescens (Agaricus blazei, Agaricus brasiliensis, himematsutake)

Agaricus subrufescens is an almond-scented mushroom first noticed being used in folk medicine in São Paulo, Brazil. In 1966, the mushroom was sent to Japan for research, which continues today.

In Japan, extracts from *Agaricus subrufescens* are the most popular complementary and alternative medicine used by cancer patients, with usage estimated at 500,000. There is some evidence for using *Agaricus subrufescens* extracts in patients undergoing chemotherapy for certain cancers, such as colorectal cancer and gynaecological cancers. Animal research showed *Agaricus subrufescens* may promote vaccination.

Agrocybe aegerita (Pioppino mushroom)

Auricularia auricula-judae (Jelly ear)

Auricularia auricula-judae has been reported as a folk remedy in numerous regions. Published research has noted possible antitumour, hypoglycemic, anticoagulant and cholesterol-lowering properties.

A lectin from *Boletus edulis* was found to inhibit several malignant cell lines and bind to the neoplastic cell specific T-antigen disaccharide, Galß1-3GalNAc.

Coprinus comatus (Shaggy mane)

An extract of *Coprinus comatus* inhibited the proliferation and viability of the androgen-sensitive human prostate adenocarcinoma cell line LNCaP.

Flammulina velutipes (Enokitake, winter mushroom)

Flammulina velutipes (cultivated vs. wild)

Flammulina velutipes contains compounds with antitumor activity, and epidemiological studies in Japan have associated the mushroom with lower cancer rates. Animal research showed the mushroom may inhibit cancer development.

Grifola frondosa (Maitake, hen-of-the-woods)

In ancient Japan, *Grifola frondosa* was worth its weight in silver. A 2009 systematic review by Massachusetts General Hospital, advocated investigating *Grifola frondosa* for possible effects on cancer, diabetes, and immune system activity. *Grifola frondosa* naturally contains an alpha glucosidase inhibitor and has been researched in a 2009 phase I/II trial. The most researched extract of *Grifola frondosa*, is known as Maitake D-fraction.

Lentinula edodes (Shiitake)

Lentinula edodes is the world's second most popular culinary mushroom, and the world's most popular mushroom that grows from wood. Research has indicated that *Lentinula edodes* may stimulate the immune system, and reduce platelet aggregation.

Lentinan, is an isolate of *Lentinula edodes*. "There have been numerous clinical trials of Lentinan in Japan, though none have been placebo-controlled and double-blinded. However, Lentinan has been approved for clinical use in Japan for many years, and is manufactured by several pharmaceutical companies. Intraperitoneal Lentinan is widely used as an adjuvant treatment for certain cancers in Japan and China."

Active Hexose Correlated Compound (AHCC), an isolate of *Lentinula edodes*, is considered an alternative medicine. Animal research suggests AHCC can help prevent influenza and the West Nile virus. A less studied isolate of *Lentinula edodes*, is known as lentinus edodes mycelia (LEM) extract.

Morchella esculenta (Morel)

Morchella esculenta contains small amounts of hydrazine and must always be cooked before consumption. A galactomannan from *Morchella esculenta* stimulated immune function *in vitro.*

Pleurotus djamor (Pink oyster mushroom)

An extract of *Pleurotus djamor* was found to inhibit proliferation of hepatoma cells and breast cancer cells *in vitro.*

Pleurotus eryngii (King oyster mushroom)

Pleurotus eryngii (left) *Pleurotus ostreatus* (right) *Sparassis crispa* (far right)

An extract of *Pleurotus eryngii* (king oyster mushroom) stimulated immune function *in vitro.*

Pleurotus ostreatus (Oyster mushroom, hiratake)

Pleurotus ostreatus naturally contains the statin lovastatin. Research with *Pleurotus ostreatus* demonstrated activity against various cancer cell lines and animals studies have shown an anticancer effect.

Sparassis crispa (Cauliflower mushroom)

Animal studies have shown *Sparassis crispa* has potential anticancer and immune enhancing activities.

Tremella fuciformis (White jelly fungus)

"*Tremella fuciformis* is commonly known as 'white jelly fungus'. It has a long historical use in traditional Chinese medicine as an immune tonic and for treating debility and exhaustion."

Tremella mesenterica (Golden jelly fungus)

Tremella mesenterica may have immuno-modulatory and anticancer activity.

Tricholoma matsutake (Matsutake)

Tricholoma matsutake is the most expensive culinary mushroom excluding truffles. Animal and cellular studies have shown the mushroom may enhance immune function. The active compound in the mushroom is thought to be an alpha-glucan polysaccharide.

Species used by tea or extraction

Antrodia camphorata

Antrodia camphorata may have immuno-modulatory and anticancer activity.

Astraeus hygrometricus (Earthstar)

Astraeus hygrometricus is a mushroom used in Chinese and Indian folk medicine. Research has shown the mushroom may contain immunomodulators. In a mouse model, the mushroom demonstrated anticancer properties.

Cordyceps spp., (Caterpillar fungus)

Cordyceps mushrooms (*C. sinensis, C. militaris, C. pruinosa, C. ophioglossoides*) are a Chinese herbal remedy with 2000 years of history. These mushrooms have traditionally been used for a variety of ailments, including cancer. Some polysaccharide components including cordycepin, have been isolated from *C. sinensis* and *C. militaris*. Limited clinical data supports the use of cordyceps for fatigue, bronchitis and coughs. Cordyceps may improve exercise performance in healthy older subjects.

Fomes fomentarius (Ice man fungus)

Fomes fomentarius is a mushroom that was found in the possession of Ötzi the Iceman. A review noted several traditional pharmacopoeias (Hungarian, Chinese, Indian) included *Fomes fomentarius*. Research with mice showed an extract of *Fomes fomentarius* altered immune function and *in vitro* research showed an anticancer effect.

Ganoderma lucidum (Língzhi, reishi, mannentake)

Ganoderma lucidum is the most well known medicinal mushroom in folk medicine. *Ganoderma* teas are described in Shennong Ben Cao Jing and Bencao Gangmu. The *Ganoderma* mushroom is occasionally seen in Chinese artwork.

Research demonstrated *Ganoderma* may have anticancer and immune system enhancing properties. Animal studies have noted *Ganoderma* may protect the liver and protect against radiation. A randomized clinical study noted *Ganoderma* improved urinary tract symptoms in men. Research has shown that *Ganoderma* contains compounds that may act as ACE inhibitors, inihibit blood platelets, and fibrosis. According to Memorial Sloan-Kettering, "in clinical studies, *Ganoderma lucidum* increased plasma antioxidant capacity and enhanced immune responses in advance-stage cancer patients."

Inonotus obliquus (Chaga mushroom)

As early as in the sixteenth century, *Inonotus obliquus* was used as an effective folk medicine in Russia and Northern Europe to treat several human malicious tumors and other diseases in the absence of any unacceptable toxic side effects.

In Russia, a medicine called Befungin is an extract of *Inonotus obliquus*.

Research has shown *Inonotus obliquus* has anticancer properties and may be able to stimulate the immune system. In one experiment, mice implanted with melanoma showed a 4-fold increase in survival rate when given an extract of *Inonotus obliquus* mushroom. *Inonotus obliquus* contains betulin, which can be converted to betulinic acid.

Peziza vesiculosa

Research has shown *Peziza vesiculosa* may have anticancer activity.

Phellinus linteus (Mesima)

Scientists have demonstrated that the extracts from fruit-bodies or mycelium of *Phellinus linteus* not only stimulate the hormonal and cell-mediated immune function and quench the inflammatory reactions caused by a variety of stimuli, but also suppress the tumor growth and metastasis. Mounting evidence from different research groups has shown that *Phellinus linteus* induces apoptosis in a host of murine and human carcinomas without causing any measurable toxic effects to their normal counterparts.

Piptoporus betulinus (Birch polypore)

Piptoporus betulinus may have anticancer properties. Ötzi the Iceman, a mummified human from 3300 BC, was found carrying *Piptoporus betulinus* wrapped in a leather string. Researchers have noted the mushroom was probably used for medicinal properties, considering Ötzi was found to be infected with the parasite *Trichuris trichiura*.

Polyporus umbellatus (Zhu-ling)

Poria cocos (Wolfiporia extensa, hoelen, fu-ling)

Schizophyllum commune (Split Gill)

"Schizophyllan (an isolate of *Schizophyllum commune*), is relatively similar to lentinan in composition and biological activity, and its mechanism of immunomoduation and anti-tumour action appears to be quite similar."

Trametes gibbosa (*Daedalea gibbosa*)

A crude extract of the mushroom *Daedalea gibbosa* inhibited chronic myeloid leukemia in a mouse model.

Trametes versicolor (coriolus versicolor, turkey tail, kawaratake, yun-zhi)

Trametes versicolor is a non-edible mushroom traditionally used as a hot water extract. Today two extracts, polysaccharide-K (PSK) and polysaccharide peptide (PSP), are made from the mushroom fruitbody and purified through fermentation methods. PSK is a best selling anticancer medicine in Japan, and is commonly used as a supplement to surgery, radiation, and chemotherapy.

"PSK was first isolated in Japan in the late 1960s while PSP was isolated about 1983 in China. Each compound has shown remarkable anticancer properties with few side effects. Remarkably by 1987 PSK accounted for more than 25 per cent of total national expenditure for anticancer agents in Japan."

Claviceps purpurea (Ergot)

Claviceps purpurea is a non-edible/poisonous fungus that can infects cereal grains. Accidental consumption of ergot can produce ergotism. Ergot has led to the discovery of several drugs. Using ergot's ergoline alkaloids, the following semi-synthetic drugs were created; ergoloid, methylergometrine, ergotamine, pergolide, cabergoline, cafergot, and lysergic acid diethylamide (LSD).

Heavy Metals

Mushrooms and plants that grow from contaminated conditions can absorb certain toxic heavy metals. Some mushroom species are known to hyper-accumulate particular heavy metals. *Agaricus bisporus* (portobello) cadmium, mercury. *Agaricus subrufescens* (agaricus blazei) cadmium, mercury. *Agaricus campestris* (meadow mushroom) cadmium, lead (10x), mercury (10x). *Boletus edulis* (porcini) cadmium (10x), radioactive cesium (Cs-137), lead, mercury (250x), copper. *Cantharellus cibarius* (chanterelle) radioactive cesium (Cs-137) (2x). *Coprinus comatus* (shaggy mane) arsenic (21x), cadmium (8x), mercury (27x). *Flammulina velutipes* (enokitake) arsenic. *Morchella* (morel) lead (70-100x). *Pleurotus ostreatus* (oyster mushroom) cadmium, mercury (65-140x). *Pleurotus pulmonarius* (indian oyster) cadmium, mercury, copper. *Trametes versicolor* (turkey tail mushroom) mercury.

CHAPTER 12 Fungiculture

Fungiculture is the process of producing food, medicine, and other products by the cultivation of mushrooms and other fungi.

The word is also commonly used to refer to the practice of cultivating fungi by leafcutter ants, termites, ambrosia beetles, and marsh periwinkles.

Introduction

Mushrooms are not plants, and require different conditions for optimal growth. Plants develop through photosynthesis, a process that converts atmospheric carbon dioxide into carbohydrates, especially cellulose. While sunlight provides an energy source for plants, mushrooms derive all of their energy and growth materials from their growth medium, through biochemical decomposition processes. This does not mean that light is an unnecessary requirement, since some fungi use light as a signal for fruiting. However, all the materials for growth must already be present in the growth medium. Mushrooms grow well at relative humidity levels of around 95-100 per cent, and substrate moisture levels of 50 to 75 per cent.

Instead of seeds, mushrooms reproduce sexually during underground growth, and asexually through spores. Either of these can be contaminated with airborne microorganisms, which will interfere with mushroom growth and prevent a healthy crop.

Mycelium, or actively growing mushroom culture, is placed on growth substrate to seed or introduce mushrooms to grow on a substrate. This is also known as inoculation, spawning or adding spawn. Its main advantages are to reduce chances of contamination while giving mushrooms a firm beginning. Spores are another inoculation option, but are less developed than established mycelium. Since they are also contaminated easily, they are only manipulated in laboratory conditions with laminar flow cabinet.

Techniques

All mushroom growing techniques require the correct combination of humidity, temperature, substrate (growth medium) and inoculum (spawn or starter culture). Wild harvests, outdoor log inoculation and indoor trays all provide these elements.

Wild Harvesting

Due to its climate, the Pacific Northwest of the USA produces commercially valuable mushrooms. Valued species include:

- American matsutake or pine mushroom (*Tricholoma magnivelare*)
- Chanterelles (*Cantharellus formosus*, *Cantharellus subalbidus*, and *Cantharellus cibarius*)
- Horn of plenty (*Craterellus cornucopioides*)
- Boletes (*Boletus edulis* and others)
- Truffles (*Tuber gibbosum* and *Leucangium carthusiana*)
- Hedgehogs/"spreading-hedgehog mushroom" (*Hydnum repandum*)
- Edible morel (*Morchella esculenta*)

- Coral tooth mushroom (*Hericium abietis*)
- Shaggy parasol (*Lepiota rhacodes*)
- Black picoa (*Picoa carthusiana*)
- Cauliflower mushroom (*Sparassis crispa*)

Mushroom gatherers have the fewest requirements to begin business. Gatherers only need to supply funds for possible park fees, knowledge for identifying mushrooms and gathering time.

There are significant disadvantages to relying on natural mushroom production. These sales may be unregulated, placing buyers at risk for buying toxic or inedible mushrooms. By honest error, harvests may include toxic or inedible species. No controls exist to regulate the quality or frequency of harvests, since gatherers rely on favorable natural conditions and weather to produce fruiting. Conflicts may arise between competing gatherers trying to harvest from the same location.

State parks in the Pacific Northwest or elsewhere may charge fees for mushroom gathering permits. Appalachia also produces edible wild mushrooms, including chanterelles and morels. Pickers may sell directly to distributors, restaurants, or sell their harvest through roadside stands wherever a natural supply of mushrooms is plentiful.

While there may be concern that harvesting wild mushrooms may exploit or damage a natural environment, harvesting wild mushrooms is different from harvesting wild plants, fishing or hunting animals. In these last three cases, removing individuals decreases the ability of a wild population to reproduce, since fewer adults remain. Removing adults leaves fewer individuals capable of reproducing and reduces genetic diversity.

Harvesting wild mushrooms removes only fruiting bodies and their attached spores. However, the fruiting bodies (mushrooms) have likely dropped spores before harvest time, or will likely drop them en route to the harvester's destination, further expanding the fungi's habitat. Arguably, the practice of mushroom harvesting may actually help the species being harvested. While truffles also represent the fruiting body of a larger underground network, they are an exception, since they rely on animal spore dispersion.

Additionally, reproduction and propagation can still occur by propagation of the parent mycelium. Harvesting removes none of the parent mycelium, which remains intact underground.

Outdoor Logs

Mushrooms can be grown on logs placed outdoors in stacks or piles, as has been done for hundreds of years. Sterilization is not performed in this method. Since production may be unpredictable and seasonal, less than 5 per cent of commercially sold mushrooms are produced this way. Here, tree logs are inoculated with spawn, then allowed to grow as they would in wild conditions. Fruiting, or pinning, is triggered by seasonal changes, or by briefly soaking the logs in cool water. Shiitake and oyster mushrooms have traditionally been produced using the outdoor log technique, although controlled techniques such as indoor tray growing or artificial logs made of compressed substrate have been substituted.

Indoor Trays

Indoor growing provides the ability to tightly regulate light, temperature and humidity while excluding contaminants and pests. This allows consistent production, regulated by spawning cycles. This is typically accomplished in windowless, purpose-built buildings, for large scale commercial production.

Indoor tray growing is the most common commercial technique, followed by containerized growing. The tray technique provides the advantages of scalability and easier harvesting. Unlike wild harvests, indoor techniques provide tight control over growing substrate composition and growing conditions. Indoor harvests are much more predictable.

According to Daniel Royse and Robert Beelman, "[Indoor] Mushroom farming consists of six steps, and although the divisions are somewhat arbitrary, these steps identify what is needed to form a production system. The six steps are phase I composting, phase II fertilizing, spawning, casing, pinning, and cropping."

Complete sterilization is not always required or performed during composting. In some cases, a pasteurization step is not included to allow some beneficial microorganisms to remain in the growth substrate.

Specific time spans and temperatures required during stages 3-6 will vary respective to species and variety. Substrate composition and the geometry of growth substrate will also affect the ideal times and temperatures.

Pinning is the trickiest part for a mushroom grower, since a combination of carbon dioxide (CO_2) concentration, temperature, light, and humidity triggers mushrooms towards fruiting. Up until the point when rhizomorphs or mushroom "pins" appear, the mycelium is an amorphous mass spread throughout the growth substrate, unrecognizable as a mushroom.

Carbon dioxide concentration becomes elevated during the vegetative growth phase, when mycelium is sealed in a gas-resistant plastic barrier or bag which traps gases produced by the growing mycelium. To induce pinning, this barrier is opened or ruptured. CO_2 concentration then decreases from about 0.08 per cent to 0.04 per cent, the ambient atmospheric level.

Substrates

Mushroom production converts raw natural ingredients into mushroom tissue, most notably the carbohydrate chitin.

An ideal substrate will contain enough nitrogen and carbohydrate for rapid mushroom growth. Common bulk substrates include:

- Wood chips or sawdust
- Mulched hay
- Strawbedded horse or poultry manure

- Corncobs
- Waste or recycled paper
- Coffee pulp or grounds
- Nut and seed hulls
- Cottonseed hulls
- Cocoa bean hulls
- Cottonseed meal
- Soybean meal
- Brewer's grain
- Ammonium nitrate
- Urea

Mushrooms metabolize complex carbohydrates in their substrate into glucose, which is then transported through the mycelium as needed for growth and energy. While it is used as a main energy source, its concentration in the growth medium should not exceed 2 per cent. For ideal fruiting, closer to 1 per cent is ideal.

Pests and Diseases

Parasitic insects, bacteria and other fungi all pose risks to indoor production. The sciarid fly or phorid fly may lay eggs in growth medium, which hatch into worms and damage developing mushrooms during all growth stages. Bacterial blotch caused by *Pseudomonas* bacteria or patches of *Trichoderma* green mold also pose a risks during the fruiting stage. Pesticides and sanitizing agents are available to use against these infestations. Biological controls for insect sciarid and phorid flies have also been proposed.

A recent epidemic of Trichoderma green mold has significantly affected mushroom production: "From 1994-96, crop losses in Pennsylvania ranged from 30 to 100 per cent".

Commercially Cultivated Fungi

- *Agaricus bisporus*, also known as champignon and the button mushroom. This species also includes the portobello and crimini mushrooms.

- *Auricularia polytricha* or *Auricularia auricula-judae* (Tree ear fungus), two closely related species of jelly fungi that are commonly used in Chinese cuisine.
- *Flammulina velutipes*, the "winter mushroom", also known as *enokitake* in Japan.
- *Hypsizygus tessulatus* (also *Hypsizygus marmoreus*), called *shimeji* in Japanese, it is a common variety of mushroom available in most markets in Japan. Known as "Beech mushroom" in Europe.
- *Lentinus edodes*, also known as shiitake, oak mushroom. *Lentinus edodes* is largely produced in Japan, China and South Korea. *Lentinus edodes* accounts for 10 per cent of world production of cultivated mushrooms. Common in Japan, China, Australia and North America.
- *Pleurotus* species are the second most important mushrooms in production in the world, accounting for 25 per cent of total world production.
- *Pleurotus* mushrooms are cultivated worldwide; China is the major producer. Several species can be grown on carbonaceous matter such as straw or newspaper. In the wild they are usually found growing on wood.
- *Pleurotus cornucopiae*
- *Pleurotus eryngii* (king trumpet mushroom)
- *Pleurotus ostreatus* (oyster mushroom)
- *Rhizopus oligosporus* - the fungal starter culture used in the production of tempeh. In tempeh the mycelia of *R. oligosporus* are consumed.
- *Sparassis crispa* - recent developments have led to this being cultivated in California.
- *Tremella fuciformis* (Snow fungus), another type of jelly fungus that is commonly used in Chinese cuisine.
- *Tuber* species, (the truffle), Truffles belong to the ascomycete grouping of fungi. The truffle fruitbodies develop underground in mycorrhizal association with certain trees e.g. oak, poplar, beech, and hazel. Being

difficult to find, trained pigs or dogs are often used to sniff them out for easy harvesting.

- *Tuber aestivum* (Summer or St. Jean truffle)
- *Tuber magnatum* (Piemont white truffle)
- *Tuber melanosporum* (Périgord truffle)
- *T.melanosporum* x *T.magnatum* (Khanaqa truffle)
- *Terfezia sp.* (Desert truffle)
- *Ustilago maydis* (Corn smut), a fungal pathogen of the maize plants. Also called the Mexican truffle, although not a true truffle.
- *Volvariella volvacea* (the "Paddy straw mushroom.") *Volvariella* mushrooms account for 16 per cent of total production of cultivated mushrooms in the world.
- Production Regions in U.S.A.

Pennsylvania is the top-producing mushroom state in the United States, and celebrates September as "Mushroom Month".

The borough of Kennett Square is a historical and present leader in mushroom production. It currently leads production of Agaricus-type mushrooms, followed by California, Florida and Michigan.

Other mushroom-producing states:

- *East:* Connecticut, Delaware, Florida, Maryland, New York, Pennsylvania, Tennessee, and Vermont.
- *Central:* Illinois, Oklahoma, Texas, and Wisconsin.
- *West:* California, Colorado, Montana, Oregon, Utah and Washington.

Vancouver, British Columbia, also has a significant number of producers — about 60 as of 1998 — mostly located in the lower Fraser Valley.

Fungi

Fungi straddle the realms of microbiology and macrobiology. They range in size from the single-celled organism we know as yeast to the largest known living organism on Earth — a 3.5-mile-wide mushroom. Dubbed "the humongous fungus," this honey mushroom (*Armillaria ostoyae*) covers some 2,200 acres in Oregon's Malheur National Forest.

The only above-ground signs of the humongous fungus are patches of dead trees and the mushrooms that form at the base of infected trees. Courtesy of the USDA Forest Service.

It started out 2400 years ago as a single spore invisible to the naked eye, then grew to gargantuan proportions by intertwining threads of cells called *hyphae.*

Under a microscope, hyphae look like a tangled mass of threads or tiny plant roots. This tangled mass is called the fungal mycelium, and is the part of the famous honey mushroom that spreads for miles underground.

If mushrooms and other fungi can get so huge, why mention them on a site about microorganisms?

Visible fungi such as mushrooms are multicellular entities, but their cells are closely connected in a way unlike that of other multicellular organisms.

Plant and animal cells are entirely separated from one another by cell walls (in plants) and cell membranes (in animals). The dividers between fungal cells, however, often have openings that allow proteins, fluids and even nuclei to flow from one cell to another. A few fungal species have no cell dividers: just a long, continuous cell dotted by multiple nuclei spread throughout.

Fungi are eukaryotic *(you-carry-ah-tick)* organisms—their DNA is enclosed in a nucleus. Many of them may look plant-like, but fungi do not make their own food from sunlight like plants do.

Friendly Fungi

Some fungi are quite useful to us. We've tapped several kinds to make antibiotics to fight bacterial infections. These antibiotics are based on natural compounds the fungi produce to compete against bacteria for nutrients and space. We use

Saccharomyces cerevisiae (sack-air-oh-my-seas sair-uh-vis-ee-ay), aka baker's yeast, to make bread rise and to brew beer. Fungi break down dead plants and animals and keep the world tidier. We're exploring ways to use natural fungal enemies of insect pests to get rid of these bugs.

Fungal Enemies

There are some nasty fungi that cause diseases in plants, animals and people. One of the most famous is *Phytophthora infestans (fie-tof-thor-uh in-fes-tuhns)*, which caused the Great Potato Famine in Ireland in the mid-1800s that resulted in a million deaths. Fungi ruin about a quarter to half of harvested fruits and vegetables annually.

Many more interesting facts about fungi can be found throughout the Microbe website, so keep clicking and reading.

Fungal Growth and Reproduction

As the "humongous fungus" shows, fungi can grow to enormous mass if unimpeded. Hyphae grow by adding cells at the tip. Hyphae are very tiny, measuring only a few microns in diameter in some cases. But they can also be incredibly strong, punching through not only the soft membranes of animal cells, but also the tough, woody walls of plant cells and the hard chitin that makes up insect bodies. Fungi usually reproduce without sex. Single-celled yeasts reproduce asexually by budding. A single yeast cell can produce up to 24 offspring. Fungi that make hyphae can reproduce asexually as well. Bits of the hyphae can break off and continue to grow as separate entities, or can form stalks containing seed-like spores. Although less common, fungi can produce spores sexually. Two mating cells from hyphae of different strains of fungi can mate by fusing together and forming a spore stalk.

When the spore caps at the end of spore stalks fully mature, they burst. The spores may simply drop in the same area, or be carried by the wind or rain to new spots.

Where they land, spores will germinate like seeds. But if they don't land on a suitable food source or in ideal conditions, the spores can survive in a dormant state for extended periods, waiting for more favorable conditions or to be carried to a better spot.

When you hear the word fungus, you probably think of mushrooms. Did you know bread mold is a kind of fungus, too? And that the itchy burning of athlete's foot is, yes, caused by another fungus? And that when you take penicillin, you're taking a medicine made by a fungus?

Fungi come in a variety of shapes and sizes and different types. They can range from individual cells to enormous chains of cells that can stretch for miles.

CHAPTER 13

Psilocybin Mushroom

Psilocybin mushrooms are fungi that contain the psychoactive compounds psilocybin and psilocin. There are multiple colloquial terms for psilocybin mushrooms, the most common being magic mushrooms or shrooms. Biological genera containing psilocybin mushrooms include *Agrocybe, Conocybe, Copelandia, Galerina, Gerronema, Gymnopilus, Hypholoma, Inocybe, Mycena, Panaeolus, Pluteus, Psilocybe* and *Weraroa*. There are approximately 190 species of psilocybin mushrooms and most of them fall in the genus *Psilocybe*.

The hallucinogenic mushrooms may have a history that dates back as far as one million years ago, originating in East Africa. He suggests that early hominids such as *Australopithecus africanus, Australopithecus boisei,* and the omnivorous *Homo habilis* expanded their original diets of fruit and small animals to include underground roots, tubers, and corms. McKenna claims that at this particular time, early hominids gathered psilocybin mushrooms off the African grasslands and ate them as part of their diet. He suggests that the psilocybin-containing mushrooms that were thought to have grown on the grasslands at that time were the *Panaeolus* species and *Stropharia cubensis,* also called *Psilocybe cubensis,* which is a famous "Magic Mushroom" widely distributed today.

There is some archaeological evidence for their use in ancient times. Several mesolithic rock paintings from Tassili n'Ajjer (a prehistoric North African site identified with the Capsian culture) have been identified by author Giorgio Samorini as possibly depicting the shamanic use of mushrooms, possibly *Psilocybe*. Hallucinogenic species of *Psilocybe* have a history of use among the native peoples of Mesoamerica for religious communion, divination, and healing, from pre-Columbian times up to the present day. Mushroom-shaped statuettes found at archaeological sites seem to indicate that ritual use of hallucinogenic mushrooms is quite ancient. Mushroom stones and motifs have been found in Mayan temple ruins in Guatemala, though there is considerable controversy as to whether these objects indicate the use of hallucinogenic mushrooms or whether they had some other significance with the mushroom shape being simply a coincidence. More concretely, a statuette dating from ca. 200 AD and depicting a mushroom strongly resembling *Psilocybe mexicana* was found in a west Mexican shaft and chamber tomb in the state of Colima. Hallucinogenic *Psilocybe* were known to the Aztecs as *teonanácatl* (literally "divine mushroom" - agglutinative form of teó (god, sacred) and nanácatl (mushroom) in Náhuatl) and were reportedly served at the coronation of the Aztec ruler Moctezuma II in 1502. Aztecs and Mazatecs referred to psilocybin mushrooms as genius mushrooms, divinatory mushrooms, and wondrous mushrooms, when translated into English.[7] Bernardino de Sahagún reported ritualistic use of teonanácatl by the Aztecs, when he traveled to Central America after the expedition of Hernán Cortés.

It's widely known that russian culture has a great influence of hallucinogenic mushrooms. One of the most widespread species of such mushrooms in Russian territory is Psilocybe semilanceata. Some historians consider that using different hallucinogenic mushrooms is an integral part of ancient culture of Rus'.

After the Spanish conquest, Catholic missionaries campaigned against the "pagan idolatry," and as a result, the use of hallucinogenic plants and mushrooms, like other pre-Christian traditions, was quickly suppressed. The Spanish believed the mushroom allowed the Aztecs and others to communicate with "devils". In converting people to Catholicism, the Spanish pushed for a switch from *teonanácatl* to the Catholic sacrament of the Eucharist. Despite this history, in some remote areas, the use of *teonanácatl* has remained.

The first mentioning of hallucinogenic mushrooms in the Western medicinal literature appeared in the London Medical and Physical Journal in 1799: a man had served *Psilocybe semilanceata* mushrooms that he had picked for breakfast in London's Green Park to his family. The doctor who treated them later described how the youngest child "was attacked with fits of immoderate laughter, nor could the threats of his father or mother refrain him."

In 1955, Valentina and R. Gordon Wasson became the first Westerners to actively participate in an indigenous mushroom ceremony. The Wassons did much to publicize their discovery, even publishing an article on their experiences in *Life* in 1957. In 1956 Roger Heim identified the hallucinogenic mushroom that the Wassons had brought back from Mexico as *Psilocybe*, and in 1958, Albert Hofmann first identified psilocin and psilocybin as the active compounds in these mushrooms.

Inspired by the Wassons' *Life* article, Timothy Leary traveled to Mexico to experience hallucinogenic mushrooms firsthand. Upon returning to Harvard in 1960, he and Richard Alpert started the Harvard Psilocybin Project, promoting psychological and religious study of psilocybin and other hallucinogenic drugs. After Leary and Alpert were dismissed by Harvard in 1963, they turned their attention toward evangelizing the psychedelic experience to the nascent hippie counterculture.

The popularization of entheogens by Wasson, Leary, authors Terence McKenna and Robert Anton Wilson, and others has led to an explosion in the use of hallucinogenic *Psilocybe* throughout the world. By the early 1970s, a number of psychoactive *Psilocybe* species were described from temperate North America, Europe, and Asia and were widely collected. Books describing methods of cultivating *Psilocybe cubensis* in large quantities were also published. The relatively easy availability of hallucinogenic *Psilocybe* from wild and cultivated sources has made it among the most widely used of the hallucinogenic drugs.

At present, hallucinogenic mushroom use has been reported among a number of groups spanning from central Mexico to Oaxaca, including groups of Nahua, Mixtecs, Mixe, Mazatecs, Zapotecs, and others.

Psilocybin mushrooms are non-addictive and rarely abused. They do create short-term increases in tolerance of users, thus making it difficult to abuse them because the more often they are taken within a short period of time, the weaker the resultant effects are. Poisonous (sometimes lethal) wild picked mushrooms can be easily mistaken for psilocybin mushrooms, but true psilocybin mushrooms are non-toxic, and the National Institute for Occupational Safety and Health, a branch of the Center for Disease Control, rated psilocybin less toxic than aspirin. When psilocybin is ingested, it is broken down to produce psilocin, which is responsible for the hallucinogenic effects. As with many psychedelic substances, the effects of psychedelic mushrooms are subjective and can vary considerably among individual users. The mind-altering effects of psilocybin-containing mushrooms typically last anywhere from 3 to 8 hours depending on dosage, preparation method, and personal metabolism. However, the effects can seem to last much longer due to psilocybin's ability to alter time perception.

Sensory

Noticeable changes to the audio, visual, and tactile senses may become apparent around an hour after ingestion. These shifts in perception, visually, include enhancement and contrasting of colours, strange light phenomena (such as auras or "halos" around light sources), increased visual acuity, surfaces that seem to ripple, shimmer, or breathe; complex open and closed eye visuals of form constants or images, objects that warp, morph, or change solid colours; a sense of melting into the environment, and trails behind moving objects. Sounds seem to be heard with increased clarity; music, for example, can often take on a profound sense of cadence and depth. Some users experience synesthesia, wherein they perceive, for example, a visualization of colour upon hearing a particular sound.

Emotional

As with other psychedelics such as LSD, the experience, or "trip," is strongly dependent upon set and setting. A negative environment could likely induce a bad trip, whereas a comfortable and familiar environment would allow for a pleasant experience. Many users find it preferable to ingest the mushrooms with friends, people they're familiar with, or people that are also 'tripping', although neither side of this binary is without exception.

Spiritual and Well-being

In 2006, the United States government funded a randomized and double-blinded study by Johns Hopkins University, which studied the spiritual effects of psilocybin mushrooms. The study involved 36 college-educated adults who had never tried psilocybin nor had a history of drug use, and had religious or spiritual interests; the average age of the participants was 46 years. The participants were closely observed for eight-hour intervals in a laboratory while under the influence of psilocybin mushrooms.

One-third of the participants reported that the experience was the single most spiritually significant moment of their lives and more than two-thirds reported it was among the top five most spiritually significant experiences. Two months after the study, 79 per cent of the participants reported increased well-being or satisfaction; friends, relatives, and associates confirmed this. They also reported anxiety and depression symptoms to be decreased or completely gone.

Despite highly controlled conditions to minimize adverse effects, 22 percent of subjects (8 of 36) had notable experiences of fear, some with paranoia. The authors, however, reported that all these instances were "readily managed with reassurance."

There have been calls for medical investigation of the use of synthetic and mushroom-derived psilocybin for the development of improved treatments of various mental conditions, including chronic cluster headaches, following numerous anecdotal reports of benefits. There are also several accounts of psilocybin mushrooms sending both obsessive-compulsive disorders ("OCD") and OCD-related clinical depression (both being widespread and debilitating mental health conditions) into complete remission immediately and for up to months at a time, compared to current medications which often have both limited efficacy and frequent undesirable side-effects. One such study states:

> "Developing drugs that are more effective and faster acting for the treatment of OCD is of utmost importance and until recently, little hope was in hand. A new potential avenue of treatment may exist. There are several reported cases concerning the beneficial effects of hallucinogenic drugs (psilocybin and LSD), potent stimulators of 5-HT2A and 5-HT2C receptors, in patients with OCD (Brandrup and Vanggaard, 1977, Rapoport, 1987, Moreno and Delgado, 1997) and related disorders such as body dysmorphic disorder (Hanes, 1996)."

"If it can be established that this class of drug can indeed lead to rapid and substantial reduction in OCD symptoms, then it opens the way for a variety of future studies with new drugs that might possibly have the anti-OCD but not the psychedelic effects. Psilocybin, LSD, and mescaline are extremely potent agonists at 5-HT2A and 5-HT2C receptors and their binding potency to these receptors is correlated with their human potency as hallucinogens (Glennon et al., 1984). The acute improvement in symptoms described in the published case reports (Brandrup and Vanggaard, 1977, Rapoport, 1987, Moreno and Delgado, 1997) suggests that interactions with 5-HT2A and 5-HT2C receptors may be an essential component of anti-OCD drug action. The observations that administration of the non-selective 5-HT antagonists metergoline or ritanserin exacerbate OCD symptoms further supports this view."

Dosage of mushrooms containing psilocybin depends on the potency of the mushroom (the total psilocybin and psilocin content of the mushrooms), which varies significantly both between species and within the same species, but is typically around 0.5-2 per cent of the dried weight of the mushroom. A typical dose of the rather common species, *Psilocybe cubensis,* is approximately 1 to 2.5 grams, while about 2.5 to 5 grams dried mushroom material is considered a strong dose. Above 5 dried grams is often considered a heavy dose.

The concentration of active psilocybin mushroom compounds varies not only from species to species, but also from mushroom to mushroom inside a given species, subspecies or variety. The same holds true even for different parts of the same mushroom. In the species *Psilocybe samuiensis* Guzmán, Bandala and Allen, the dried cap of the mushroom contains the most psilocybin at about 0.23 per cent–0.90 per cent. The mycelia contain about 0.24 per cent–0.32 per cent.

Legality

Psilocybin and psilocin are listed as Schedule I drugs under the United Nations 1971 Convention on Psychotropic Substances. Schedule I drugs are deemed to have a high potential for abuse and are not recognized for medical use. However, psilocybin mushrooms themselves are not covered by UN drug treaties.

From a letter, dated Sept 13, 2001, from Herbert Schaepe, Secretary of the UN International Narcotics Control Board, to the Dutch Ministry of Health.

As you are aware, mushrooms containing the above substances are collected and used for their hallucinogenic effects. As a matter of international law, no plants (natural material) containing psilocine and psilocybin are at present controlled under the Convention on Psychotropic Substances of 1971. Consequently, preparations made of these plants are not under international control and, therefore, not subject of the articles of the 1971 Convention. It should be noted, however, that criminal cases are decided with reference to domestic law, which may otherwise provide for controls over mushrooms containing psilocine and psilocybin.

Psilocybin mushrooms are regulated or prohibited in many countries, often carrying severe legal penalties (for example, the US Psychotropic Substances Act, the UK Misuse of Drugs Act 1971 and Drugs Act 2005, and the Canadian Controlled Drugs and Substances Act).

The prohibition of psilocybin mushrooms has come under criticism because psilocybin mushrooms are considered soft drugs with a low potential for abuse, very low toxicity, and no risk of addiction.

Magic Mushrooms in their fresh form still remain legal in some countries including Spain, Austria, and Canada. On November 29, 2008, The Netherlands announced it would ban the cultivation and use of psilocybin-containing fungi beginning December 1, 2008. The UK ban on fresh mushrooms (dried ones were illegal as they were considered a psilocybin-containing preparation) introduced in 2005 came under much criticism, but was rushed through at the end of the 2001-2005 Parliament; until then Magic Mushrooms had been sold in the UK.

New Mexico appeals court ruled on June 14, 2005, that growing psilocybin mushrooms for personal consumption could not be considered "manufacturing a controlled substance" under state law. However it still remains illegal under federal law.

CHAPTER 14

Fomes Fomentarius (*Tinder Fungus*)

Fomes fomentarius (commonly known as the Tinder Fungus, Hoof Fungus, Tinder Conk, Tinder Polypore or Ice Man Fungus) is a species of fungal plant pathogen found in Europe, Asia, Africa and North America. The species produces very large fruit bodies which are shaped like a horse's hoof and vary in colour from a silvery grey to almost black, though they are normally brown. It grows on the side of various species of tree, which it infects through broken bark, causing rot. The species typically continues to live on trees long after they have died, changing from a parasite to a detritivore.

Though inedible, *F. fomentarius* has traditionally seen use as the main ingredient of amadou, a material used primarily as tinder, but also used to make clothing and other items. The 5,000-year-old Ötzi the Iceman carried four pieces of *F. fomentarius*, concluded to be for use as tinder. It also has medicinal and other uses. The species is both a pest and useful in timber production.

The first scientific description of the fungus appeared in the literature in the 1753 *Species Plantarum* by Carl Linnaeus; he called it *Boletus fomentarius*. The specific name *fomentarius* is from the Latin *fomentum*, referring to tinder. The species has been described as a member of numerous different genera.

In 1783, Jean-Baptiste Lamarck named the species *Agaricus fomentarius* in his *Encyclopédie Méthodique: Botanique*. In 1818, Georg Friedrich Wilhelm Meyer described *Polyporus fomentarius* in his *Primitiae Florae Essequeboensis*, and this name was sanctioned by Elias Magnus Fries in the 1821 publication of the first volume of his *Systema Mycologicum*. Fries later, in his 1849 *Summa vegetabilium Scandinaviae*, moved the species to the genus *Fomes*. Subsequent attempts to change the genus of the species have been unsuccessful; the species was named *Placodes fomentarius* by Lucien Quélet in 1886, *Ochroporus fomentarius* by Joseph Schröter in 1888 and *Scindalma fomentarium* by Otto Kuntze in 1898.

In the twentieth century, Narcisse Théophile Patouillard named the species *Ungulina fomentaria* in 1900, and William Murrill twice reallocated the species; in 1903, he named it *Elfvingia fomentaria* and in 1914, he named it *Elfvingiella fomentaria*. In 1963, Shu Chün Teng named it *Pyropolyporus fomentarius*. These names are considered obligate synonyms; that is, different names for the same species based on a single description or specimen. In addition to the obligate synonyms, there are a number of taxonomic synonyms, whereby names have been described as separate species, but have come to be considered synonymous. The species is commonly known as the Tinder Fungus, Hoof Fungus, Tinder Polypore or Ice Man Fungus.

Fomes fomentarius has a fruit body of between 5 and 45 centimetres (2.0 and 18 in) across, 3 and 25 cm (1.2 and 9.8 in) wide and 2 and 25 cm (0.8 and 9.8 in) thick, which attaches broadly to the tree on which the fungus is growing. While typically shaped like a horse's hoof, it can also be more bracket-like with an umbonate attachment to the substrate.

The species typically has broad, concentric ridges, with a blunt and rounded margin. The flesh is hard and fibrous, and a cinnamon brown colour. The upper surface is tough, bumpy, hard and woody, varying in colour, usually a light brown or grey. The margin is whitish during periods of growth.

The hard crust is from 1 to 2 mm (0.04 to 0.08 in) thick, and covers the tough flesh. The underside has round pores of a cream colour when new, maturing to brown, though they darken when handled. The pores are circular, and there are 2-3 per millimetre. The tubes are 2 to 7 mm (0.08 to 0.28 in) long and a rusty brown colour.

The colouration and size of the fruit body can vary based on where the specimen has grown. Silvery-white, greyish and nearly black specimens have been known. The darkest fruit bodies were previously classified as *Fomes nigricans*, but this is now recognised as a synonym of *Fomes fomentarius*.

The colour is typically lighter at lower latitudes and altitudes, as well as on fruit bodies in the Northern Hemisphere that grow on the south side of trees. However, studies have concluded that there is no reliable way to differentiate varieties; instead, the phenotypic differences can "be attributed either to different ecotypes or to interactions between the genotype and its environment".

The spores are lemon-yellow in colour, and oblong-ellipsoid in shape. They measure 15-20 by 5-7 μm. The species has a trimitic hyphal structure (meaning that it has generative, skeletal and binding hyphae), with generative hyphae (hyphae that are relatively undifferentiated and can develop reproductive structures) with clamp connections.

Similar Species

Fomes fomentarius can easily be confused with *Phellinus igniarius*, species from the genus *Ganoderma* and *Fomitopsis pinicola*. An easy way to differentiate *F. fomentarius* is by adding a drop of potassium hydroxide onto a small piece of the fruit body from the upper surface. The solution will turn a dark blood red if the specimen is *F. fomentarius*, due to the presence of the chemical fomentariol.

Habitat and Distribution

F. fomentarius has a circumboreal distribution, being found in both northern and southern Africa, throughout Asia and into eastern North America, and throughout Europe, and is frequently encountered. The optimal temperature for the species's growth is between 27 and 30 °C (81 and 86 °F) and the maximum is between 34 and 38 °C (93 and 100 °F). *F. fomentarius* typically grows alone, but multiple fruit bodies can sometimes be found upon the same host trunk.

The species most typically grows upon hardwoods. In northern areas, it is most common on birch, while, in the south, beech is more typical. In the Mediterranean, oak is the typical host. The species has also been known to grow upon maple, cherry, hickory, lime tree, poplar, willow, alder, hornbeam, sycamore, and even, exceptionally, softwoods, such as conifers.

Fomes fomentarius is a stem decay plant pathogen. The species' mycelium penetrates the wood of trees through damaged bark or broken branches, causing rot in the host. It can grow on the bark wound, or even directly onto the bark of older or dead trees.

The decayed wood shows black lines in the lightly coloured decayed areas; these are known as pseudosclerotic layers or demarcation lines. The lines are caused by enzymes called phenoloxidases, converting either fungus or plant matter into melanin. The lines are not an absolute identifier, as they can also occur in plants infected by *Ustulina deusta* and some *Armillaria* species. Despite beginning as a parasite, the species is able to survive for a time (hastening decomposition) on fallen or felled trees as a saprotrophic feeder, and typically lives there for years, until the log is completely destroyed.

It is also capable of colonising and breaking down pollen grains, giving it a second food source which is particular high in nitrogen. Infected trees become very brittle, and cracks can occur in the affected tree due to wind. *F. fomentarius* is particularly adept at moving between cracks on the tree without interruption. However, in addition to the obviously infected damaged trees, *F. fomentarius* is known to be an endophyte, meaning that healthy trees which are not sporting *F. fomentarius* fruit bodies could still be infected.

The fruit bodies are perennial, surviving for up to thirty years. The strongest growth period is between early summer and autumn. The yearly growth always occurs on the bottom of the fungus, meaning that the lowest layer is the youngest.

This occurs even if the host tree has been laid on the forest floor, which can happen because of the white rot induced by the fungus. This is a process known as positive gravitropism. Very large numbers of spores are produced, particularly in spring, with up to 887 million basidiospores an hour being produced by some fruit bodies. Spore production also takes place in autumn, though not nearly as heavily. The spores are released at comparatively low temperatures. In dry weather, the spores are visible as a white powder.

The species is not considered edible; the flesh has an acrid taste, with a slightly fruity smell. The fungus has economic significance as it removes any timber value of infected trees. As *Fomes fomentarius* infects trees through damaged bark, it will often infect trees already weakened from beech bark disease. However, it is too weakly parasitic to infect healthy trees, and so can be regarded merely as an aspect of the ecosystem, with the important and useful role of decomposing unusable timber.

Amadou

The species is well known for its uses in making fire. This species, as well as others, such as *Phellinus igniarius*, can be used to make amadou, a tinder. Amadou is produced from the flesh of the fruit bodies. The young fruit bodies are soaked in water before being cut into strips, and are then beaten and stretched, separating the fibres. The resulting material is referred to as "red amadou". The addition of gunpowder or nitre produced an even more potent tinder. The flesh was further used to produce clothing, including caps, gloves and breeches. Amadou was used medicinally by dentists, who used it to dry teeth, and surgeons, who used it as a styptic. It is still used today in fly fishing for drying the flies. Other items of clothing and even picture frames and ornaments have been known to be made from the fungus in Europe, particularly Bohemia. The fungus is known to have been used as a firestarter in Hedeby, and it is known that the fungus was used as early as 3000 BCE. When found, the 5,000-year-old Ötzi the Iceman was carrying four pieces of *F. fomentarius* fruit body. Chemical tests led to the conclusion that he carried it for use as tinder.

CHAPTER 15

Ascomycota

The Ascomycota are a Division/Phylum of the kingdom Fungi, and sub-kingdom Dikarya. Its members are commonly known as the Sac fungi. They are the largest phylum of Fungi, with over 64,000 species. The defining feature of this fungal group is the "ascus" (from Greek: (*askos*), meaning "sac" or "wineskin"), a microscopic sexual structure in which nonmotile spores, called ascospores, are formed. However, some species of the Ascomycota are asexual, meaning that they do not have a sexual cycle and thus do not form asci or ascospores. Previously placed in the Deuteromycota along with asexual species from other fungal taxa, asexual (or anamorphic) ascomycetes are now identified and classified based on morphological or physiological similarities to ascus-bearing taxa, and by phylogenetic analyses of DNA sequences.

The ascomycetes are a monophyletic group, i.e., all of its members trace back to one common ancestor. This group is of particular relevance to humans as sources for medicinally important compounds, such as antibiotics and for making bread, alcoholic beverages, and cheese, but also as pathogens of humans and plants. Familiar examples of sac fungi include morels, truffles, brewer's yeast and baker's yeast, Dead

Man's Fingers, and cup fungi. The fungal symbionts in the majority of lichens (loosely termed "ascolichens") such as *Cladonia* belong to the Ascomycota. There are many plant-pathogenic ascomycetes, including apple scab, rice blast, the ergot fungi, black knot, and the powdery mildews. Several species of ascomycetes are biological model organisms in laboratory research. Most famously *Neurospora crassa*, several species of yeasts, and *Aspergillus* species are used in many genetics and cell biology studies. *Penicillium* species on cheeses and those producing antibiotics for treating bacterial infectious diseases are examples of taxa that belong to the Ascomycota.

Before the recognition of the fungal kingdom, the sac fungi were considered to be a *Class*, not a *Phylum*. The original collective term for these taxa was "Ascomycetes", which was first coined in the 1800s for a rankless nonlichenized taxon that possessed asci. The names Ascomycota, Ascomycetes, and others with the same root are based upon the term "ascus". "Ascomycetes" was soon used to include lichenized taxa, and became the standard term, at the class level, for all ascus-bearing species, just as the term "Basidiomycetes" became used for their basidium-bearing counterparts. Elevation of the taxonomic rank of the Ascomycetes resulted in the names Ascomycetae, Ascomycotina, and finally Ascomycota. Together, the Ascomycota and the Basidiomycota form the subkingdom Dikarya. The more familiar term, Ascomycetes, is still loosely used, e.g. at fungal forays it is often said of a fungus, such as *Peziza*, "It is an ascomycete, not a basidiomycete" in reference to their sexual reproductive mode. The terms are further abbreviated to "ascos" and "basidos" which are not officially sanctioned technical names.

Modern Classification of Ascomycota

There are three subphyla that are described and accepted:

- The *Pezizomycotina* is the largest subphylum and contains all ascomycetes that produce ascocarps (fruiting bodies), except for one genus, *Neolecta*, in the Taphrinomycotina. It is roughly equivalent to the previous taxon,

Euascomycetes. The Pezizomycotina includes most macroscopic "ascos" such as truffles, ergot, ascolichens, cup fungi (discomycetes), pyrenomycetes, lorchels, and caterpillar fungus. It also contains microscopic fungi such as powdery mildews, dermatophytic fungi, and Laboulbeniales.

- The *Saccharomycotina* comprises most of the "true" yeasts, such as baker's yeast and *Candida* which are single-celled (unicellular) fungi, which reproduce vegetatively by budding. Most of these species were previously classified in a taxon called *Hemiascomycetes*.
- The *Taphrinomycotina* includes a disparate and basal group within the Ascomycota that was recognized following molecular (DNA) analyses. The taxon was originally named *Archiascomycetes* (or *Archaeascomycetes*). It includes both hyphal fungi (*Neolecta, Taphrina*), fission yeasts (*Schizosaccharomyces*), and the mammalian lung parasite, *Pneumocystis*.

Ribosomal RNA gene sequencing of soil suggests that there may be a fourth subphylum of Ascomycota (termed Soil Clone Group I or SCGI), that has not been described in cultures or based on fruiting bodies. SCGI organisms are only known from DNA sequences found in soils worldwide and are placed between the Taphriomycotina and the Saccharomycotina.

Outdated Taxon Names

Several outdated taxon names—based on morphological features—are still occasionally used for species of the Ascomycota. These include the following sexual (teleomorphic) groups, defined by the structures of their sexual fruiting bodies: the Discomycetes, which included all species forming apothecia; the Pyrenomycetes, which included all sac fungi that formed perithecia or pseudothecia, or any structure resembling these morphological structures; and the Plectomycetes, which included those species that form cleistothecia. Hemiascomycetes included the yeasts and yeast-like fungi that have now been placed into the

Saccharomycotina or Taphrinomycotina, while the Euascomycetes included the remaining species of the Ascomycota which are now in the Pezizomycotina, and the Neolecta which are in the Taphrinomycotina.

Some ascomycetes do not reproduce sexually or are not known to produce asci and are therefore anamorphic species. Those anamorphs that produce conidia (mitospores) were previously described as Mitosporic Ascomycota. Some taxonomists placed this group into a separate artificial phylum, the Deuteromycota (or "Fungi Imperfecti"). Where recent molecular analyses have identified close relationships with ascus-bearing taxa, anamorphic species have been grouped into the Ascomycota, despite the absence of the defining ascus. Sexual and asexual isolates of the same species commonly carry different binomial species names, as, for example, *Aspergillus nidulans* and *Emericella nidulans*, for asexual and sexual isolates, respectively, of the same species.

Species of the Deuteromycota were classified as Coelomycetes if they produced their conidia in minute flask- or saucer-shaped conidiomata, known technically as *pycnidia* and *acervuli*. The Hyphomycetes were those species where the conidiophores (*i.e.*, the hyphal structures that carry conidia-forming cells at the end) are free or loosely organized. They are mostly isolated but sometimes also appear as bundles of cells aligned in parallel (described as *synnematal*) or as cushion-shaped masses (described as *sporodochial*).

Morphology

Most species grow as filamentous, microscopic structures called hyphae. Many interconnected hyphae form a mycelium, which—when visible to the naked eye (macroscopic)—is commonly called mold (or, in botanical terminology, thallus). During sexual reproduction, many Ascomycota typically produce large numbers of asci. The asci is often contained in a multicellular, occasionally readily visible fruiting structure, the ascocarp (also called an *ascoma*). Ascocarps come in a very large variety of shapes: cup-shaped, club-shaped, potato-like, spongy, seed-like, oozing and pimple-like, coral-like, nit-like, golf-ball-shaped, perforated tennis ball-like, cushion-shaped, plated and feathered in miniature (Laboulbeniales), microscopic classic Greek shield-shaped, stalked or sessile. They can appear solitary or clustered. Their texture can likewise be very variable, including fleshy, like charcoal (carbonaceous), leathery, rubbery, gelatinous, slimy, powdery, or cob-web-like. Ascocarps come in multiple colors such as red, orange, yellow, brown, black, or, more rarely, green or blue. Some ascomyceous fungi, such as *Saccharomyces cerevisiae*, grow as single-celled yeasts, which—during sexual reproduction—develop into an ascus, and do not form fruiting bodies.

In lichenized species, the thallus of the fungus defines the shape of the symbiotic colony. Some dimorphic species, such as *Candida albicans*, can switch between growth as single cells and as filamentous, multicellular hyphae. Other species are pleomorphic, exhibiting asexual (anamorphic) as well as a sexual (teleomorphic) growth forms.

Except for lichens, the non-reproductive (vegetative) mycelium of most ascomycetes is usually inconspicuous because it is commonly embedded in the substrate, such as soil, or grows on or inside a living host, and only the ascoma may be seen when fruiting. Pigmentation, such as melanin in hyphal walls, along with prolific growth on surfaces can result in visible mold colonies; examples include *Cladosporium* species, which form black spots on bathroom caulking and other moist areas. Many ascomycetes cause food spoilage, and, therefore, the pellicles or moldy layers that develop on jams, juices, and other foods are the mycelia of these species or occasionally Mucoromycotina and almost never Basidiomycota. Sooty molds that develop on plants, especially in the tropics are the thalli of many species.

Large masses of yeast cells, asci or ascus-like cells, or conidia can also form macroscopic structures. For example. *Pneumocystis* species can colonize lung cavities (visible in x-rays), causing a form of pneumonia. Asci of *Ascosphaera* fill honey bee larvae and pupae causing mummification with a chalk-like appearance, hence the name "chalkbrood". Yeasts for small colonies in vitro and in vivo, and excessive growth of*Candida* species in the mouth or vagina causes "thrush", a form of candidiasis.

The cell walls of the ascomycetes almost always contain chitin and ß-glucans, and divisions within the hyphae, called "septa", are the internal boundaries of individual cells (or compartments). The cell wall and septa give stability and rigidity to the hyphae and may prevent loss of cytoplasm in case of local damage to cell wall and cell membrane. The septa commonly have a small opening in the center, which functions as a cytoplasmic connection between adjacent cells, also sometimes allowing cell-to-cell movement of nuclei within a hypha. Vegetative hyphae of most ascomycetes contain only one nucleus per cell (*uninucleate* hyphae), but multinucleate cells—especially in the apical regions of growing hyphae—can also be present.

In common with other fungal phyla, the Ascomycota are heterotrophic organisms that require organic molecules as energy sources. These are obtained by feeding on a variety of organic substrates including dead matter, foodstuffs, or as symbionts in or on other living organisms. To obtain these nutrients from their surroundings, ascomycetous fungi secrete powerful digestive enzymes which break down organic substances into smaller molecules, which are then taken up into the cell. Many species live on dead plant material such as leaves, twigs, or logs. Several species colonize plants, animals, or other fungi as parasites or mutualistic symbionts and derive all their metabolic energy in form of nutrients from the tissues of their hosts.

Owing to their long evolutionary history, the Ascomycota have evolved the capacity to break down almost every organic substance. Unlike most organisms, they are able to use their own enzymes to digest plant biopolymers such as cellulose or lignin. Collagen, an abundant structural protein in animals, and keratin—a protein that forms hair and nails—, can also serve as food sources. Unusual examples include *Aureobasidium pullulans*, which feeds on wall paint, and the kerosene fungus *Amorphotheca resinae*, which feeds on aircraft fuel (causing occasional problems for the airline industry), and may sometimes block fuel pipes. Other species can resist high osmotic stress and grow, for example, on salted fish, and a few ascomycetes are aquatic.

The Ascomycota is characterized by a high degree of specialization; for instance, certain species of Laboulbeniales attack only one particular leg of one particular insect species. Many Ascomycota engage in symbiotic relationships such as in lichens—symbiotic associations with green algae or cyanobacteria—in which the fungal symbiont directly obtains products of photosynthesis. In common with many basidiomycetes and Glomeromycota, some ascomycetes form symbioses with plants by colonizing the roots to form mycorrhizal associations. The Ascomycota also represents several carnivorous fungi, which have developed hyphal traps to capture small protists such as amoebae, as well as roundworms (*Nematoda*), rotifers, tardigrades, and small arthropods such as springtails (*Collembola*).

The Ascomycota are represented in all land ecosystems worldwide, occurring on all continents including Antarctica. Spores and hyphal fragments are dispersed through the atmosphere and freshwater environments, as well as ocean beaches and tidal zones. The distribution of species is variable; while some are found on all continents, others, as for example the white truffle *Tuber magnatum*, only occur in isolated locations in Italy and Eastern Europe. The distribution of plant-parasitic species is often restricted by host distributions; for example, *Cyttaria* is only found on *Nothofagus* (Southern Beech) in the Southern Hemisphere.

REPRODUCTION

Asexual Reproduction

Asexual reproduction is the dominant form of propagation in the Ascomycota, and is responsible for the rapid spread of these fungi into new areas. It occurs through vegetative reproductive spores, the conidia. The conidiospores commonly contain one nucleus and are products of mitotic cell divisions and thus are sometimes call mitospores, which are genetically identical to the mycelium from which they originate. They are typically formed at the ends of specialized hyphae, the *conidiophores*. Depending on the species they may be dispersed by wind or water, or by animals.

Asexual Spores

Different types of asexual spores can be identified by colour, shape, and how they are released as individual spores. Spore types can be used as taxonomic characters in the classification within the Ascomycota. The most frequent types are the single-celled spores, which are designated *amerospores*. If the spore is divided into two by a cross-wall (septum), it is called a *didymospore*.

When there are two or more cross-walls, the classification depends on spore shape. If the septa are *transversal*, like the rungs of a ladder, it is a *phragmospore*, and if they possess a net-like structure it is a *dictyospore*. In *staurospores* ray-like arms radiate from a central body; in others (*helicospores*) the entire spore is wound up in a spiral like a spring. Very long worm-like spores with a length-to-diameter ratio of more than 15:1, are called *scolecospores*.

Conidiogenesis and Dehiscence

Important characteristics of the anamorphs of the Ascomycota are *conidiogenesis*, which includes spore formation and dehiscence (separation from the parent structure). Conidiogenesis corresponds to Embryology in animals and plants and can be divided into two fundamental forms of development: *blastic* conidiogenesis, where the spore is already evident before it separates from the conidiogenic hypha, and *thallic* conidiogenesis, during which a cross-wall forms and the newly created cell develops into a spore. The spores may or may not be generated in a large-scale specialized structure which helps to spread them.

These two basic types can be further classified as follows:

- *blastic-acropetal* (repeated budding at the tip of the conidiogenic hypha, so that a chain of spores is formed with the youngest spores at the tip);
- *blastic-synchronous* (simultaneous spore formation from a central cell, sometimes with secondary acropetal chains forming from the initial spores);
- *blastic-sympodial* (repeated sideways spore formation from behind the leading spore, so that the oldest spore is at the main tip);
- *blastic-annellidic* (each spore separates and leaves a ring-shaped scar which is inside the scar left by the previous spore);
- *blastic-phialidic* (the spores arise and are ejected from the open ends of special conidiogenic cells called phialides which remain constant in length);
- *basauxic* (where a chain of conidia, in successively younger stages of development, is emitted from the mother cell);
- *blastic-retrogressive* (spores separate by formation of crosswalls near the tip of the conidiogenic hypha, which thus becomes progressively shorter);
- *thallic-arthric* (double cell walls split the conidiogenic hypha into cells which develop into short, cylindrical spores called *arthroconidia*; sometimes every second cell dies off, leaving the arthroconidia free);
- *thallic-solitary* (a large bulging cell separates from the conidiogenic hypha, forms internal walls, and develops to a *phragmospore*).

Sometimes the conidia are produced in structures visible to the naked eye, which help to distribute the spores. These structures are called "conidiomata" (singular: conidioma), and may take the form of *pycnidia* (which are flask-shaped and arise in the fungal tissue) or *acervuli* (which are cushion-shaped and arise in host tissue).

Dehiscence happens in two ways. In *schizolytic* dehiscence, a double-dividing wall with a central lamella (layer) forms between the cells; the central layer then breaks down thereby releasing the spores. In*rhexolytic* dehiscence, the cell wall which joins the spores on the outside degenerates and releases the conidia.

Heterokaryosis and Parasexuality

Several Ascomycota species are not known to have a sexual cycle. Such asexual species may be able to undergo genetic recombination between individuals by processes involving *heterokaryosis* and *parasexual* events.

Parasexuality refers to the process of heterokaryosis, caused by merging of two hyphae belonging to different individuals, by a process called *anastomosis*, followed by a series of events resulting in genetically different cell nuclei in the mycelium. The merging of nuclei is not followed by meiotic events, such as gamete formation and results in an increased number of chromosomes per nuclei. *Mitotic crossover* may enable recombination, i.e., an exchange of genetic material between homologous chromosomes. The chromosome number may then be restored to its haploid state by nuclear division, with each daughter nuclei being genetically different from the original parent nuclei. Alternatively, nuclei may lose some chromosomes, resulting in aneuploid cells.

Sexual Reproduction

Sexual reproduction in the Ascomycota leads to the formation of the *ascus*, the structure that defines this fungal group and distinguishes it from other fungal phyla. The ascus is a tube-shaped vessel, a *meiosporangium*, which contains the sexual spores produced by meiosis and which are called *ascospores.*

Apart from a few exceptions, such as *Candida albicans*, most ascomycetes are haploid, i.e., they contain one set of chromosomes per nuclei. During sexual reproduction there is a diploid phase which commonly is very short, and meiosis restores the haploid state.

Formation of Sexual Spores

The sexual part of the life cycle commences when two hyphal structures mate. In the case of *homothallic* species, mating is enabled between hyphae of the same fungal clone, whereas in *heterothallic* species, the two hyphae must originate from fungal clones that differ genetically, i.e., those that are of a different mating type. Mating types are typical of the fungi and correspond roughly to the sexes in plants and animals; however one species may have more than two mating types, resulting in sometimes complex vegetative incompatibility systems.

Gametangia are sexual structures formed from hyphae, and are the generative cells. A very fine hypha, called trichogyne emerges from one gametangium, the *ascogonium*, and merges with a gametangium (the *antheridium*) of the other fungal isolate. The nuclei in the antheridium then migrate into the ascogonium, and plasmogamy—the mixing of the cytoplasm—occurs. Unlike in animals and plants, plasmogamy is not immediately followed by the merging of the nuclei (called *karyogamy*). Instead, the nuclei from the two hyphae form pairs, initiating the *dikaryophase* of the sexual cycle, during which time the pairs of nuclei synchronously divide. Fusion of the paired nuclei leads to mixing of the genetic material and recombination and is followed by meiosis. A similar sexual cycle is present in the red algae (Rhodophyta).

From the fertilized ascogonium, *dinucleate* hyphae emerge in which each cell contains two nuclei. These hyphae are called *ascogenous* or fertile hyphae. They are supported by the vegetative mycelium containing uni– (or mono–) nucleate hyphae, which are sterile. The mycelium containing both sterile and fertile hyphae may grows into fruiting body, the *ascocarp*, which may contain millions of fertile hyphae.

The sexual structures are formed in the fruiting layer of the ascocarp, the hymenium. At one end of ascogenous hyphae, characteristic U-shaped hooks develop, which curve back opposite to the growth direction of the hyphae. The two nuclei contained in the apical part of each hypha divide in such a way that the threads of their mitotic spindles run parallel, creating two pairs of genetically different nuclei. One daughter nucleus migrates close to the hook, while the other daughter nucleus locates to the basal part of the hypha. The formation of two parallel cross-walls then divides the hypha into three sections: one at the hook with one nucleus, one at the basal of the original hypha that contains one nucleus, and one that separates the U-shaped part which contains the other two nuclei.

Fusion of the nuclei (karyogamy) takes place in the U-shaped cells in the hymenium, and results in the formation of a diploid zygote. The zygote grows into the ascus, an elongated tube-shaped or cylinder-shaped capsule. Meiosis then gives rise to four haploid nuclei, usually followed by a further mitotic division that results in eight nuclei in each ascus. The nuclei along with some cytoplasma become enclosed within membranes and a cell wall to give rise to ascospores that are aligned inside the ascus like peas in a pod.

Upon opening of the ascus, ascospores may be dispersed by the wind, while in some cases the spores are forcibly ejected form the ascus; certain species have evolved spore cannons, which can eject ascospores up to 30 cm. away. When the spores reach a suitable substrate, they germinate, form new hyphae, which restarts the fungal life cycle.

The form of the ascus is important for classification and is divided into four basic types: unitunicate-operculate, unitunicate-inoperculate, bitunicate, or prototunicate.

Ecology

The Ascomycota fulfil a central role in most land-based ecosystems. They are important decomposers which break down organic materials, such as dead leaves and animals, and help the detritivores (animals which feed on decomposing material) to obtain their nutrients. Ascomycetes along with other fungi can break down large molecules such as cellulose or lignin, and thus have important roles in nutrient cycling such as the carbon cycle.

The fruiting bodies of the Ascomycota provide food for many animals ranging from insects and slugs and snails (*Gastropoda*) to rodents and larger mammals such as deer and wild boars.

Many ascomycetes also form symbiotic relationships with other organisms, including plants and animals.

Lichens

Probably since early in their evolutionary history, the Ascomycota have formed symbiotic associations with green algae (*Chlorophyta*), and other types of algae and cyanobacteria. These mutualistic associations are commonly known as lichens, and can grow and persist in terrestrial regions of the earth that are inhospitable to other organisms and characterized by extremes in temperature and humidity, including the Arctic, the Antarctic, deserts, and mountaintops. While the photoautotrophic algal partner generates metabolic energy through photosynthesis, the fungus offers a stable, supportive matrix and protects cells from radiation and dehydration. Around 42 per cent of the Ascomycota (about 18,000 species) form lichens, and almost all the fungal partners of lichens belong to the Ascomycota.

Mycorrhizal Fungi and Endophytes

Members of the Ascomycota form two important types of relationship with plants: as mycorrhizal fungi and as endophytes. Mycorrhiza are symbiotic associations of fungi with the root systems of the plants, which can be of vital importance for growth and persistence for the plant. The fine mycelial network of the fungus enables the increased uptake of mineral salts that occur at low levels in the soil. In return, the plant provides the fungus with metabolic energy in the form of photosynthetic products.

Endophytic fungi live inside plants, and those that form mutualistic or commensal associations with their host, do not damage their hosts. The exact nature of the relationship between endophytic fungus and host depends on the species involved, and in some cases fungal colonization of plants can bestow a higher resistance against insects, roundworms (nematodes), and bacteria; in the case of grass endophytes the fungal symbiont produces poisonous alkaloids, which can affect the health of plant-eating (herbivorous) mammals and deter or kill insect herbivores.

Symbiotic Relationships with Animals

Several ascomycetes of the genus *Xylaria* colonize the nests of leafcutter ants and other fungus-growing ants of the tribe Attini, and the fungal gardens of termites (Isoptera). Since they do not generate fruiting bodies until the insects have left the nests, it is suspected that, as confirmed in several cases of Basidiomycota species, they may be cultivated.

Bark beetles (family Scolytidae) are important symbiotic partners of ascomycetes. The female beetles transport fungal spores to new hosts in characteristic tucks in their skin, the *mycetangia*. The beetle tunnels into the wood and into large chambers in which they lay their eggs. Spores released from the mycetangia germinate into hyphae, which can break down the wood. The beetle larvae then feed on the fungal mycelium, and, on reaching maturity, carry new spores with them to renew the cycle of infection. A well-known example of this is Dutch elm disease, caused by *Ophiostoma ulmi*, which is carried by the European elm bark beetle, *Scolytus multistriatus*.

Importance for Humans

Tree attacked by the Bluestain fungus, *Ophiostoma minus* Ascomycetes make many contributions to the good of humanity, and also have many ill effects.

Harmful Interactions

One of their most harmful roles is as the agent of many plant diseases. For instance:

- Dutch Elm Disease, caused by the closely related species *Ophiostoma ulmi* and *Ophiostoma novo-ulmi*, has led to the death of many elms in Europe and North America.
- *Claviceps purpurea* on rye (*Secale cereale*)

- The originally Asian *Cryphonectria parasitica* is responsible for attacking Sweet Chestnuts (*Castanea sativa*), and virtually eliminated the once-widespread American Chestnut (*Castanea dentata*)
- A disease of Maize (*Zea mays*), which is especially prevalent in North America, is brought about by *Cochliobolus heterostrophus*.
- *Taphrina deformans* causes leaf curl of peach.
- *Uncinula necator* is responsible for the disease Powdery mildew, which attacks grapevines.
- Species of *Monilia* cause brown rot of stone fruit such as peaches (*Prunus persica*) and sour cherries (*Prunus ceranus*).
- Members of the Ascomycota such as *tachybotrys chartarum* are responsible for fading of woollen textiles, which is a common problem especially in the tropics.
- Blue-green, red and brown moulds attack and spoil foodstuffs - for instance *Penicillium italicum* rots oranges.
- Cereals infected with *Fusarium graminearum* contain mycotoxins like deoxynivalenol (DON), which can lead to skin and mucous membrane lesions when eaten by pigs.
- Ergot (*Claviceps purpurea*) is a direct menace to humans when it attacks wheat or rye and produces highly poisonous and carcinogenic alkaloids, causing ergotism if consumed. Symptoms include hallucinations, stomach cramp, and a burning sensation in the limbs ("Saint Anthony's Fire").
- *Aspergillus flavus*, which grows on peanuts and other hosts, generates aflatoxin, which damages the liver and is highly carcinogenic.
- *Candida albicans*, a yeast which attacks the mucous membranes, can cause an infection of the mouth or vagina called thrush or candidiasis, and is also blamed for "yeast allergies".
- Fungi like *Epidermophyton* cause skin infections but are not very dangerous for people with healthy immune

systems. However if the immune system is damaged they can be life-threatening; for instance, *Pneumocystis jiroveci* is responsible for severe lung infections which occur in AIDS patients.

Positive Effects

On the other hand, ascus fungi have brought some important benefits to humanity.

The most famous case may be that of the mould *Penicillium chrysogenum* (formerly *Penicillium notatum*), which, probably to attack competing bacteria, produces an antibiotic which, under the name of Penicillin, triggered a revolution in the treatment of bacterial infectious diseases in the 20th century.

- The medical importance of *Tolypocladium niveum* as an immunosuppressor can hardly be exaggerated. It excretes Ciclosporin, which, as well as being given during organ transplants to prevent rejection, is also prescribed for auto-immune diseases such as multiple sclerosis, although there is some doubt over the long-term side-effects of the treatment.
- Some ascomycete fungi can be altered relatively easily through genetic engineering procedures. They can then produce useful proteins such as insulin, human growth hormone, or TPa, which is employed to dissolve blood clots.
- Several species are common model organisms in biology, including *Saccharomyces cerevisiae*, *Schizosaccharomyces pombe*, and *Neurospora crassa*. The genomes of a number of ascomycete fungi have been fully sequenced.
- Baker's Yeast (*Saccharomyces cerevisiae*) is used to make bread, beer and wine, during which process sugars such as glucose or sucrose are fermented to make ethanol and carbon dioxide. Bakers use the fungus for the carbon dioxide production, causing the bread to rise, with the ethanol boiling off during cooking. Most vintners use it for the ethanol production, with the carbon dioxide being

released into the atmosphere during fermentation. Brewers and traditional producers of sparkling wine use both, with a primary fermentation for the alcohol and a secondary one to produce the carbon dioxide bubbles that provide the drinks with "sparkling" texture in the case of wine and the desirable foam in the case of beer.

- Enzymes of *Penicillium camemberti* play a role in the manufacture of the cheeses Camembert and Brie, while those of *Penicillium roqueforti* do the same for Gorgonzola, Roquefort and Stilton.
- In Asia *Aspergillus oryzae* is added to a pulp of soaked soya beans to make soy sauce.
- Finally, some members of the Ascomycota are eaten with relish; morelss (*Morchella*) and truffles (*Tuber*) are some of the most sought-after fungus delicacies.

CHAPTER 16

Mushroom Cultivation

At present 3 mushrooms are being cultivated in India. These are: the white mushroom (*Agaricus bisporus*), the paddy-straw mushroom (*Volvariella vovvacea*) and the oyster mushroom (*Pleurotus sajor-caju*). Of these, A. bisporus is the most popular and economically sound to grow and is extensively cultivated throughout the world. However, due to its low temperature requirement, its cultivation is restricted to the cool climatic areas and to the winter in the plains of Northen India. In summer, the tropical paddy-straw mushroom is suitable for growing in most parts of India. Even then it is less attractive commercially owing to very low yield per unit weight of the substrate and an extremely short shelf-life. But, as a kitchen-garden crop it is preferred because it isvery delicious and nutritous.

Oyster mushroom can grow at moderate temperature ranging from 22° to 28°C. therefore, it is suitable for most of the places of India. It is a familiar item in the menu of most hotels in Bangalore where it is being grown commercially in north India, the climate conditions prevailing during different seasons can be exploited for growing mushroom throughout the year. To this a year-wise production schedule is suggested:

Mid-November to Mid-March	:	*Agaricus bisporus*
February to Mid-April	:	*Pleurotus sajor-caju*
Mid-June to Mid-September	:	*Volvariella volvacea*
September to November	:	*Pleurotus sajor-caju*

CULTIVATION

Selection of Strains

For successful mushroom production, it is necessary for each grower to produce as economically and efficiently as possible the highest quality of mushrooms. This can be accomplished among other requirements, by selecting the best strains which should be high yielding , visually attractive, having desirable flavour, and resistance to adverse climate and pests and diseases. Presently, there are many strains of white, cream and brown varieties in cultivation. The brown variety is the natural mushroom and considered to be the most vigorous form. It tolerates and adverse conditions better than the white variety. A snow white mushroom first appeared amongst a bed of mushroom in the USA and ever since the variety has dominated the mushroom industry throughout the world, although it has a very high limited shelf-life. Where growing conditions tend to be on the dry side and humidity cannot be correctly controlled the brown mushroom should be grown. New superior strains are through selection, hybridization and induced mutations continually introduced by mushroom research laboratories and spawn makers. In India, S 11, S 649 and S791 are the good strains available. These strains were originally introduced from reowned commercial spawn makers, Somycel and darlington. Now these strains are well adapted in the Indian climate and are very popular with the growers.

Maintenance of Strains

Three methods are known by which strains can be propagate. these are multispore culture, tissue culture and mycelium transfer. By periodic subculturing of the mycelium on a suitable agar medium, the span strains can be kept for many years in a fairly good state. However, the frequent subculturing of the strain may result in its degeneration. Maintenence of strain by multisporous culture is only possible if new multispore cultures are compared with the original strain before the original multisporous culture would show much genetic variation. In the tissue culture, small pieces of fruit bodies are cut under sterile conditions and inoculated on a nutrient medium. Mycelium growing out of these tissue can provide the starting point for subsequent spawn production. However, it is commonly observed that tissue cultures often give lower yields than the original cultures. Of these 3 methods, mycelium transfer is most reliable but it is essential that the performance of the mycelium is continually checked in order to detect any degeneration-like slow-growing matted mycelium or fluffy mycelium with abnormal growth rate.

Spawn

The propogating material used by the mushroom growers for planting beds is called spawn. The spawn is equivalent to vegetative seed of higher plant. Quality of spawn is basic for the successful mushroom cultivation. At present, the pure culture spawn has been the basis of modern spawn production units all over the world. The manufacture of the pure culture spawn is done under scientifically controlled conditions which demand a standard of hygiene as in a hospital operation theatre. Equipment and substrate used for spawn are autoclaved and filtered air is passed during the inocluation ensures complete freedom from contamination.

Manure Spawn

Both composted horse-dung or synthetic compost may be used. The composted manure is thoroughly washed to remove such substance in compost which retard growth. The excess water is squeezed out and moisture content adjusted to 60 per cent. The manure is packed in half-litre milk bottles or heat-resistant polypropylene bags os suitable size. The bottles or bags plugged with non-absorbant cotton-wool and sterlized in an autoculave at 121°C for 2 hr or on 2 consecutive days for an hour each. They are then inoculated with a large bit of agar-containing mycelium and incubated at 22°-24°C in a dark place. the spawn can be used to inoculate fresh bottles or bags to obtain the second generation spawn.

Grain Spawn

Ten kilograms of wheat grains are boiled for 15 min in 15 litres of water and then allowed to soak for another 15 min without heating. the excess water is drained off and the grains are colled in sieves. Turn the grains several times with a spoon for quick cooling. The colled grains, are mixed with calcium carbonate. the gypsum ($CaSO_4.2H_2O$) and 30 g fo calcium carbonate. The gypsum prevents the grains from sticking together and calcium carbonate is necessary to correct the pH. the prepared grains are filled into half-litre milk bottles or polypropylene bags (at the rate of 150-200 g per bottle or bag) and autocalved for 2 hr at 121°C. After sterlization, the material should have a pH value of 6.5 to 6.7. the bottles are inoculated with grains spawn or with bits of agar medium colonized with mycelium and incubated at 22°-24°C in a dark place. the mycelium completely permeates the grains in about 2 weeks. Other grains like sorghum and pearlmillet can also be used for spawn making.

Perlite Spawn

This was developed by Lemke (1971). Perlite is a mineral which expands at temperature more than 1000°C. The ingredients, of the spawn are : Perlite (1,450 g), wheat-bran (1,650 g), gypsum (200 g), calcium carbonate (50 g), and water (665 cc). The gredients are mixed, filled in bottles and sterlized. Thereafter, the process is the same as for grain spawn. Perlite spawn is easy to disperse and can be produced at a cheaper cost. This spawn can be stored for a long time.

Compost

The white-button mushroom is grown on a select substrate which provides adequate levels of nutrients to support the crop so that it can successfully complete with other microorganisms. Traditionally, partially-decomposed horse-manure has been the principal medium for providing the required nutrients in artificial cultivation of the mushroom and it is only in recent times that other materials have also been used successfully.

Materials and Their functions

(i) *Base materials:* These includes wheat straw, maize cobs and Conventionally wheat straw either alone or mixed with horse-manure is the most widely used base material. When wheat straw is not available, straws of the other cereals, like rice of barely may be used. the chief function is to provide cellulose, hemicellulose and lignin in bulk. These materials also provide proper physical structure to the mixture to ensure the necessary aeration for the build up of microbial population and the subsequent spawn growth in the compost. Rice and barley straws are quite soft and decompose quickly, leaving only a little fibre for imparting a proper physical structure to the compost. Therefore the types and quantity of supplement should be discretely utilized at the proper time.

(ii) *Supplements:* These are for activating fermentation and can be categorised as: Animal dungs. These include horse- and chicken-manure, the extremely variable manures in composition. Nitrogen cantent may vary from 1 to almost 5 per cent . In addition to nutrients, they contribute greatly to the final bulk density of the compost. cow manure is not considered suitable.

Carbohydrate Nutrients

From molasses, wet brewers' grain and malt sprouts, carbohydrates are readily available. Concentration meals. These materials are usually used for animal feeds and include wheat or rice bran, dried brewer's grain, the seed meals of cotton, soya, castor and linseed. In these, both nitrogen and carbohydrate are available rather slowly. Nitrogen content may vary from 3-12 per cent. The oil and mineral content of some of these may be significance in mushroom nutrition. Nitrogen fertilizers. Nitrogen in chemical fertilizers (ammonium sulphate, calcium ammonium nitrate and urea) is rapidly released for the quick growth of microbial population. Materials to correct mineral deficiencies. These are muriate of potash and calcium superphosphate. Materials to correct greasiness. Gypsum and calcium carbonate serve to precipitate suspended colloidal materials and neutralize greasiness.

The choice of materials within each category is largely determined by cost-factors and their availability locally. Compost prepared from horse-dung mixed with straw are termed as 'natural', whereas they are called synthetic if the base material is used is mainly straw without bulk animal-manure.

Wheat Straw

Straw protected from rain is preferred. One year old straw which is no longer bright yellow and shiny, can be used only if it is tough. Full-length straw must be chopped to smaller size, about 8-10cm length, or else the heap would be less compact. Such a heap would not be able to retain moisture and termentation would be slower. The reverse, if the straw is too short, the heap would be compact and with very little air space inside allowing anaerobic fermentation. Straw, as is sold in the market for cattle feed is quite suitable. Composting is a microbial process requiring biological changes in all parts of the straw tissues and for this, it is essential that the straw tissue be accessible to the appropriate bacteria and fungal enzymes. Microbial action starts as soon as the straw is wetted and stacked in a heap. If the straw is short, fragile and damp, all parts of it will become exposed to microorganisms in a short time ans composting will start early and proceed fairly uniformly. If the straw is long, tough and dry, cut ends and few broken points may start microbial activity, leaving other parts untouched until later, to result in uneven composting. To include speed and uniformly, it needs much more mechanical breakage and wetting treatment at the beginning of the preparation. Horse-manure Stable manure with wheat, barley and hay-bedding must be collected regularly from the stables at intervals not more than a fortnight. Manure that has been collected over a long period of time will not ferment properly. It should be an even mixture of droppings and straw well-soaked in urine. Care should be taken that there is no admixture of manure of other animals, garbage or other trash. There should not be excess water because very wet manure cannot be stored satisfactory.

Composting Theory

Composting for mushroom cultivation has 3 basic purposes:

(i) it transforms the horse-manure and straw into the substrate more suitable for the growth of Agaricus bisporus mycelium than for the many microorganisms whose presence in such a substratum cannot be avoided;

(ii) to create a favourable medium for the unfavourable microbial flora which does not inhibit the growth of A. bisporus. Protein in the countless dead bacteria and other microorganisms is a vital item in mushroom nutrition; and

(iii) its fermentation temperature is high enough to eliminate most harmful pests and diseases.

Composting is accomplished by pilling up wetted inputs in the heap. When this is done properly the temperature inside the heap begins to rise due to the aerobic fermentation brought about by bacteria and other microorganisms. It is not unusual to reach a temperature of 70°-74°C, in the center of the heap on the third of composting. Because of the high temperatures which build up in composting heaps, thermophillic and the thermotolerant organisms quickly dominate over the mesophiles. In the early stages, the natural mesophile flora subside but the population of the thermophiles and thermotolerants increases. Bacterial population dominates and their rapid increase in numbers coincides with maximum heat generation—consequently, the temperature build up. This is followed by a relatively prolonged stage dominated by thermophiles mainly thermophilic actinomycetes. As the fermenting organisms require both water and oxygen, the heap is watered frequently and aerated by 'turning'. If there is unsufficient moisture, the microorganisms require cannot function properly. If there is an excess of moisture much oxygen is excluded and anaerobic fermentation sets in resulting in a soggy and stinking compost. In such a compost mushroom spawn will not grow.

During composting, ammonia gas is liberated and some of it is lost to atmosphere, but some is consumed by bacteria to produce nitrogenous intermediates which are eventually converted into protein by another kind of bacteria. Composting more than necessary results in loss of valuable nitrogen and cellulose.

Formulations

There is no standard pattern in the compost fromulations. However, 3 basic formulations for preparing compost are in use. The horsedung compost is all horse-manure. Synthetic compost is mainly a combination of straw, carbohydrate source (wheat bran), chicken litter and chemical fertilizer. The main objective of computing the formulation being to achieve some of the balance between carbon and nitrogen. The nitrogen level of compost at stacking is adjusted to 1.5 per cent of the dry matter and the carbon-nitrogen ratio at the same time is 25-30 : 1. the compost should have 2.0-2.3 per cent N at the completion of the process, which corresponds to 17:1, C-N ratio. There are so many variations in compost formulations. The basis of primarily the cost of availability of the ingredients and suitable supplements in the particular growing states. Some recommended formulae are: *(i)* Natural compost Basic formula (IARI)Synthetic compost is comparable with natural compost because it is capable of producing perfectly normal yields, sometimes even superior yields because of better aeration within the bed. However, horse-manure compost because it is cheaper is still the most-favoured substrate with the growing units in Europe and America. The main drawback in horse-manure is that its quality varies and this results in inconsistent yields. The natural compost is not pasteurized as per requirements, will tend to build up temperature within the bed which is detrimental to spawn run; also pests and diseases become active in such a compost. With the scarcity of horsedung, the synthetic compost is bocoming increasingly popular in many mushroom-growing countries, especially in the far-East. Synthetic compost is more uniform in quality and texture and supports better spawn run, since the bed is bettet aerated. However, such a compost tends to dry up rather quickly when the atmosphere turns dry. The actual time of composting a synthetic compost is about a week longer than that required for composting horse-manure in the normal way by the long method.

Method of Composting

There are two methods for preparing mushroom compost, the long and short method. The 'long method' is considered primitive and unsuitable for commercial cultivation. The 'short method' is quick and a definite advance over the earlier technology. However, the 'long method' is still relevant for the growers in India who cannot afford the expensive technology required for the short method. Composting yard. The compost should be prepared near the growing site, on clean concrete or pucca floor at a higher level to prevent the run-off water collecting near the heap. Composting is usually done in the open, but it has to be protected from rain, by covering it with polythylene sheet. It can also be carried out in a shed with open sides to shelter it from rain.

Composting Procedure by Long Method

(i) *Wetting the straw:* The first step in the composting process is to wet straw. Fresh dry straw resists water absorption, and unless it is persuaded to absorp water, it will not soften; and unless it softens it will not take more water later. In practice, the straw is spread thinly over the entire floor of the composting yard. It is then gradually wetted by sprinkling water, gently, till the straw takes no more water. The straw is then turned for even wetting. Again water is sprinkled till it can absorb no more. At this stage, the water content is 75 per cent and for the composts this point is reached when the compost is just saturated and before any run-off occurs. One ton of dry straw will requirealmost 5,000 litres of water to bring it into saturation.

(ii) Mixing and heaping: After the straw is wetted, the supplements excluding the gypsum are uniformally scattered over the straw and mixed. Some growers prefer to mix half the supplements at the beginning of composting, and the remaining half after the first turn. It is not known whether this practice is in any way beneficial. After mixing, the mixture is finally stacked in a heap. A heap one meter high, one meter wide and of indefinite length has been found to be suitable for Delhi during September-October. The straw can be stacked manually or with a stack mould. The straw should be firmly but not compactly compressed into the mould. The dimensions of the heap can be adjusted according to the size of straw and air temperature. The principle is that longer the straw, bigger the heap. If composting is done in the cooler months when the temperature ranges between 10° and 18°C, a small heap would be unable to retain heat and moisture and the composting would be unsatisfactory. During the hot weather generally and in particular in tropical and sub-tropical regions, the temperature difference between inside of the compost and the surrounding air is too small to produce chimney-effect necessary for compost ventilation. Core ventilation does not take place. as a rule undesirable acid zones occur inside the compost. In such cases, relatively narrow heaps would be more suitable.

(iii) Turning schedule: It is important to ensure that the heap attains sufficiently high temperatures (70°-75°C) to bring about the correct composting, otherwise the compost will lack the necessary nutritive value so essential for a good

crop. Care must also be taken to see that overcomposting does not take place. Open the heap and make it a number of times and for this purpose, the time schedule is suggested is:

Day zero	Wet, mix the stack the heap
4th day	First turning
8th day	Second turning
12th day	Third turning
16th day	Fourth turning
20th day	Final turning and filling of the trays

Nitrogeneous supplements and carbohydrates are mixed on day zero. Gypsum is usually mixed at the third and forth turning in quantities. During the final turning, 40 ml Malathion diluted in 20 litres of water is sprinkled. any other available insecticide, like DDT, BHC or Lindane can also be used. The above schedule has been worked out on the basis of author's experience and can be altered if the conditions within the heap so require. The guiding principle is that the heap should be opened when the temperature within rises no further. For horsedung manure, the final turning is given is given on day rather than on day 20.

Composting by Short Method

The method which was developed by Sinden and Hauser (1950) constitutes a general advance in controlled composting. The short method consists of two phases : phase I and phase II. The procedure for phase I is similar to the initial stages of the long method except, thatturnings are given sooner, the first on day 3, the second on day 6 and the third day on 9 or 10 when gypsum is added. The compost is now ready for the phase II or the peak heating.This is recognised as the microbial-composting stage and is an integral part of the total composting process. One aspect of the phase II is to promote such conditions in which the pasteurization of the compost. BY heating the compost and the surrounding air, for a brief periodof temperatures of about 60°C, virtually all important parasites and pathogens can be eliminated.

CHAPTER

17 Different Types of Mushrooms

Currently there are over 10,000 known types of mushrooms. That may seem like a large number but mycologists suspect that this is only a fraction of what's out there! We can put these various species in one of 4 categories: saprotrophic, mycorrhizal, parasitic, and endophytic. These categories describe how the the organism feeds itself.

Saprotrophs — Thriving on Decay

Saprotrophic mushrooms are decomposers. They release acids and enzymes that break down dead tissue into smaller molecules they can absorb. Thus decaying wood, plants, and even animals can become food for a saprotroph.

Think of all the dead matter on the ground. Now imagine what would become of it if there were fewer organisms to recycle it into compost or soil. You can easily see how important saprotrophs are to the food chain! It's no wonder this category includes so many gourmet and medicinal types of mushrooms. Some examples are below:

- Morels (*Morchella angusticeps, Morchella esculenta,* etc.) - These elusive, delicious species are very popular with mushroom hunters. Known to be mycorrhizal as well.

- Reishi (*Ganoderma lucidum*) - Highly prized in Chinese medicine, this mushroom is now the subject of many medical studies.
- Shiitake (*Lentinula edodes*) - Famous for both its great taste and medicinal properties.
- Portobello/Button (*Agaricus bisporus*) - Common in supermarkets all over the world.
- Cremini (*Agaricus bisporus*) - Another Agaricus bisporus strain that's a great edible. Come learn the real difference between a cremini and a portobello.
- Oyster (*Pleurotus ostreatus*) - Another popular edible, also known for its cholesterol-reducing effects.
- Maitake (*Grifola frondosa*) - Edible, known anti-tumor properties, and it looks like a brain!
- Turkey Tail (*Trametes versicolor*) - Although too tough to be edible in any manner other than a tea, this is one of the most well-studied medicinal mushrooms.
- Giant Puffball (*Calvatia gigantea*) - These large mushrooms are only edible when young.
- Chicken of the Woods (*Laetiporus sulphureus*) - Younger specimens are known to taste similar to, you guessed it, chicken. Also known to be parasitic.
- Enokitake (*Flammulina velutipes*) - Easy to cultivate and often used in soups.
- Shaggy Mane (*Coprinus comatus*) - This unique looking mushroom has antibiotic properties.
- Black Trumpet (*Craterellus cornucopioides*) - The best tasting edible mushroom out there!
- Yellow Houseplant Mushroom (*Leucocoprinus birnbaumii*) - Famous for popping up in potted houseplants.

Mycorrhizae — Successful Partnering with Plants

Mycorrhizal mushrooms have a fascinating relationship with trees and other plants. The mycelia of these fungi enter into a beneficial union with the roots of plants by either weaving into the root cells (endomycorrhizal) or wrapping around the roots themselves (ectomycorrhizal).

How is this beneficial? The mycelia bring in additional moisture, phosphorous, and other nutrients to their hosts. In return they gain access to sugars (such as glucose) that the hosts produce. This allows plants to grow bigger, faster, and stronger than their nonmycorrhizal counterparts. Many farmers and gardeners will inoculate their crops with a mycorrhizal fungus for better growth.

An estimated 95 per cent of plants form mycorrhizal partnerships with fungi. The types of mushrooms these fungi produce are difficult to cultivate and are often found only in nature. The ones below make a delicious treat if you can find them:

- Porcini (*Boletus edulis*) - Often used in soups and sauces, this mushroom can grow quite large.
- Truffles (*Tuber melanosporum,* Tuber magnatum, etc.) - These gourmet delights are very expensive.
- Chanterelles (*Cantharellus cibarius, Cantharellus formosus,* etc) - Another prized edible found on many continents.
- Matsutake (*Tricholoma matsutake*) - Highly sought after for their flavor and aroma in cooking.

Parasites — Feeding on the Weak

Parasitic types of mushrooms also take plant hosts. Although in this case the relationship is one-sided. These fungi will infect the host and eventually kill it.

Sometimes the line between parasitic and saprotrophic is not so clear. The honey mushroom is a known parasite yet it will also continue to live saprotrophically on the dead wood of its host. Most true parasitic fungi do not produce mushrooms and are too small to be noticed on a tree until it's too late. Some notable types of mushroom producing parasites are:

- Honey Fungus (*Armillaria mellea, Armillaria ostoyae,* etc.) - Some species in the Armillaria genus are edible, some are bioluminescent, and one colony is suspected to be the largest organism on the planet!

- Caterpillar Fungus (*Cordyceps sinensis*) - A true parasite that preys on insects. This interesting mushroom may just be my favorite.
- Lion's Mane (*Hericium erinaceus*) - This strange specimen possesses spiny teeth instead of the traditional cap. In addition to being edible, it's also suspected to help heal nerve tissue!

Endophytes — A Mysterious Symbiosis

Endophytic fungi deserve their own category due to their behavior. Endophytes partner with plants by invading the host tissue. However, unlike with parasitic fungi, the host remains healthy and seem to benefit with increased nutrient absorption and resistance to pathogens. Unlike mycorrhizal fungi, most endophytes can be easily cultivated in a lab without their host present.

Successful cultivation aside, much is still unknown about this category of fungi. Many species do not produce mushrooms and their partnership with plants is not fully understood. Some mycologists suspect that certain parasitic and saprophytic fungi will reveal themselves as endophytes as the field expands. Time will tell what discoveries will emerge as this group is studied further.

There are roughly 2000 types of known mushrooms on the planet. These fungi come in a variety of shapes, sizes and colours, and they can be nutritious, poisonous or medicinal. Knowing the difference between common types of mushrooms will back you know what you are looking at.

- *Bearded tooth mushrooms* grow on trees or logs and resemble tufts of white hair, although over time they take on a yellow hue. It is best to eat them when they are white since the older mushrooms have a slightly sour flavor. These mushrooms are edible and part of the tooth fungus group. Fortunately, no other mushrooms resemble bearded tooth mushrooms, so they cannot be confused with a poisonous variety.

- *Oyster mushrooms* are another common type of edible mushroom. They also grow on logs and trees, and have a shape that resembles a shell. Both the cap and the gills of these mushrooms are white. This variety is more easily found in grocery stores because it is popular with commercial growers. No poisonous types of mushrooms resemble these, but some other imposters have a terrible taste.
- *Destroying Angel mushrooms* are a common white variety of mushroom, but this variety is poisonous. They are very similar to common white mushrooms, but they contain the toxin amanitin, which displays symptoms within a single day. Never eat a mushroom unless you are obvious what type it is.
- *The Jack-O-Lantern mushroom* is a common poisonous mushroom type. They actually glow in the murky and have an orange colour. Although these mushrooms do have a pleasant taste, they also contain muscarine, which is a toxin that affects the digestion and cardio/respiratory function. These mushroom are not typically deadly, but the results of eating them can be bad.
- A popular medicinal type of mushroom that is gaining popularity is the maitake. Typically found at the below hardwood trees in Japan, maitake mushrooms are now carefully cultivated. They are believed to act as natural antioxidants that benefit the immune system. They also help control blood sugar, lower cholesterol, act as an antiviral and possibly prevent cancer.
- *Winter Mushroom,* also known as Enoki/Enokitake, is another type of mushroom commonly used for medicinal reasons. They are small white mushrooms with long slender stems. They are used to lop blood pressure and cholesterol, and they benefit the immune system. Winter mushrooms may also fight tumors and lymphoma.

The promising mushroom types and species which can be cultivated in warm subtropical regions are oyster mushroom (*Pleurotus* spp.), paddy straw mushroom (*Volvariella volvacea*) and milky mushroom (*Calocybe indica*). In the present investigation, five different mushroom species, viz., *Pleurotus sajor-caju*, *P. flabellatus*, *P. florida*, *V. volvacea* and *C. indica*, of all three categories have been cultivated successfully with the use of different agricultural residues in Tripura . All three oyster mushroom species have been found to grow throughout the year under in house condition but their productivity is only high and considerable during the period of September to January. The paddy straw mushroom (*V. volvacea*) developing gray to light brown fruit bodies and salmon coloured spore print on white paper, grows well during the period, April to November. However, the months starting from June to October are more favourable for fruit body production than others. Milky mushroom, also known as 'Dudh Chhata', can be cultivated during the period from April to October in Tripura. However, the productivity is considerably high during the period April to August in this warm subtropical region.

Agricultural residues, such as, black gram haulms, black gram pod shell, brinjal stem, paddy straw, pea haulms, saw dust, sesame stick with pod shell, toria (mustard) stick and maize stalk are more or less equally good substrates for oyster mushroom cultivation. Paddy straw mushroom, on the other hand, prefers paddy straw, pea pod shell and rajmash pod shell for fruit body formation, while, milky mushroom grows well on arhar pod shell, paddy straw, pea haulms and tomato haulms.

Mushrooms have been used for thousands of years both as food and for medicinal purposes. They are often classified as a vegetable or a herb, but they are actually fungi. While there are over 14,000 mushrooms, only about 3,000 are edible, about 700 have known medicinal properties, and fewer than one percent are recognized as poisonous.

Many people enjoy going to the woods to pick their own mushrooms. However, identifying mushrooms can be a real challenge. The colour, shape and size of the fruiting body can vary tremendously. It is important to properly identify the mushroom that is collected, so as to avoid a poisonous species.

The Pharaohs prized mushrooms as a delicacy, and the Greeks believed that mushrooms provided strength for warriors in battle. The Romans regarded mushrooms as a gift from God and served them only on festive occasions, while the Chinese treasured them as a health food.

Today, mushrooms are enjoyed for their flavor and texture. They can impart their own flavor to food or take on the flavor of other ingredients. Their flavor normally intensifies during cooking, and their texture holds up well to usual cooking methods, including stir-frying and sauteing.

It is popular to add mushrooms to soups, salads, and sandwiches, or to use them as an appetizer. They also add an appealing touch to vegetable-based casseroles and stews. In the US, mushroom extracts are increasingly being used in nutraceutical products and sports drinks.

Mushrooms contain about 80 to 90 percent water, and are very low in calories (only 100 cal/oz). They have very little sodium and fat, and 8 to 10 percent of the dry weight is fiber. Hence, they are an ideal food for persons following a weight management program or a diet for hypertensives.

Mushrooms are an excellent source of potassium, a mineral that helps lower elevated blood pressure and reduces the risk of stroke. One medium portabella mushroom has even more potassium than a banana or a glass of orange juice. One serving of mushrooms also provides about 20 to 40 percent of the daily value of copper, a mineral that has cardioprotective properties.

Mushrooms are a rich source of riboflavin, niacin, and selenium. Selenium is an antioxidant that works with vitamin E to protect cells from the damaging effects of free radicals. Male health professionals who consumed twice the recommended daily intake of selenium cut their risk of prostate cancer by 65 per cent. In the Baltimore study on Aging, men with the lowest blood selenium levels were 4 to 5 times more likely to have prostate cancer compared to those with the highest selenium levels.

The most commonly consumed mushroom in the United States is *Agaricus bisporus* or the white button mushroom. A. bisporus has two other forms - *Crimini* or brown mushrooms with a more earthy flavor and firmer texture, and *Portabella* mushrooms with a large umbrella-shaped cap and meaty flavour.

All three mushrooms, but especially the fresh button mushrooms, possess substances that inhibit the activity of aromatase (an enzyme involved in estrogen production), and 5-alpha-reductase (an enzyme that converts testosterone to DHT). The latest findings show that white button mushrooms can reduce the risk of breast cancer and prostate cancer. An extract of white button mushrooms decreased cell proliferation and decreased tumor size in a dose-dependent manner. The chemoprotective effect can be seen with an intake of about 100 grams (3.5 ozs) of mushrooms per day.

Shiitake mushrooms have been used for centuries by the Chinese and Japanese to treat colds and flu. *Lentinan*, a beta-glucan isolated from the fruiting body of shiitake mushrooms, appears to stimulate the immune system, help fight infection, and demonstrates anti-tumor activity.

CHAPTER 18

Nutritive Value of Mushrooms

Mushrooms, a group known as fungi, lacks chlorophyll and cannot therefore make its own food. It grows on dead organic matter either parasitically or symbiotically with other living organisms. Among the various mushroom species, button mushroom (*Agaricus bisporus*), oyster mushroom (*Pleurotus* spp.), paddy straw (*Volvariella* spp.), milky mushroom (*Calocybe Indica*) are most popular among the commercial growers.

Mushrooms are a rich source of nutrients, particularly proteins, minerals and vitamins such as Vitamin B, C and D. The content of the anti-pellagra vitamin, niacin is comparable to its levels found in pork or beef, which are the richest known sources of this vitamin. Mushroom cultivation is the only major fermentation industry, which involves the bio-conversion of cellulose wastes into edible biomass. According to an estimate, yield of mushroom per unit area, as such or in terms of proteins is 100-1000 times more than conventional agriculture like production of paddy, wheat, pulses and cereals etc., hence, mushrooms are considered to be the best alternative to supply the masses with vegetable protein rich food. Mushrooms are also good source of minerals. They are rich in phosphorus, potassium and iron but are low in sodium. About one third of the total iron in mushrooms is in the available form. Mushrooms are good sources of several vitamins and excel many fruits and vegetables on this account. They are particularly rich in thiamine (B_1), riboflavin (B_2), niacin, biotin, ascorbic acid, vitamin K and vitamin E.

In addition to these, some other interesting features in the nutritional quantities of mushrooms are:

1. lack of starch;
2. low fat high fiber content.

Hence, they are said to be the 'delight of diabetics'.

Cultivation Technologies of Edible Mushrooms

Four types of mushrooms *viz.*, white button, oyster, paddy straw and milky mushrooms have been adopted by farmers/ entrepreneurs at marginal and commercial scale in different parts of the country at present. The cultivation technologies of some of these mushrooms are being described here in brief.

Cultivation of White button mushroom (*Agaricus Bisporus*)

It is popularly known as European or Temperate mushroom and is extensively cultivated throughout the world. It requires a temperature of 14-18°C during cropping hence its cultivation has become popular in the cooler hilly regions of our country. One crop can easily be taken during the winter season in the plains of north India and maximum two cro s can be grown in hilly areas. This mushroom (both fresh and canned) has better market acceptability. Unlike other cultivated species its cultivation needs more technical skill, which can be acquired by training. The steps involved in its cultivation are given below:

1. **Compost Preparation:** It is grown on a specially prepared substrate called compost. This is prepared by mixing various raw materials in specific proportions either by long or short method of composting. Straw based compost involves the use of wheat or paddy straw or sugarcane bagasse as base material, whereas horse dung

is used for preparation of natural compost. In both cases the base materials are supplemented with some activators (chicken manure, molasses, wheat bran and nitrogen sources - organic/inorganic fertilizers cakes). The nitrogen content is adjusted at 1.5 per cent of the dry weight of the base materials, activators and nitrogenous sources.

2. **Spawning and spawn run:** Spawning means seeding of the compost. Pure and productive spawn is procured from a reliable source a few days prior to seeding. Fresh spawn should be used always. Three methods are generally employed:

   (a) **Surface spawning:** Spreading the spawn in top layer of compost and mixing to a depth of 3-5 cm and it is then covered with thin layer of compost.

   (b) **Layer spawning:** Spawn is mixed with the compost in 2-3 layers and pressed. Bags are spawned while filling.

   (c) **Through spawning:** In this method, spawn is mixed in the compost thoroughly and then spawned compost is filled in the bags.

   Rate of spawning is important in getting optimum yield. It is generally calculated per unit bed area or according to the quantity of compost to be spawned. Generally, 500-750 g spawn is sufficient for one qt of compost, thus spawning rate comes to 0.5-0.75 per cent of compost. More spawn is required for layer or through spawning than in surface spawning. After spawning the compost is pressed hard to make it compact.

   The trays are then arranged in cropping room in tiers and are covered with newspaper sheets sprayed with 2 per cent formalin. Presently, cultivation in polythene bags is in use as an alternate to old tray cultivation method. The temperature during spawn run should be maintained between 22-25°C. In case of tray method, the trays are covered with newspaper. Changing consumer demand should be sprinkled with water at least twice daily to prevent drying of compost and to provide 90-95 per cent RH in the room. The compost is impregnated with mycelial threads completely within 15-20 days showing whitish strands. The dark brown colour of compost changes to light brown. Little ventilation is required during spawn run.

3. **Casing:** It means covering the spawn run compost with a layer of sterilized or pasteurized casing soil of any other materials. The following mixtures are used with success in India:
   - *(a)* Mixture of 2 years old FYM and 2 years old spent compost (1:1).
   - *(b)* Garden soil and sand mixture (4:1 by volume).
   - *(c)* Decomposed FYM and loam soil (1:1 by volume).

   Casing soil is treated either by steam at 60°C for 4 hours or by drenching with formaldehyde or formalin (40%) at the rate of 3 litres in 40 litres of water per m^3. The pH of casing soil is adjusted between 7-8 with the addition of chalk (calcium carbonate). Casing soil should be porous and allow good gaseous exchange. Before casing newspapers are removed and the trays or bags are covered with a layer of casing material (3-4 cm) depth. The humidity in the room is maintained at 95 per cent and temperature 22-25°C. Not much aeration is required during the first week. The beds are kept moist.

4. **Cropping:** One week after casing, the room temperature is lowered to 14-18°C and the pinheads start appearing within 7-10 days. Good ventilation is required at this stage. The carbon dioxide concentration in the room should remain below 0.1 per cent and 2-4 air changes per hour are required. The air-bed ratio should be 6:1 if forced air circulation is not used. More watering is required during the production of flushes. Pinheads appear within 12-15 days of casing.

   Cropping continues for 6-8 weeks. At pea size stage, heavy mist spraying should be done. Mushrooms appear in flushes every 7-10 days. Periodicity of flushes depends on temperature in the room.

5. **Harvesting of mushroom and marketing:** Mushrooms are harvested while still in button stage (cap tightly closed over the stem 2.5-3.5 cm dia). These are collected in small baskets. Soil particles and mycelial strands sticking to the base of stalk are removed carefully and fruit bodies are cleaned with a soft cloth and washed in EDTA solution (0.125 g/l of water) before sending them for marketing. An average yield of 10-20 kg/100 kg compost is generally obtained by good growers within a period of 8-10 weeks. This, however, depends on the quality of compost and spawn along with other management factors. This mushroom is consumed mostly fresh due to its short shelf-life. It can be stored in polythene bags at <5°C up to 3 days. Storage at high temperature results in browning and rotting.
6. **Economics of cultivation:** Cost of cultivation varies from place to place depending upon the price of raw material, labour wages, environmental conditions at the site and marketing opportunities.

Cultivation of Oyster or Tropical Mushroom

(*Pleurotus* spp.)

Oyster mushroom is the 3rd largest cultivated mushroom in the world and it is being cultivated in about 25 countries. n India, it is being produced in the States like Orissa, Karnataka, Maharashtra, A.P., M.P., West Bengal, Meghalaya, Manipur, Mizoram, Assam, etc.

Many species of *Pleurotus* grow wild on dead decaying tree logs, stumps, or dead branches of living trees or on dead decaying organic matter mostly during the rainy season. All these species of oyster mushroo are edible except *P. olearius* and *P. nidiformis*. There are thirty eight species reported in this genus, out of which only 25 species are commercially cultivated in the world. Different substrates like wheat and paddy straw, saw dust, maize stalks, dried leaves, waste from food industries and synthetic compost (used for European mushroom) are used for its cultivation. It can also grow on dried logs of soft wood trees and roots of water hyacinth, paper waste and shelled maize cobs.

Different species need different temperature ranges between 20-30°C for their growth. Hence they are ideally suited for cultivation at different times of the year in various regions. This mushroom has better prospects in our country, especially as the technology for its cultivation is simple and cheap. Further, the produce has a longer shelf life, and it can be dried easily. Artificial cultivation involves the following steps:

1. **Preparation of substrate:** This mushroom proliferates equally well on both paddy as well as wheat straw. It should preferably be fresh or not more than a year old using 3-6 cm cut pieces.
2. **Chemical sterilization of substrate:** The straw or any other recommended substrate is steeped in a solution of Bavistin and formalin (Bavistin 75 ppm and Formaldehyde 500 ppm) for a period of 18 hours. This can be prepared by mixing 7.5 g of Bavistin (50% WP) and 125 ml of Formaldehyde (40%) in 100 litres of water (approximately 10 buckets) in a 200 lit. Capacity drum or a tub or a tank. This solution is sufficient to steep 20 kg of dry straw in 2 lots of 10 kg each. Treated straw is put on a sieve for 30 minutes for removal of extra solution. It is then spawned.
3. **Hot water treatment of substrate:** The substrate can also be sterilized by boiling in water (80°C for 40 minutes). If pasteurization facilities are available, bulk pasteurization can be carried out after over-night wetting at 60-65°C for 2 hours:
   (a) **Spawning and Spawn run:** As soon as the substrate is free from excess of chemical solution and has cooled down to 25-30°C, it is filled in polythene bags (size 30 × 40 cm) or other container after mixing the spawn @ 2-3 per cent by wet weight of substrate

(i.e. 200-300 g in 10 kg). The moisture content of substrate should be 65-70 per cent. Fresh grain spawn not more than a month old should be used. The bags should be perforated at 15cm regular intervals for gaseous exchange with a nail. These are then arranged on raised platform or shelves in a room or shed. And 20-25°C temperature and 70-85 per cent RH is maintained for spawn run.

(*b*) **Removal of bags for production of mushrooms:** As soon as the substrate is fully covered with the mycelium, the polythene bags are removed from the substrate. The spawn run bags are then arranged on a wooden platform or shelves at a distance of 15-20 cm between the bags. Watering is done twice a day or as required to ensure 70-80 per cent RH. Walls and floor of the room are also sprinkled with water. Fresh air is also given once or twice a day during cropping. Sufficient amount of diffused light is required for normal fruit body formation. Mushroom pinheads will appear within 7-10 days which can be harvested after 2-3 days. The right stage of picking is prior to the up curving of the margin of the pileus, before they over-mature. Younger fruit bodies have longer shelf life. Three to four flushes appear within a period of 4-5 weeks.

4. **Harvesting and Yield:** The fruit bodies may arise singly or in clumps and form tiers on the substrate. They are variable in size, shape and colour. They should be harvested carefully to avoid any disturbance to other pinheads as much as possible. The debris from the lower portion of stalk is removed before marketing. These are then packed in perforated polythene bags for sale in fresh form. Surplus produce can be sun-dried or dehydrated at 50-55°C and stored in sealed/closed polythene bags for later use or can be pickled in absence of market. Its yield per unit substrate and area is good which varies from 2.5-3 kg per 10 kg of wet substrate.

5. **Economics of cultivation:** As this mushroom can grow on a wide variety of agricultural wastes, which are easily available and cheap, its cost of production is lower than that of others.

Canning: Canning is technique by which the mushrooms can be stored for longer periods up to a year and most of the international trade in mushrooms is done in this form. The canning process can be divided into various unit operations namely cleaning, blanching, filling, sterilization, cooling, labeling and packaging. In order to produce good quality canned mushrooms, these should be processed as soon as possible after the harvest. In case a delay is inevitable, mushrooms should be stored at 4 to 5ºC till processed. The mushrooms with a stem length of one cm are preferred and are canned whole, sliced and stems-andpieces as per demand. Longitudinal (mushroom shape) slicing is common.

Cleaning: The mushrooms are sorted to remove diseased, damaged, bruised and browned ones. Fresh mushrooms white in colour, without dark marks in either cap or stem are preferred for canning. The veil should be in tight closed condition and not stretched otherwise the mushroom will open in the blanching and will be rejected in can-filling process. Grading based on cap diameter is also followed. Then the whole mushrooms are washed 3-4 times in cold running water to remove adhering substances. Use of iron free water with 0.1 per cent citric acid prevents discolouration. Hydration with jets before blanching is now a common practice in the industry; it washes as well as hydrates the mushrooms to reduce weight-loss in canning.

Blanching: Blanching is normally done to inhibit polyphenol oxidase enzyme activity and to inactivate micro organisms. It also removes the gases from the mushroom tissue and reduces bacterial counts. Mushrooms are blanched in stainless steel kettles filled with a boiling solution of 0.1 per cent citric acid and 1 per cent common salt. The blanching time ranges from 4-6 min at 95-100ºC. Some plants blanch the mushrooms in slightly acidified water to improve the colour of the canned product. The foam developed during blanching should be removed constantly. The loss of weight during blanching is about 20-25 per cent of the fresh weight of the product. If blanching time is reduced to restrict weight loss, the loss of weight at sterilization will be accordingly higher. Six minute blanching is common to give proper drained weight of the final product especially in A-2½ cans. Over blanching can cause poor quality of colour and texture with loss of free amino acids and sugars. Different blanching times should be used for the various sizes to prevent over-blanching and shrinkage. A short spray of cold water should follow the blanching process to cool the mushrooms to 36°C or lower.

Filling: Mushrooms after blanching are manually filled in tin cans; it takes care of the rejection of mushrooms broken and opened during blanching (rejection is almost 10 % of the original weight). The size of the can depends on the amount of produce to be filled in them as per the requirements of the customer. In our country generally A-2½ and A-1 tall can sizes containing approximately 440 and 220 g drained weight respectively are preferred. However, for export A-10 (3 kg with drained weight of 1.96 kg) is preferred. The cans are thoroughly washed to remove any adhering dust or foreign matter. All the cans are sterilized before use. Mushrooms can be filled in the cans either manually or mechanically in case of automatic can filling machines.

Lidding or Clinching: The cans after being filled are covered loosely with the lid and passed through exhaust box. In large-scale process, this has certain disadvantages such as spilling of the contents, toppling of the lids etc. Lidding has now been modernized by the clinching process in which the lid is partially seamed to the can by a single first roller action of a double seamer. The lid remains sufficiently loose to permit the escape of dissolved as well as free air from the contents and also the vapour formed during the exhaust process.

Exhausting: Before sealing, it is necessary to remove all air from the contents. The process by which this is achieved is known as exhausting. By removing air, risk of corrosion of the tin plate, pinholing during storage and discolouration of the products are reduced; because oxidation is prevented. The exhausting process will also assist in avoiding overfilling or underfilling of can, which normally happens due to the tendency of expanding or shriveling during heating. The other advantages of the exhaust process are: prevention of bulging of the can when stored at high altitudes or in hot climates, reduction of chemical reaction between the container and contents; and prevention of excessive pressure as well as strain during sterilization. Cans are exhausted in the exhaust box where filled cans are passed through a hot steam at about 100°C on a moving chain conveyor through a covered double jacketed steam box. The time of exhaust varies from 10 to 15 min. At the end of the exhaust box, the temperature at the centre of the can should be about 80°C.

Sterilization: Sterilization is the process of heating the cans to prevent the spoilage by microorganisms during storage. Two procedures are preferred for common sterilizing of the cans:

(a) A continuous process called 'steriflame' in which cans are treated by passing them over gas burners. This process lasts for 3-8 min.

(b) A batch process, in which the cans are placed in an autoclave and sterilized for 25-30 min, under 15 lb/sq inch (1.06 kg/sq cm) (time and pressure varies with can and mushroom size). The sterilization temperature should not be above 118°C to avoid discolouration and burnt taste.

Cooling: The cans are cooled immediately after sterilization process to stop over-cooking and to prevent stack-burning. Cooling can be done by placing the cans in a cold-water tank. It also gives an abrupt shock to the microorganisms to get rid of their adverse activities.

Labelling and Packing: The outer surface of the can should be completely dry as even small traces of moisture are likely to cause rusting. The clean and dry cans are labeled manually or mechanically and packed in strong wooden crates or corrugated cardboard cartons. The cans are stored in a cool and dry place before dispatch. In a hot country like India, where the ambient temperatures are high during several months in a year, basement stores are useful, especially during the summer months. Very high loss in weight of the mushrooms is the most serious problem in the canning. This is also known as 'shrinkage', which is caused by the removal of water as well as solids from the mushrooms during processing operations. The losses vary from 35-40 per cent and seriously affect the profitability of the cannery. To ameliorate this problem, various methods have been tried to varied degrees of success. Water binding additives *viz.*, sodium polyphosphate, sodium alginate, Agar-agar, methyl cellulose, carboxy methyl cellulose, pectin and pectin-calcium chloride have been used by various workers in increasing the drained weight (reducing the shrinkage) of canned products. The shrinkage losses can also be decreased by the vacuum treatment of the fresh mushroom, cutting the blanching time and also prehydration treatments.

Setting up of a canning unit: Among the various preservation methods followed, canning is the extensively used method for storage and trade of mushrooms. The process of sealing foodstuffs hermetically in containers and sterilizing them by heat for long term storage is called canning or appertization. Canning is the most popular method of preserving the mushrooms for more than a period of one year.

Many Asian countries like India, China, Taiwan, Korea, *etc.*, export their produce to the American and European Countries in the form of canned mushrooms This canning unit can be used for canning any produce and the capacity of most of the machine is one ton mushroom per shift of 8 hours (3 tons per day). Bigger, automated, imported and FDA approved canning units are established in 100 per cent EOU big mushroom commercial units in India.

Lid-Embossing machine: This machine is used to emboss the lids with the required reference letter or figures like date of manufacture, date of expiry, rate, batch number, brand name and quantity. This machine is operated by a foot treadle which, when depressed, embosses the lid by virtue of marker dies, without piercing it.

Can reformer: This is simple machine, which makes the flattened can bodies to round, prior to flanging. The flattened can is mounted on to the rubber roller and on depressing the pedal, it presses the can against the rotating steel roller there by giving it a round shape. The capacity of the can reformer varies from 600 to 800 cans per hour.

Can flanger: This simple hand operated machine, shown in the Figure is used for simultaneous flanging of both sides of the round can obtained from canreformer. A toggle motion balanced hand-lever enables the machine to be operated with minimum exertion.

Flange rectifier: This is a simple hand operated machine the Fig. used for rectification of misshaped flanges of cans. The misshaped flanged can is placed on the die and by simple application of the handle the flange is rectified.

Steam jacketed kettle: This machinethe is mounted on a heavy duty mild steel stand with tilting arrangement. The pan has a double jacket for maximum steam utilization and efficiency. Both the pan and jacket are made up of high quality stainless steel. This is mainly used for batch heating and blanching of mushrooms in brine solution. The capacity of the steam jacketed kettle is 100 Gallons. It is also available in the smaller capacity of 25 and 50 Gallons.

Exhaust box: This machine consists of a chain conveyor moving at low rpm to keep the cans filled with mushrooms to contact with steam for 1 to 2 min to get it sterilized. It can pass two A-2½ size cans at a time and the overall length of the exhaust box varies from 14, 16 and 18 feet.

Double-seamer: This is a semi-automatic machine most suitable for seaming processed cans as well as flanged cans with the embossed lids on both sides. The capacity of the double seaming machine is approximately 600 cans per hour and heavy-duty double seamers also available at the capacity of about 2000 cans per hour.

Canning retort: This equipment is used for sterilization of cans under pressure, after filling and seaming. It is equipped with pressure gauge and safety valve. The capacity of the canning retort is 280 to 300 cans of A-2½ size and it is also available in the smaller capacities like 21, 75-80, 90-100 cans of A-2½ size.

Mushroom production should be encouraged in the country and it is a peculiar agricultural activity suited to the country for varied reasons such as:

1. Mushroom production is indoor activity hence do not need agricultural land, thus suited to small farmers and landless labourers.
2. Many agricultural wastes can be utilized to produce quality food and organic manure for field crops. Besides mushroom have high bio-efficiency i.e., conversion of dry substrate into fresh mushroom.
3. Spent mushroom substrate can be used to produce organic manure.
4. It can generate self employment.
5. Families living below poverty line can be brought above poverty line through mushroom production and improving their socio-economic status.
6. It can provide nutritional security particularly to poor people through incorporating mushrooms in their diets.

It is expected that with the above advantages, the day is not too far when the government, entrepreneurs, farmers and funding and marketing agencies truly realise the potential of the venture and come forward in a big way to solve the problems of poverty, unemployment and malnutrition prevalent in the country.

CHAPTER 19

Mushroom Industry in India

India is not a major producer of any of the mushroom varieties, but it does cultivate mushrooms and has great potential as an important producer in the future. From a production standpoint, the white button mushroom has the highest growth rate and potential for production.

However, the cultivation of oyster mushrooms has been more common since the end of the last century, when the infrastructure of oyster mushroom growing was much improved and therefore capital requirements went way down in comparison with the requirements for white button mushroom cultivation.

Though India's present share in the world production and trade of oyster mushroom is meager, being only an estimated 2000 tons, the potential for the future is rated as high for a variety of reasons. India has a very large availability of various types of raw substrate material such as wheat straw, paddy straw, bagasse, chicken manure, gypsum, tea waste, de-oiled cakes and so forth in almost all the regions and these materials are relatively inexpensive when compared with international prices. In 2001-2002, the production of wheat and paddy in India was estimated to be 73.53-90.75 million tons respectively. Although the residue straws are commonly used as fodder, almost 50 per cent of the crop residues are still potentially available for the growing of mushrooms.

India has large number of agro-climatic regions that offer congenial climatic conditions for mushroom cultivation. India also has a good combination of both the technical and non-technical manpower needed to operate and manage the mushroom growing operations. The supply and demand gap in the world trade of mushrooms and the shrinkage of production in countries like Taiwan and South Korea due to high labor costs would result in better market prices for Indian mushroom producers.

The costs of building materials and other inputs related to construction costs are much lower in India than in many other countries. This keeps the investment cost per unit weight of mushroom produced more advantageous in India.

India is also developing its infrastructure rapidly and therefore enjoys a large and well-organized distribution network that facilitates the marketing of products in order to meet domestic consumer demands.

From a dietary standpoint mushrooms are a particularly favorable food in vegetarian-predominant India. With a domestic population of more than one billion, India itself is a large market for mushrooms. The per capita consumption of mushrooms in India is currently only about 25g per year although there has been a steady increase in the consumption of exotic mushrooms including oyster mushrooms in addition to the use of regular button mushrooms. This increase can be seen as a highly encouraging sign coming from the potential mushroom consumers in India. Cultivated mushrooms are available today in all common vegetable shops, grocery stores, department stores in both small and big towns in India. One final reason for optimism concerning India's potential as a major mushroom producer is its strategic geographical location with respect to exportation, making it convenient to export oyster mushrooms to the Middle East, Europe, the United States, Africa, and Southeast Asia.

Benefits of Oyster Mushroom Growing

There are many remarkable ecological advantages in the cultivation of edible fungi. One major advantage is the efficient re-integration of agricultural residues such as horse and chicken manure, cereal straw, bagasse and others.

The spent mushroom substrate can then be used either as animal feed or as compost for application in farm fields. The cost of oyster mushroom cultivation varies according to regions and the specific type of cultivation, but generally, the growing of oyster mushrooms is less expensive than that of other cash crops. The major reason for this is it requires little space and inexpensive raw materials. Oyster mushroom cultivation is economically efficient for the farmers of other crops, who do not have to buy the raw materials for substrate and can use low cost structures for mushroom cultivation on seasonal basis. would provide a view on the cost-benefitrelationships of oyster mushroom cultivation in India. there are two most likely situations. Some growers are growing mushrooms with purchased raw materials, while others are growing mushrooms with their own raw materials. If the substrate materials are from the owner's own fields, this produces maximum profits. To obtain the maximum benefit mushroom growers should be farmers of other crops or young farmers in rural areas. The Indian agencies involved in the promotion of oyster mushroom growing are using this information to promote self-employment among rural youth. This particular aspect holds good for all developing nations in which rural youth are migrating to industrialized cities in search of employment.

The oyster mushroom has various species and each has its own characteristics. Therefore, each geographic region in India chooses the appropriate species for its climate and environment. In addition, the substrate materials used and growing methods are also different according to species and regions. aspects of various species of oyster mushroom.

How to Grow Oyster Mushroom in India

Substrate Preparation and Treatment

The wheat or paddy straw is chopped in 3-5cm long by hand or mechanically. The chopped wheat straw is filled into gunny bags for 12- 24 hours of soaking, while paddy straw is treated in boiled water for 15-25 minutes. The wheat straw is also treated with boiled water. This decision is purely based on the capacity of straw to absorb and retain the moisture. In some cases, bavistin (carbendasim) is used instead of the boiled water treatment. The hours of treatment vary according to the substrate or substrate composition.

Spawn Preparation

10kg of wheat grains are boiled for 15 minutes in 15L of water and then allowed to soak for another 15 minutes without heating. The excess water is drained off and the grains are cooled in sieves. The grains should be turned several times with a spoon for quick cooling. The cooled grains are mixed with the gypsum ($C_aSO_4 \bullet 2H_2O$) and 30g of calcium carbonate ($CaCO_3$). The gypsum prevents the grains from sticking together and the calcium carbonate is necessary to correct the pH. The prepared grains are filled into half-liter milk bottles or polypropylene bags (150-200g per bottle or bag) and autoclaved for 2 hours at 21°C. After sterilization, the material should have a pH value of 7. The bottles are inoculated with grains or bits of agar medium colonized with mycelium, and then incubated at 22-24°C in a dark place. The mycelium completely spreads through the grains in about 2 weeks.

Substrate Inoculation

The cooled substrate is inoculated with spawn by layers at a rate of 2 per cent on a wet basis to make the blocks. The procedure of block making is as follows:

1. The wooden frame of 60 × 45cm is placed on a smooth floor.
2. The jute ropes and poly sheet are placed on the frame.

3. The frame is filled with approximately 5cm of cooled pre-treated straw and compressed by the wooden lid.
4. The spawn is sprinkled over the whole surface.
5. The same procedure is repeated five times to achieve a depth of 25-30cm.
6. The plastic sheet is folded over the top of the frame and tied down with help of ropes previously placed below the plastic. The frame is removed from the block.
7. Small holes of approximately 2mm in diameter are punched in the block for breathing. The blocks are later placed on the shelves in single layer for incubation.

Spawn Run and Pin Initiation

The block temperature is maintained at 25°C for 12-15 days. Once the blocks are fully colonized, they are hung, after removing the polythene, in a room where the relative humidity is maintained above 85 per cent. The humidity is normally maintained by frequent spraying of water on the blocks and on the floor. The pins are visible 9 days after the opening of the blocks.

A high relative humidity and proper ventilation is maintained in the growing room during pinning and fruitbody development. The mushrooms are usually picked for fresh market sales.

Most of the growers take three flushes. Mushrooms picked in the third flush are mostly used for sun drying, where maximum dry matter is achieved. Most growers in India are self-employed and operating small-scale farms. They have different backgrounds with low or no knowledge of running small biological enterprises. Many short-sighted and non-committed growers are getting out of mushroom growing enterprises due to small setbacks they encounter before they accumulate enough experience in mushroom cultivation management. This situation creates fluctuations in the total number of oyster mushrooms growing units and causes an inconsistent supply-demand curve in the marketplace. This in turn causes the market price for oyster mushroom producing growers to fluctuate. As such, the market of oyster mushroom is highly localized with individual traders having great control on prices. The retail price of fresh oyster mushroom varies in India from INR*30-120 (USD0.66-2.65) per kg.

To make the oyster mushroom growing business more profitable, the following efforts should be made:

- The present growers must join hands to form co-operative societies in order to share the technical information on day to day growing and spawn production, and in order to control the price of mushrooms in the market place. The idea of co-operative formation among growers is already proposed among the grower communities but no leader has emerged to date.
- The costs of production should be maintained as low as possible by utilizing the local agricultural residue.
- Introduction of value-added products like oyster mushroom powder for soups, and oyster mushroom pizza should be made.
- Mature and committed entrepreneurs should be encouraged to become involved in the mushroom industry.
- The Indian government sectors must take the initiative in assisting in the marketing of fresh and processed oyster mushrooms for export by purchasing crops from the small scale mushroom farms.
- The revenue from this process can later be utilized in improving the rural infrastructure.

The food markets in most of the developed economies are currently in the middle of a revolution. Most households are devoting a much larger percentage of their consumer outlay on precooked and pre-packed foods generally known as "convenience foods". The share of convenience foods in total food intake is bound to increase further with households looking for more nutritious foods and greater variety. Other factors that are accelerating the demand for pre-packed off-the shell foods include shift in eating habits, rising personal incomes and consumer spending, housewife's desire to spend less time in the kitchen, growing sophistication of consumer taste, marked advances in food technology, transportation and distribution methods andavailability and use of better marketing and advertising techniques. The conversion of increased demand for convenience foods into an effective marketing opportunity will depend upon weakening of several deterrents that are currently in operation in this area.

High levels of excise duty or state taxes such as sales conducive to multiplication of the market for packaged foods. Also packaging materials are either not available or too expensive in relation to the value of the content and over all retail price. Furthermore unemployment, full or disguised, places enough time at the disposal of Indian housewives to continue to attend to their family food requirements through their own kitchens. The excessive reliance on homemade foods is in part conditioned by a partial lack of trust in the quality of pre-cooked and pre-packed food products as available in the market.

This distrust arises either from some individual past experience or a general distrust of all foods processed by unknown persons or from inputs of unknown quality. In short, the quality of packaged foods is, as yet, not taken for granted.

But now we will start a series of new investment opportunities for the weaker sections so that they can start their business on a small-scale level with techno-economical methods utilizing their rural level resources in a very effective manner. Thus, there are at the consumption end two upward pulls on the demand for processed products. First, rural households will tend to catch up with their urban counterparts in the corresponding consumer expenditure groups. Secondly, the bottom consumer expenditure group in the rural or the urban sector will tend to catch up with the next higher expenditure group in its own strata till it reaches almost the same levels of consumption as currently experienced by the top expenditure groups. With these two factors pulling the demand for processed items upward scope for substantially larger food market than currently experienced exists. As we know that Food Industry is in its inception stage. The Future will demand a Strong Food Industry in the Nation and will call for added vigor in Food Science and Technology. The pressing need will be concerted effort to Transfer Modern Food Technology to Small and Medium sized Enterprises.

Mushroom farming is being practised in more that 100 countries and its production is increasing at the rate of 7 per cent per annum. Production of mushroom has already crossed 5 million metric tons annually in the world and is expected to reach around 7 million metric ton in next ten years. India had been known world over for its exotic mushrooms. Total mushroom production in India was 48,000.00 tones in 2005. Punjab alone produces 20-25 per cent mushrooms out of the total production in India.

There are around 38,000 mushroom varieties known to exist but only 100 of these are considered to be edible. The variety which had been exported in dried form i.e. Moral or Black mushrooms (*Morchella* spp) commonly known as 'Guchhi' is collected as wild growth from coniferous forests of Himachal Pradesh, Jammu and Kashmir and Uttar Pradesh. Most acceptable varieties among cultivated type are *Agaricus Bisporus., Auricularia spp., Flemulina Velutipes., Lentinus edodes., Tramella* spp., *Volvariella* spp., *Plerotus* spp. The Food and Agriculture Organization have recognized mushrooms as food contributing protein nutrition to the countries depending largely on cereals. In addition folic acid and vitamin B12, which are absent in most of the vegetables, are also present in mushrooms. Mushrooms are praised and priced for its characteristic meaty biting texture and flavour. Mushroom cultivation is now a big industry in the industrialized countries of the west. There is a very considerable export potential for mushrooms and climatic conditions in various states offer congenial environment for cultivation, if modern technology is adopted. It is also realized that merely producing mushroom is of no use unless these are properly preserved, keeping in view the export objectives and for internal market. Mushroom production has increased many folds during the recent past. Mushrooms have found a definite place in the food consumption habits of common masses and there is a constant demand for it throughout the year.

Freshly harvested mushrooms are highly perishable because of high moisture content, metabolism and susceptibility to enzymatic browning. Its quality starts declining soon after harvesting, rendering the produce unsaleable.

Hence, the development of appropriate storage and processing technology in order to extend their marketability and availability to the consumers in fresh or processed form is of great significance. Drying, canning and freezing are initially accepted methods of mushroom preservation. Drying being cheaper can be employed on commercial scale.

Food processing in India is not only far behind the developed countries of the world but is much less than developing countries like Philippines and China where value addition is 45 per cent and 23 per cent, respectively as compared with 7 per cent in India. Linked with the issue of fostering relationship between processor and farmer is the need to develop varieties that are suitable for processing. The food-processing sector has tremendous potential to promote direct and indirect employment.

Freshly harvested mushroom is susceptible to deterioration by the enzyme system and by the decay, which develops very fast around the bruised portion caused during handling. Due to high respiration rate, there is a build up of temperature, which very adversely affects the delicate flavour principles in mushrooms, which ultimately results in short post-harvest life. It also results in the Grey colour formation by the polyphenoloxidase enzymes which are quite active in mushroom hence the preservation and processing of mushrooms have received considerable attention over the years that's why for satisfactory results, freshly harvested mushrooms should be immediately processed by any of the following technique:

1. Short term storage
2. Long term storage

The shelf life of mushrooms may vary from 1 day to 2 weeks at 1-4°C. Low temperature is effective in short-term preservation because it retards the growth of microorganisms, reduce the rate of post harvest metabolic activities of the mushroom tissues and minimizes moisture loss. Straw mushrooms may be picked in wooden cases and transported by road, rail or sea.

The case is divided into three compartments; ice is placed in the central compartment and the mushrooms are packed in the two other sections. Mushrooms may also be packed in bamboo baskets and transported by airfreight. An aeration channel is formed at the center of the basket and dry ice, wrapped in paper, is placed above the mushrooms.

Storage of straw mushrooms in a closed plastic box with 95 per cent CO_2 accelerates deterioration even at 15-20°C, the temperature range most suitable for their storage under normal circumstances. On the other hand, mushrooms stored in a perforated plastic box at 10-15°C have excellent keeping quality for up to 4 days and the loss of moisture is less than 5 per cent. When straw mushrooms are stored at 30°C, under similar conditions, the veils are fully open and vegetative mycelia develop after only 2 days. In closed bags, liquefication and microbial spoilage may occur rapidly.

Straw mushroom can be stored more effectively at button stage than at any other stage. At temperatures below 10°C, however, the mushrooms liquify rapidly, irrespective of type of packaging and stage of development (button or umbrella stage) due to chilling injury.

Canning, pickling, and drying processes are employed for long term storage. These processes are not always suitable for all types of mushrooms. The quality of the finished product is rarely comparable with that of fresh mushrooms.

Canning

Canning is the most common process for preserving mushrooms, particularly *Agaricus*mushrooms. Canning is divided into six basic operations: cleaning, blanching, canning, sterilization, cooling, labeling and packing.

Trimming the steps immediately after harvest can reduce Browning and blemishing of Agaricus. If the mushrooms are not canned immediately before processing then, refrigeration at 15°C along with high RH will help in retaining colour and texture. Soaking for 30 minutes prior to canning may increase canning yield. At this stage, an appropriate level of sodium metabisulphite or ascorbate is incorporated for colour retention. The mushrooms are then rinsed and blanched for 2 minutes. Blanching is used to reduce the activity of enzymes. After blanching, the mushrooms are placed in cans containing 2.5 per cent sodium chloride and 0.25–0.5 per cent citric acid. The cans are then sealed and sterilized. Sterilization methods vary according to the type of equipment used. The most commonly used method is the batch process in which the cans are placed in an autoclave and sterilized for on hour at 12°-10°C.

Drying

Mushrooms are dehydrated in India as such in the sun. The products available in the market are of sub-standard quality. Not only there is contamination with sand, but also the products are highly discoloured. But on the other hand dried mushrooms are convenient for long term storage and transportation. Mushrooms preserved by drying have a good flavour and the drying prevents deterioration. The moisture content of fresh mushrooms varies in the range of 70-90 per cent depending upon the harvest time and environmental conditions while that of dried mushrooms is about 10-13 per cent.

Mushrooms can be dried by sun drying and thermal power drying. For general drying, the picked mushrooms are cut off at the basal part of the stalk and arranged in single layers on shelves and exposed to the sun or placed within a drying oven. Usually about 2-4 days under continuous daily sunshine is adequate for sun drying. This process of thermal power drying begins at a relatively low temperature. Mushrooms grown during sunny days are dried at an initial temperature of 35°C while mushrooms grown during damp days are dried at an initial temperature of 30°C. In addition to preserving the product, drying enhances the flavour and appearance of the mushrooms.

Dried mushrooms are highly hygroscopic and are apt to absorb moisture from the air, they should be properly stored. If moisture content of the mushrooms reaches about 20 per cent, insects and molds will infest the mushrooms. The gloss of the cap surface may also fade. In addition, mushrooms may develop a white powdery surface and the gills may turn brownish from their original yellowish white. The dried mushrooms should therefore, be put into polyethylene bags, sealed, and kept in a dry, cool, and dark place. For prolonged storage, mushrooms should be packed in cartons or wooden boxes and kept at 2-5°C in a low temperature store.

Some work has been done at the Central Food Technological Research Institute (CFTRI), Mysore, on this aspect of the preservation of mushrooms. It is reported that mushrooms in the fresh condition may be possible to preserve for about 10 days at room temperature by steeping in a solution containing 2.5 per cent common salt, 0.2 per cent citric acid, 0.1 per cent ascorbic acid, 0.1 per cent sodium bicarbonate and 0.1 percent potassium metabisulphite. The blanched mushrooms and steeped solution of (1:2) are put into clean glass containers, which are covered with lids and sealed with paraffin wax and stored at room temperature (21-28°C). This method of preservation can be used at places where facilities for canning, freezing and dehydration do not exist.

Mushroom a fungus fruit body has been considered a delicacy all over the world. The cultivation of mushroom under controlled condition is of recent origin in India. For climatic condition of Assam cultivation of Oyster mushroom is most suitable. It is very rich in protein and resembles meat, when we chew it. The vegetarian people like the taste of it as other soybean products.

Mushrooms are delicacy with definite food value. It has already acquired commercial status almost all over the world. Mushroom cultivation has been declared as a major thrust area by Government of India. Mushroom dish is a common item in all the big hotels.

Rice straws first cut into 4-5″ pieces, is then soaked in water for 12 hr. After soaking the straw is boiled. Treated straw is spread on a cement floor for 15 min to drain excess water. Now these straws are put in polythene bags of 40 × 60 cm size. This can hold 3 kg of wet straw. There should be holes in the bags. Now put 10-cm layer of the straw in the bags and press it. From the spawn bottle sprinkle spawn in the layer. Fill the bags to 3/4th capacity with alternate layers of staw and spawn. Tie the bag and place in spawn running room. These bags are kept in a dark room at 20 to 30°C for 12-15 days. A cottony growth proliferates through straw. The bed is taken out by inverting the bag. The open bed is transferred to cropping room. Direct sunlight should not fall on cropping room. Small pinheads surface come out from beds after 3-6 days of opening. Three flushes of mushroom can be harvested at weekly intervals. Water should be sprayed three times a day.

There is no specification for mushroom cultivation.

Mushroom can be stored for a maximum of 7 days in a refrigerator. Dehydrated mushrooms can be preserved for two months. It is proposed to market the Mushroom in polypack of 250 grams through various shops who sale various canned fish, pork etc.

Bibliography

Ainsworth, GC. (1976). *Introduction to the History of Mycology*. Cambridge, UK: Cambridge University Press.

Alexopoulos, CJ, Mims CW, Blackwell M. (1996). *Introductory Mycology*. John Wiley and Sons. ISBN 0-471-52229-5. Deacon J. (2005). *Fungal Biology*. Cambridge, MA: Blackwell Publishers.

Alexopoulos, CJ, Mims CW, Blackwell M. (1996). *Introductory Mycology*. John Wiley and Sons.

All That the Rain Promises, and More (1991).

Ammirati, JF, Traquair JA, Horgen PA. (1985). *Poisonous Mushrooms of Canada: Including other Inedible Fungi*. Markham, Ontario: Fitzhenry & Whiteside in Cooperation with Agriculture Canada and the Canadian Government Publishing Centre, Supply and Services Canada.

Deacon, J. (2005). *Fungal Biology*. Cambridge, MA: Blackwell Publishers.

Edible and Medicinal Mushrooms of New England and Eastern Canada (2009)

Edible Wild Mushrooms of North America: A Field-to-kitchen Guide (1992).

Hall, IR, Stephenson SL, Buchanan PK, Yun W, Cole ALJ. (2003). *Edible and Poisonous Mushrooms of the World*. Portland, Oregon: Timber Press.

Hall, IR. (2003). *Edible and Poisonous Mushrooms of the World*. Portland, Oregon: Timber Press. ISBN 0-88192-586-1. Hanson JR. (2008). *The Chemistry of Fungi*. Royal Society Of Chemistry.

How to Identify Edible Mushrooms (2007).

Jennings DH, Lysek G. (1996). *Fungal Biology: Understanding the Fungal Lifestyle*. Guildford, UK: Bios Scientific Publishers Ltd.

Kirk, PM, Cannon PF, Minter DW, Stalpers JA. (2008). *Dictionary of the Fungi. 10th ed.* Wallingford: CABI.

Mushrooms Demystified: A Comprehensive Guide to the Fleshy Fungi (1986).

Mushrooms of Northeastern North America (1997).

Mushrooming Without Fear (2007).

North American Mushrooms: A Field Guide to Edible and Inedible Fungi (2006).

Stuntz, DE, Largent DL, Thiers HD, Johnson DJ, Watling R. (1978). *How to Identify Mushrooms to Genus I*. Eureka, California: Mad River Press.

Taylor, EL, Taylor TN. (1993). *The Biology and Evolution of Fossil Plants*. Englewood Cliffs, N.J: Prentice Hall..

100 Edible Mushrooms: With Tested Recipes (2007).

Index

A

A.bisporus, 8
Agaricoid fungus, 56
Agaricus bisporus, 71, 118, 119, 186
Agaricus subrufescens, 119
Agaricus, 1, 3, 210
Allwerstein Laboratories Nutrient, 43
Amanita Dill, 72
Amanita muscaia, 4, 11
Amanita, 5, 89, 95
Amanitaphalloides, 82
Amoebozoa, 30
Anthurus, 77
Aporophallus, 77
Armillaria gallica, 66
Armillaria, 17, 20, 62
Ascocarp, 54-57
  basidiocarp, 55-57
  classification of ascocarps, 54-55
    apothecium, 54
    cleistothecium, 55
    perithecium, 55
    pseudothecium, 55
Ascomycota, 151-167
  modern classification of ascomycota, 152-153
  morphology, 154-157
  outdated taxon names, 153-154
Aspergillus, 24, 33, 152
Assam cultivation of oyster mushroom, 212
Australopithecus boisei, 137

B

Ballistospores, 24
Basidiomycota, 58-66
  agaricomycotina, 59
  pucciniomycotina, 59
  rusts, 63-64
  smuts, 64-66
  typical life-cycle, 60-62
  ustilaginomycotina, 60
  variations in life-cycles, 62-63
Berkeley, Miles Joseph, 40
Big white mushrooms, 91
Boletus fomentarius, 145
Brettanomyces, 46

C

C. albicans, 53
C. glabrata, 53
Calocybe indica, 187
Calvatia gigantean, 68
Canadian Controlled Drugs and Substances Act, 144

Candida, 33, 52
Candida albicans, 41
Cantharelloid fungus, 56
Cantharellus cibarius, 125
Centennial Exposition in 1876, 43
Central Food Technological Research Institute (CFTRI), 211
China, 9
Choanozoa, 30
Cladonia, 152
Clathrus columnatus, 80
Club fungus, 56
Collembolan, 157
Conocybe filaris, 94
Coprinopsis altramentaria, 86
Coprinus comatus, 120
Coprinus plicatlis, 7
Craterellus, 62
Cryptococcus neoformans, 52
Cryptococcus, 58
Cultivation, 169
  carbohydrate nutrients, 172-173
  compost, 171-172
  composting by short method, 178
  – procedure by long method, 176-178
  – theory, 174-175
  formulations, 175-176
  maintenance of strains, 169-170
  materials and their functions, 172
  method of composting, 176
  selection of strains, 169
  spawn, 170-171
  wheat straw, 173-174
Czech Republic, 91

D

DDT, 178
Different types of mushrooms, 179-186
  endophutes, 182-186
  mycorrhizae, 180-181
  parasites, 181-182
  saprotrophs, 179-180
DNA, 16
Drugs Act 2005, 144

E

Ecovative Design LLC, 12, 75
Edible mushrooms, 81-88
  commercially cultivates, 83-84
  conditionally edible species, 86-87
  current culinary use, 82
  – medical use, 87
  other edible wild species, 85-86
  preparing wild edibles, 87-88
Elias Magnus Fries, 15
Eumycota, 14

F

F. fomentarius, 148
False truffle, 56
Filobasidiella, 64
Flammulina velutipes, 118, 120
Fomes fomentarius, 39, 122, 145-150
  amadou, 149-150
  habitat and distribution, 147-149
  similar species, 147
Frogstooles, 4
Fungal evolution, 24
Fungi, 12

Fungiculture, 126-136
  commercially cultivated fungi, 131-133
  friendly fungi, 134-135
  fungal enemies, 135
  fungal growth and reproduction, 135-136
  fungi, 133-134
  indoor trays, 129-130
  introduction, 126-127
  outdoor logs, 129
  pests and diseases, 131
  substrates, 130-131
  techniques, 127
  wild harvesting, 127-129
Fusarium, 29

G

Gasteromycetes, 6
Gastroid fungus, 56
Glomeromycota, 22
Gomphus, 3
Government of India, 212
Grain spawn, 171
Grifola frondosa, 114, 120
Guignardia aesculi, 55

H

Hericium erinaceus, 115
Histoplasma, 33
Hypomyces lactifluorum, 3

I

Iberiam peninsula, 92
India, 200
Inonotus obliquus, 123
Introduction, 1-12

J

Jelly fungus, 56

K

Kingdoms, 30

L

Lactarius delicious, 86
Lactarius, 3
Lentinula edodes, 120
Lepiota, 5
Lloyd, Curtis G., 40

M

Magic Mushroom, 137
Malheur National Forest, 7
Manipur, 191
Manure spawn, 170
Medicinal mushrooms, 113-125
  antihormone activity, 117
  anti-inflammatory activity, 117-118
  antioxidant activity, 118
  antiviral, antibacterial, antifungal, and antimicrobial activities, 116-117
  edible species, 119-122
  effect on
    blood sugar, 118
    cholesterol, 115
    cognition, 115-116
  epidemiological research, 118-119
  heavy metals, 125
  immune system and cancer, 114-115
  species used by tea or extraction,

122-125
statins, 115
vitamin D2 and conjugated linoleic acid, 118
Meghalaya, 191
Memoire sur la fermentation alcoolique, 42
Monophyletic group, 14
Monterey Mushrooms Company, 88
Morchella esculenta, 121
Morchella, 54
Mushroom cultivation, 168-178
Mushroom industry in India, 200-212
benefits of oyster mushroom growing, 202
canning, 210
drying, 210-212
how to grow oyster mushroom in India, 203
spawn preparation, 203
spawn run and pin initiation, 204-210
substrate inoculation, 203-204
Mushroom poisoning, 100-112
causes of poisonings, 102-105
folk traditions, 101-102
other causes of poisoning, 111-112
poisonous mushrooms, 109-111
toxins and their symptoms, 105-109
Mushrooming, 89-99
agaricaceae, 95-96
basket of morels, 97
boletaceae, 96
Cantharellus cibarius, 96-97
commonly gathered mushrooms, 95
eating poisonous species, 94-95
guidelines for mushroom picking, 94
helvellaceae, 97
lactarius, 97-98
lepiotaceae, 97
little brown mushrooms, 90-91
psychotropics, 91-93
radiation, 93-94
russulaceae, 98
tricholomataceae, 98-99
Mycelium, 74-80
phallaceae, 76-80

N

Nectria, 55
Nematode, 157
Neocallimastigomycota, 28
Neurospora crassa, 152
Nova plantarum genera, 39
Nutritive value of mushrooms, 187-199
cultivation of oyster or tropical mushroom, 191-199
chemical sterilization of substrate, 192
economics of cultivation, 194
harvesting and yield, 193
hot water treatment of substrate, 192-193
preparation of substrate, 192
cultivation of white button mushroom, 188-191

cultivation technologies of edible mushrooms, 188

O

Omphalotus, 5
Ophiostoma ulmi, 32
Orissa, 191

P

P. nidiformis, 191
Paecilomyces lilacinus, 20
Paleozoic Era, 25
Panus, 5
Parasola plicatilis, 7
Penicillium, 24, 152
Perlite spawn, 171
Phallus ravenelii, 79
Phellinus igniarius, 149
Pleurotus eryngii, 122
Pleurotus, 191
Pleurotus, 5
Pneumocystis, 33
Psalliota, 71
Pseudomonas, 131
Psilocybe, 138
Psilocybin mushroom, 137-144
emotional, 141
legality, 143-144
sensory, 140-141
spiritual and well-being, 141-143
Psychoactive mushrooms, 10
Puffball, 67-73
agaricus, 71-72
classification, 69-71
edibility, 73
false puffballs, 69
phylogenetics, 72
sections, 72-73
stalked puffballs, 69
true puffballs, 69

R

Reproduction, 157
asexual reproduction, 157-158
asexual spores, 158
conidiogenesis and dehiscence, 158-160
ecology, 162-164
formation of sexual spores, 161-162
heterokaryosis and parasexuality, 160
important for humans, 164-167
sexual reproduction, 160
Rhizopus, 29
Rotten mushrooms, 112

S

S. carlsbergensis, 46
Saccharomyces cerevisiae, 41, 166
Scecotioid fungus, 56
Schwamm, 15
Septobasidium, 59
Source of penicillin, 113
Sparassis crispa, 121
Sporocarp, 13-40
characteristics, 16
cultured foods, 34-35
drugs, 33-34
edible and poisonous species, 35-36
evolution, 24-27
history, 39-40

model organisms, 37-38
mycology, 39
mycotoxins, 38-39
others, 38
pest control, 36-37
reproduction, 21
reproduction: a sexual reproduction, 22
reproduction: other sexual processes, 24
reproduction: sexual reproduction, 22-24
shared features, 16-17
symbiosis, 30
taxonomic groups, 27-30
unique faturs, 17-21
with plants, 30-33
Statismospores, 67

T

Tadstoles, 4
Tinder fungus, 145
Todesstuhl, 4
Tooth fungus, 56
Trametes gibbosa, 124
Trichosporon cutaneum, 44
Tuber magnatus, 157

U

UK Misuse of Drugs Act 1971, 144
United States, 42
US Psychotropic Substances Act, 144
Ustilago maydis, 64
Ustulina deusta, 148

V

Volvariella, 187

W

West Bengal, 191
World War I, 42
World War II, 48

X

Xerula, 62
Xylaria, 55

Y

Yeast, 41-53
alcoholic beverages, 45-48
aquarium hobby, 50-53
bioremediation, 48-50
food spoilage, 53
probiotics, 50

Z

Zygomycota, 29